AUTOMOBILE QUARTERLY'S

WORLD OF CARS

AUTOMOBILE QUARTERLY'S
WORLD

PRODUCED BY THE EDITOR
The Connoisseur's Magazine of Mo

OF CARS

F AUTOMOBILE QUARTERLY,
ng Today, Yesterday and Tomorrow

BONANZA BOOKS · NEW YORK

STAFF FOR THIS BOOK

PUBLISHER AND EXECUTIVE EDITOR
L. Scott Bailey

BOOK EDITOR
Richard M. Langworth

CREATIVE DIRECTOR
Theodore R. F. Hall

PRODUCTION EDITOR
Courtlandt van Rooten

PRODUCTION MANAGER
Chester R. DeTurk

AN INTERNATIONAL ROSTER OF CONTRIBUTORS

Nuccio Bertone • Russ Catlin • Nicolás Franco, Jr. • Charles A. Friedric • Jeffrey I. Godshall

Maurice D. Hendry • Mervyn Kaufman • Beverly Rae Kimes • Richard M. Langworth • Karl E. Ludvigsen

Tom Mahoney • Dennis May • Raymond L. Perrin • Ken W. Purdy • José Rodriguez de la Viña

Gianni Rogliatti • Cullen Thomas • Don Vorderman • G. P. K. Wheaton • Raymond A. Wolff

This edition is published by Bonanza Books,
a division of Crown Publishers, Inc.,
by arrangement with AUTOMOBILE *Quarterly* Publications.
h g f e d c b a
BONANZA 1981 EDITION

Typesetting by Kutztown Publishing Co., Kutztown, PA
Separations by Litho-Art, Inc., New York, NY
Printed and bound in Hong Kong
by South China Printing Co.

Library of Congress Cataloging in Publication Data
Main entry under title:

Automobile quarterly's world of cars.

Bibliography: pp. 220-221
1. Automobiles—Addresses, essays, lectures.
I. Automobile quarterly. II. Title: World of cars.
TL155.A8   1981   629.2'222   81-6115
ISBN 0-517-34818-7   AACR2

CONTENTS

INTRODUCTION

*This is a rather special book about automobiles.
Instead of confining its contents to one particular marque, or a specific era or
type of car, this book takes you on a tour through all those realms,
and the result is a rich and wonderfully varied selection of automotive lore.
It has been prepared by the same staff who produce* AUTOMOBILE *Quarterly, and it
features the work of our international staff of writers, researchers and photographers.*

*AUTOMOBILE Quarterly's world of cars knows no limits.
Through the years we've pursued the automotive idea all the way from an English
clergyman's suggestion for a carriage propelled by a windmill
in the mid-1600's to our own predictions of the modes of land travel
which may be commonplace in the Twenty-first Century. Between that distant
past and not-so-distant future lie the automobile's beginnings,
the antiques, the classics and the special-interest variety;
cars that are flamboyant, cars that are utilitarian; racing cars, sports cars,
luxury cars, record cars, Model T's and Type 35B's.
Thousands of cars—and each with a fascinating story of its own well worth the telling.*

Pursuing these stories has been AUTOMOBILE *Quarterly's mission
since our magazine's founding twenty years ago. We've talked to engineers, designers
and racing drivers who contributed to the development of the automobile,
and the sport, during the Teens, Twenties and Thirties,
who have survived to see their endeavors become part of our automotive heritage.
We've gone to the source to determine the background of countless automobiles from
the men who designed them, built them, raced them, or who were there when it happened.*

*An automobile, we feel, can only be properly appreciated
when skillfully photographed—in color. But to photograph a car one must first find it
—and in the case of rare historic cars this is often no small task.
It has not been unusual for an* AUTOMOBILE *Quarterly marque history to feature cars*

photographed in as many as five different countries.
Our photographic assignments continually take us all over the world—to museums and
private collections, to factories and coachbuilding studios,
to test tracks and racing circuits—wherever automobiles are
preserved, produced or put to the task of proving themselves.

Over the last twenty years, then, we have covered a lot of territory.
From that considerable volume of material this book has been prepared. The selection
of the cars to be featured here was pure pleasure,
as it brings together in one volume the high points of our years of publication,
visually representing what the automobile has been, is, and might be all about.

For their intriguing design and technological interest
we chose the Ruxton, the Chadwick, the Doble, the Marmon; for its aesthetic approach
to engineering, the unforgettable Bugatti; for the fascinating stories
of how a car became an industry, the Chrysler and the Chevrolet;
for a study of two generations' answer to how sporting an automobile can be,
the Stutz and the Allard J2X. For a sampling of the nostalgic,
there's the Model T Ford and M.G. TC; for the utterly sensational, the Hispano-Suiza
and Lago-Talbot; for the whimsical, the Adams-Farwell and Pungs-Finch.
For a look at the sort of vehicle that inventors thought road-worthy in the
Nineteenth Century, there's the Taylor Steam Buggy and the Balzer;
for a glance at the variety of vehicle available to American drivers of the Twenties
and Thirties, there's the Pierce-Arrow, the Auburn and the Plymouth;
for a look at the automobile as it may well be tomorrow, there's the Carabo
and the Modulo. And there's Duesenberg, Packard, Rolls-Royce—and a great deal more.

You might best define this as a book for anyone who loves cars.
I also hope you will find it a useful addition to your
automotive library. But most importantly, I sincerely hope you will enjoy reading it.

THE SAGA
OF
STUTZ
America's Greatest Sports Car

A 1912 Series A Bearcat.

"safety" Stutz. Each was the product of a different era, and a different approach to automobile design. The Stutz story is essentially that of the two men who created these cars: Harry C. Stutz and Fred E. Moskovics.

Moskovics was foreign-born, brilliantly educated and financially comfortable. Stutz was American-born, unlettered beyond the three R's and, until his Thirties, extremely poor. Yet as different as each man was, and as varied as were his automotive ideas, each produced a car which, in retrospect, could have been nothing but a Stutz. Perhaps that is the proper stuff of legend. For all the tangible and intangibles for which Stutz might be remembered today, it is happiest to recall what the company represented: a sporting tradition as grand as their cars. From Bearcat to Black Hawk to Bearcat, there was always beauty in the beast — and always a bit of beast in the beauty. It was called then "America's most worthy sports car." It seems no less today.

Carrying the beauty/beast analogy into the Stutz saga, it should be admitted straightaway that the beauty part was given rather short shrift during the Harry Stutz era. That was exactly the way Harry Stutz wanted it. Aesthetics weren't his motivation; winning races was. A farm boy of Pennsylvania Dutch stock, he was born in Ansonia, Ohio. Very early he displayed his preference for repairing farm machinery rather than operating it, and by his eighteenth year he had already decided on a mechanical career. In 1903, when he was twenty-seven, he settled in Indianapolis, where he would work for several automobile and automotive parts companies and as an engineer and officer of the Marion Motor Car Company. It was during the latter venture that he met Gil Anderson, a big Swede who had grown up on the Chicago waterfront as a genial tough who could bring just about any personal dispute to a successful conclusion with his fists. Still he was happy-go-lucky, easygoing and had a friendly nature that made him universally liked. Anderson never considered himself anything other than a journeyman mechanic, and it was as such that Stutz met his future driving ace when both were employed at the Marion factory. The friendship between these two men ripened and, undoubtedly, with his future in mind, Stutz induced Anderson to try his hand at race driving. On May 30th, 1909, Anderson drove a Marion in a fifty-mile race at the brand-new Indianapolis Motor Speedway. He finished fifth, and Stutz knew he had his future driver. From that race until the end of a very successful competition career, Anderson's driving technique mirrored the style that would have been the little Dutchman's had he been behind the wheel. He was steady, reliable, rarely got into trouble and finished more races than he retired from. To say that this type of performance was unspectacular is true, but Harry Stutz could counter with the clincher, "but let's look at the record," after which no excuses were needed.

Later in 1909 the Speedway was closed down to be paved with brick, and this was followed by

Mention the Stutz Bearcat and in the same breath — or the next one — someone will say "Roaring Twenties." Indeed that's how most people remember the Stutz: as part and parcel of the decade of the frantic flapper. The original Bearcat, however, was better than a half decade old before the first roar of the Twenties, and the Stutz company devoted at least half of that decade to building cars that were its antithesis. Still the legend persists.

It is significant that the Stutz is thus remembered. The history of the automobile has

provided us with a number of legends, but few have become so tenacious a part of our folklore as the Stutz, and the results are interesting. Even the most sophisticated of automobile enthusiasts have occasionally fallen prey to the Stutz lore, and among those who have not are more than a few who believe it their divine mission to debunk it. They've not had an easy time of that. A car of controversy the Stutz may be, but it's not a car one can discredit.

To put it as simply as possible, the Stutz was really two cars — the "sturdy" Stutz and the an announcement that the first big race to inaugurate the Brickyard would be a 500-mile extravaganza in 1911. Harry Stutz wanted to be there — with a car of his own. What better way to launch a new automobile? The publicity value was inestimable, and besides that Harry Stutz was a firm believer in racing as the ultimate proving ground for any automobile.

In 1910 he was in business for himself, with the Stutz Auto Parts Company, ostensibly formed for the manufacture of axles and transmissions for companies already producing automobiles. But even now Harry Stutz was devoting most of his time and energy to the building of a sturdy T-head four-cylinder car for the Indianapolis event. Its transmission, combining differential and gearbox into one compact, rigid unit was a special Stutz design — and the whole package was neat, tidy, and fast. Meanwhile the Stutz plant — with money from a group of Indianapolis financiers — was being tooled to produce 500 cars a year.

But the first one remained foremost in Harry Stutz' mind. It was completed in May of 1911 and delivered directly to the Indianapolis Speedway, along with Gil Anderson. A mere recital of how the Stutz did that race day — it finished eleventh — doesn't sound particularly impressive. But considering that this was the maiden Stutz car, that it performed flawlessly without a single pit stop for a mechanical adjustment (pit stops for persistent tire problems were its downfall) and that its overall race average was 68 mph — one should sit up and take notice. Everyone in Indianapolis did. Harry Stutz decided that his was "The Car That Made Good in a Day." This slogan was to remain with Stutz throughout its life.

Orders poured into the fledgling factory, and here Harry Stutz was at his best. He personally supervised the construction of every car and guaranteed its quality. He worked day and night. His daughter recalls that a regular ritual was performed on Sunday. First there was church, following which a family tour of the factory took place. Here Stutz inspected for cleanliness and orderliness — and woe betide the worker who had left a tool in the wrong place or failed to tidy up his bench.

In spite of this first flush of success, Harry Stutz did not forget his obligations to auto racing. He sent Gil Anderson to the post twice more in 1911, the big Swede finishing second to Louis Disbrow's formidable National at Fairmount Park — and he dispatched another car to the West Coast to be driven in the Santa Monica road races by Dave Lewis. The car accredited itself admirably, but perhaps its most notable accomplishment was in attracting the attention of a young professional driver by the name of Earl Cooper. Cooper was then driving for Maxwell and had quite a bit to offer. He was an established professional with an impressive record on the West Coast and possessed a riding mechanic of considerable reputation named Reeves Dutton. Placing his resumé on the line, Cooper advised Stutz he would be receptive to

A 1913 Series B Bearcat.

an offer to join the Stutz racing team. Stutz refused him, in spite of his gilt-edged credentials, with the conservative reasoning that the company was not yet ready to support a race team on two fronts and that what factory representing needed to be done on the race track Gil Anderson could handle. Somewhat startled, Cooper appealed to the West Coast Stutz distributor Walter Brown, and under the pressure that developed, Stutz agreed to sell Cooper a car. The conditions regarding the sale

and the races which followed during this alliance were quite exacting and unique. Cooper had to sign an agreement that he would not publicize or acknowledge in any manner any official connection with the Stutz factory! Furthermore, he agreed never to race east of the Mississippi River, as that lucrative territory was reserved for Anderson. All parts to be replaced had to be stock parts ordered directly from Indianapolis and installed only with the permission of Harry C. Stutz.

Now Stutz was ready for the 1912 racing season. The Stutz colors would fly in the East under the marquee of the factory, Gil Anderson starring, and on the West Coast as an independent operation, Earl Cooper driving. As usual the Dutchman concentrated on the Indianapolis 500 and added two drivers to his stable, Charlie Merz, the son of an Indianapolis policeman, and Len Zengel, a veteran eastern driver. Both had excellent reputations in competition.

The 1912 Indy 500 was won by Joe Dawson in the huge National. After Anderson wrecked his car on the eightieth lap — one of the few times of his career — Merz brought his Stutz into fourth and Zengel moved into sixth, where they finished. From Indy the team journeyed to Illinois for the famous Elgin road races. On August 30th, in the 203-mile Illinois Trophy, Merz won and Anderson was second. Only ninety seconds separated the two cars. On the following day, in the Elgin National Trophy, Merz was

third and Anderson fifth. That fall, in the ill-fated Vanderbilt Cup at Milwaukee, Anderson placed fourth behind winner Ralph De Palma and his racing Mercedes, and two days later in the gruelling 410-mile Grand Prize he finished third to Caleb Bragg's giant Fiat and Erwin Bergdoll's 120 hp Benz. Remember, of course, that the Stutz was a pigmy compared to those big-engined European racing cars. The audacious American competitor was well making its presence felt.

Meanwhile on the West Coast, Cooper bloodied his Stutz in his first championship race at Santa Monica, California. He finished the 350-mile event in fifth place; Dave Lewis, who had managed to wrangle another Stutz, was just ahead of him. Two months later, over the July 4th holiday, Cooper won the 150-miler at Tacoma, Washington, and was flagged in fifth place at the finish of the 250-miler.

But the peak had yet to be reached. The com-ing 1913 season would see the first Stutz high-water mark. As usual the factory prepared for the Indianapolis 500. Meanwhile Cooper, back on the West Coast, entered a 200-mile race at San Diego, finishing second. It was to be the last time in 1913 that Cooper would finish anywhere but in first place.

At Indianapolis Jules Goux made a mockery of his competitors, winning by thirteen minutes in his French Peugeot from Spencer Wishart in a Mercer. However, Charlie Merz gave his usua good performance and finished third, while Gi Anderson was well up in the money until his ca quit some thirty-five miles from the finish Although the eastern half of the Stutz stable wa raced many times that summer, Harry Stut busied himself only with the big national events aiming for a national championship. The nex time he sent Anderson to the post was at the Elgin National Trophy Race on August 30th

A 1927 Custom Series AA Black Hawk by Robbins.

This time Anderson won — and spectacularly. Vanquished by no less than seven minutes was a Mason, by ten minutes a Mercer, an Italian Isotta and a Marmon. Over the difficult course Anderson and his Stutz had averaged 71.4 mph.

Back on the West Coast Cooper and the Stutz journeyed to Tacoma over the July 4th holiday and won the Potlach Trophy by sixteen minutes from Bob Burman in the then-popular Keeton. Two days later he won the Montamarathon Trophy over the same course, this time defeating Dave Lewis in a Fiat. A month later, back in Santa Monica, Cooper won a 400-mile road race, besting none other than Barney Oldfield in a Mercer. In September, at Corona, California, every name driver and car had been entered in a racing program over a unique circular paved course set in the heart of the city. Here the little Stutz and Cooper won their class easily at two hundred and fifty miles and continued to take the free-for-all by eight minutes over Frank Verbeck's Fiat. Those vanquished that day included not only Oldfield, but De Palma, Wishart and "Terrible Teddy" Tetzlaff, the top Fiat driver of the day.

In ten premier events in 1913 Stutz had been victorious in eight. At the close of the season Cooper was acclaimed National Champion with a record total of 2610 points. Anderson was ranked sixth. The Stutz was a runaway success.

13

In 1913, too, Harry Stutz had combined his Stutz Auto Parts Company with its subsidiary, the Ideal Motor Car Company, to form the Stutz Motor Car Company.

Factory orders for the championship car were on a year-wait basis by now, causing some sales losses to the Mercer factory in Trenton, New Jersey. Mercer was Stutz' principal rival, both in sales and in competition — and partisan owners were equally spirited; so legend has it, rhymes of "worser" and "Mercer," "Stutz" and "nuts" were heard across the land.

One seldom hears much about the more

"practical" Stutz cars of this era — though Stutz did produce them. What is remembered today — and what was most talked about then — was the Bearcat, introduced in 1914 and patterned very closely on the victorious "White Squadron" racers of the year previous. Available with either a four- or six-cylinder engine, it was a no-nonsense machine. Unlike the racer, it had fenders, running boards and lights — and that, combined with two bucket seats, a luggage trunk, outside mounted spare tires and rear-mounted fuel tank just about sums up the Bearcat's coachwork. The Bearcat was perhaps

less aesthetically pleasing than its rival Mercer Raceabout — that anyway is the oft-put-forward conclusion of contemporary Mercer fans: The Stutz-Mercer rivalry has happily endured through the passing years. Yet one can scarcely resist the straightforward appeal of the Bearcat. It was designed to give anyone with a sporting flair hour upon hour of exhilaratingly fast motoring, and for the passenger, that grand feeling of having been driven, not merely transported. And that is beautiful.

In Indianapolis Stutz continued to be besieged with orders from the sporting gentry through

Above and page following: A 1928 Series BB Black Hawk speedster.

Howdy Wilcox — with a creditable second place in both events.

The public, of course, was anxious for a meeting on equal ground between Cooper and Anderson. Not that they were to get it, of course. Harry Stutz was too smart for that. At Indianapolis the Stutz team finished third and fourth, Harry Stutz seeing to it that his original star, Anderson, finished in front. It is noteworthy to know that Cooper made no protest. Neither, of course, did Anderson. One month later, at the new Chicago board speedway, Cooper was fourth in the gala 500-mile race, and Anderson sixth. The public remained unsatisfied with these Mexican stand-offs.

The Elgin road races were the next big events on the schedule, and again Stutz entered his two aces. Here, perhaps, their teamwork was at its best. In the first race, a 300-miler, Cooper was the four-minute winner over Anderson. The next day in the National Trophy contest Anderson won by three minutes over Cooper. Clearly, both races had been prearranged by the Stutz factory and the public was still not happy. Harry Stutz was, though. His cars had finished first and second in both national events. Afterwards he stated, not surprisingly, that it's the horse, not the jockey, that wins.

Perhaps there has never been a more thrilling finish in championship auto racing than the one at the new Minneapolis two-mile concrete speedway held on Labor Day of 1915. It was a 500-mile event, contested by the estimable likes of Eddie O'Donnell, Tom Alley, Barney Oldfield, Ralph De Palma, Bob Burman, Ralph Mulford, Dario Resta — and of course, Anderson and Cooper. The race was a brutal one. Oldfield retired after changing twenty tires. Shock absorbers and/or suspensions gave way, and finally, late in the race, it became apparent that Stutz would be the winner. Anderson and Cooper were storming around hub to hub, one lap apart, or so it seemed. Harry Stutz was puzzled. Although scoring in those days was as good as it is today, errors did creep in — and at the 450-mile mark, Stutz decided to check with the scoring stand, and to his horror discovered his two aces were running on the same lap! Returning to his pit, Harry Stutz made a decision. Racing law demanded that drivers be kept informed of their positions at all times, yet Stutz knew, the temperament of his two drivers being as it was, that should he tell them they were tied for the lead, both would throw caution to the wind and probably end up against or over the wall. He waited until the two cars were tearing down the straightaway to begin their last lap and then held the signal board aloft. It read: "Position?" Earl Cooper tells it this way: "I thought I was a lap behind, and yet I noted the inactivity in our pits. That was unusual. As we neared the pit to start the last lap I read the sign and I reacted before Anderson. We both pushed our throttles to the floor and in that manner we completed the last lap. My initial momentum had given me a wheel-length advantage and I won the race, five hundred miles

914, although that year had seen a Stutz slump in the competition arena. The company came back the following season, however, with a new single overhead camshaft, sixteen-valve engine, and its competition prowess was heartily demonstrated that year.

Cooper opened the 1915 season for Stutz by winning at San Diego. Then something occurred that shook the racing world to its roots. Stutz announced that he would take Anderson to the West Coast to meet Cooper in the championship races — the Vanderbilt and the Grand Prize — then attendant to the San Francisco Exposition.

Quietly, too, he finally signed Earl Cooper to a factory contract. The thinking behind this move became clear at the San Francisco fair. Stutz would manipulate his two drivers so they wouldn't have to compete with each other. The results were not initially successful. Anderson failed miserably in the Vanderbilt, although he did come in fourth in the Grand Prize. Cooper disappeared after only four laps in the former event, and his car was declared unrepairable for the next race. Ironically, it was another member of the Stutz team who put up the best performance in the San Francisco contests —

at an average speed of 86 mph, 25 one-hundredths of a second in front of Gil."

The rest of the 1915 season was almost anticlimactic. Anderson won a 350-mile board track race at Sheepshead Bay, while Cooper returned to the West Coast, taking a hundred-mile road race at Phoenix and winning another at San Francisco. At the season's end Cooper was again the National Champion, this time by a tremendous total of 3780 points. Anderson placed third.

Everything seemed to be going Stutz' way.

When, in the spring of 1915, a disgruntled Stutz owner had the temerity to turn his car in to the New York dealer with the complaint that its motor was "no good," even that was turned to advantage. Stutz mechanics asked for the engine, looked it over, found absolutely nothing wrong with it, plopped it into a stock Bearcat, shipped the car to San Diego and, amid a hoopla of publicity, told Erwin G. "Cannonball" Baker to drive it across the country, solo. Baker, after removing the car's fenders, proceeded to do just that. Over the abysmal roads of that era he

drove, averaging four hours of sleep a night, putting up an astounding 592 miles in one driving day, and arriving in New York 11 days 7 hours 15 minutes after he had left California. Every existing record for motor travel across the country was broken. For Baker, of motorcycle renown, it must have been an especially rewarding feat — because this cross country trip represented practically all the four-wheel driving he had ever done. And for Stutz, it was an equal triumph; the car finished in astonishingly good shape, having broken only a shoc

absorber clip en route. All in all, it had been a very good trip.

The competition triumphs of 1915 really did it for the Stutz factory. They were swamped with orders. Success, of course, always has its pitfalls — and Harry Stutz was about to stumble into a big one. His factory couldn't accommodate the deluge, and he decided to expand. Surprisingly, he decided, too, to give up racing — perhaps like Alexander there was little left for him to conquer. He acquired a second factory, prepared to increase production from 500 cars a year to

3500, and to finance the expansion he ventured into the New York Stock Exchange. Rather quickly it was proven this was not his ball game; a stock manipulator by the name of Alan A. Ryan secured control of the company and in 1919 Harry Stutz left. It was the end of an era for the Stutz Motor Company.

The following few years were financially disastrous for the company. The notorious Stutz "corner" in 1920 became a national scandal and resulted in the suspension of the stock from the market. In 1922 Charles Schwab, president of

Bethlehem Steel, and a group of his associates bought Ryan's holdings and tried to pick up the pieces. The Bearcat was still being produced, though by this time it was a rather more genteel roadster with a top, side panels and other refinements. It was not the car virtually everyone associates with the Twenties — and there may be a partial explanation. The original Bearcat was obviously a youth-oriented car, but at $2000-plus, its market had been limited. Its identification with college youngsters of the Twenties may indeed have some validity. No 17

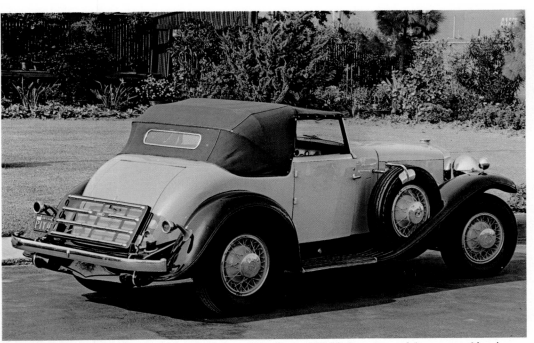

doubt scores of racoon-coated blades across the country snapped up used ones whenever available, and together they roared into American folklore. In any case, this was of little value to the Stutz firm who were, after all, in the business of making new cars, not selling used ones. The company cut prices on their entire line, placed all their hopes in a new model called the Speedway Six and optimistically set a target of 10,000 units for its first production year, 1924. The disconcerting result was the loss of over a half million dollars. Quite properly, Charles Schwab was worried. Then he hired a Hungarian-born engineer by the name of Fred Moskovics.

Frederic Ewan Moskovics (the spelling he preferred for his oft-misspelled name) had been born in 1880 in Budapest, arriving in this country with his parents at age four, later studying engineering at Armour Institute in Chicago and thereafter embarking on a remarkably prolific

The Super Bearcat, a lighter, truncated version of the Series DV-32 Bearcat model, was capable of more than 100 mph. The 1932 example pictured above carries coachwork by Murray.
Among the more popular SV-16 models was the 1931 boattailed speedster by Le Baron shown below.

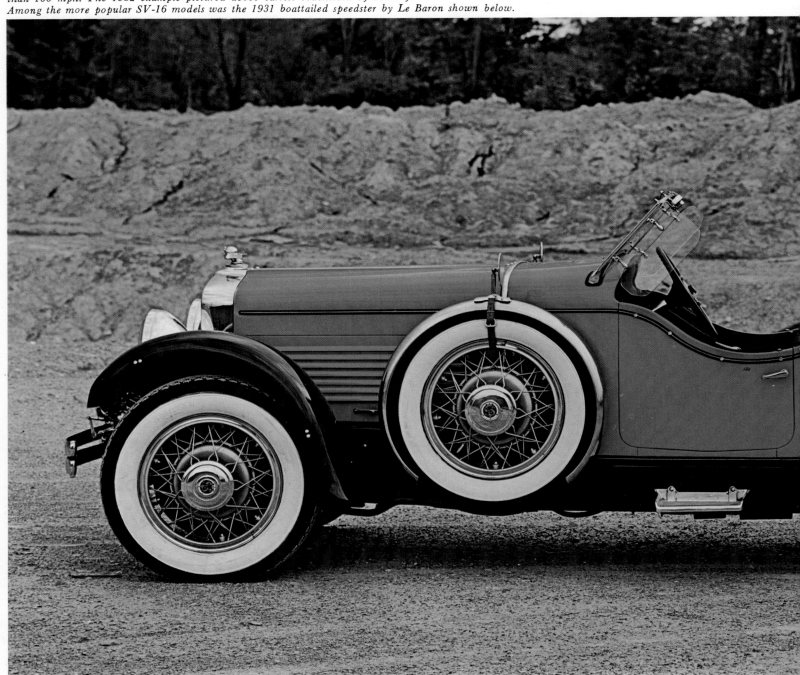

career which included work with Daimler in Germany and, in the United States, such assorted companies as Brandenberg Brothers, Frayer-Miller, Acme Motor Company, Allen-Kingston, Bristol Engineering Company, Remy Electric, Nordyke and Marmon, and H. H. Franklin.

Moskovics came to Stutz with twenty years experience in the automotive field, a new car design he was sure couldn't miss, and an answer to the question of why Stutz sales had slumped so disastrously. "People have put the Stutz down as a sporty, high speed automobile," he said, "We are now going to appeal to safety, beauty and comfort." The car that would do that was the Vertical Eight with Safety Chassis. The Stutz company laid out a million dollars on its development — it was well spent. The car's straight-eight engine was distinguished by a chain-driven single overhead camshaft which directly actuated the sixteen valves. It was an

engine of high speed and high efficiency, and its cast iron block with integral crankcase was rigid and durable. Moskovics was particularly happy with the Link Belt chain drive, a pet design of his: With its automatic tensioners, it was silent, reliable and maintenance free. The chassis was a marvel too. With "double dropped" frame rails, it was extremely low, this because of its underslung worm-driven rear axle, which allowed lowering of the floorboards by some five inches, while at the same time maintaining 8½ inches road clearance under the worm gear housing.

The new Safety Stutz caused a sensation at the 1926 New York show — and all shows that followed it. From a virtual standstill the Stutz line went up to full production — 5000 cars annually. Stutz dealerships took a new lease on life, the technical press was enthusiastic, and the car aroused international interest.

The Stutz now was a luxury car — with price tags and snobbish model names to match. One

could order a Stutz Aix-Les-Bains, if one wished — or a Deauville or Biarritz, or any of a number of luxurious custom coachbuilt body styles. But it's doubtful many were fooled into believing the Stutz basically was anything less than it had always been — a first rate high performance automobile. The very idea behind the new Stutz — high efficiency engine, low center of gravity — in itself added up to performance.

Even Fred Moskovics didn't fall for his own promotional line. In downplaying Stutz sporty image for the safety-comfort-beauty angle, he had said "if our car has got speed, the buyer will find it out." So would Fred. Enterprising Indianapolis reporters frequently spied him storming around the Indy Speedway trying out something new, at "something up around 90." He would explain that "greater top speed is not so much for the sake of the high speeds but rather to make the low speeds sweeter." MMmmm, perhaps. . .

Finally Fred Moskovics admitted his sporting instinct. In 1927 the Black Hawk speedster appeared. So-called "speedsters" had been listed in the 1926 line, but they were indistinguishable from touring or phaeton models of other marques. The Black Hawk, on the other hand, was designed with sports and competition drivers in mind. Frettish at anything below fifty miles an hour, only the open highway and far away places held challenge. On the race track, it had the legs of almost any sports car made anywhere. Set on a wheelbase of 131 inches, the Black Hawk was fourteen inches shorter and a whopping 1377 pounds lighter than the Stutz sedans, which were no mean performers themselves. In addition the Black Hawk carried a "high compression" head, boosting the power of its 4.9-liter engine from the standard 115 hp to around 125. This may not seem like much today but combine that with its impressive torque, and the superb handling characteristics inherent in its splendid chassis design — and the Black Hawk had to be a winner.

Fred Moskovics decided to prove it. Apparently the opportunity to continue Stutz racing tradition by capitalizing on the high performance potential of his new car was too good to pass up. Stock car racing had been pretty much in limbo in the United States for some years previous, but the AAA Contest Board had recently drawn up a comprehensive set of competition rules and was encouraging its revival with a number of important events sanctioned around the country. Supporting this move, Fred Moskovics determined to revive the Stutz racing team and enter works cars in the 1927 AAA events.

The first competition success, however, was chalked up by a completely standard five-passenger sedan, under conditions that were, in part, even more stringent than those of AAA stock car races. Early in 1927 American automobile pioneer Samuel B. Stevens had donated a handsome trophy to be awarded to the regular production sedan that could maintain the highest average speed over twenty-four hours

on the Indianapolis track. On April 11th, Moskovics announced that Stutz had filed an entry, and ten days later three cars, a stock-bodied five-passenger sedan, Moskovics' own Weymann-bodied sedan, and a stripped Black Hawk set off to circle the track for a day and a night at full throttle. The three cars averaged 68.44, 67.18 and 71.36 mph respectively, despite gusty winds and alternate snow and rain storms. The cars were carefully inspected before and after the run by technical committees from the SAE and the AAA, and the two sedans were found to be

completely standard in all aspects, including such items as valve lift, timing and clearance, ignition timing, gear ratios, standard muffler, standard fuel and oil — nothing was overlooked. Thomas J. Litle, chief engineer of Marmon, was chairman of the technical committee and Chester S. Ricker of the AAA directed the electrical timing and scoring. The Trophy's first award went to Stutz without argument.

The stripped Black Hawk had not been eligible for trophy consideration. It had run for an evaluation of comparative performance and had

shown a best lap some 13 mph faster than the standard sedan. Moskovics was satisfied.

Veteran employees of the Stutz factory must have been delighted at the competition revival of Stutz, for returning with it was Gil Anderson. He, together with Tom Rooney and L. L. Corum, took Stutz racing again. They did very well.

On May 7th the trio took part in a seventy-five-mile stock car race over the one and a half miles of board track at Amatol, New Jersey. Rooney drove a convertible coupé, Anderson a Weymann sedan, Corum a regular sedan.

*A 1933
Series DV-32
convertible
victoria
by Rollston.*

at Le Mans that year must have been heartening news. (Until the recent Ford victories, the Stutz performance would stand as America's finest hour in that European classic.) But earlier the ill-fated Stutz-Hispano match race and the death of Frank Lockhart in a Stutz-sponsored land speed record attempt at Daytona had consumed much of Moskovics' sporting spirit, and administratively he was not having an easy time of it either. Late in 1928 new financiers came into the company, they and Moskovics were unable to get along, and in January, 1929, he resigned.

It is singularly satisfying that Moskovics' exit from Stutz didn't change the marque's course — satisfying, in effect, that the Stutz went out as it came in. E. S. Gorrell, a Moskovics man, took over the presidency. The stock market crashed. The Pennsylvania Stutz distributor went out of business, and a number of creditors with trivial claims decided, prematurely, that Stutz should too. But Charlie Schwab again came through with additional financing. Stutz got a reprieve, for one last memorable endeavor.

The new Stutz DV-32, introduced for 1931, carried the same basic engine and chassis combination as the Vertical Eight, but with a new cylinder head design featuring twin overhead camshafts, four valves per cylinder and a single spark plug centered in a polished hemispherical combustion chamber. It was fabulous. And it was for the DV-32 that the legendary Bearcat name was revived. Commanding 156 hp and 300 foot-pounds of torque, this new Bearcat was guaranteed to have done at least 100 mph before delivery. Even better performance was promised from the Super Bearcat, a lighter version on a 116-inch wheelbase — the Bearcat's was 134.5, a dimension it shared with some twenty other body styles. A 145-inch chassis provided the basis for more than thirty custom models of unabashed luxury, with prices to match. Stutz had a car for everyone — everyone, that is, with three to nine thousand available dollars.

All this was, in purely fiscal terms, tragically wasted effort. Despite the delighted handsprings journalists were doing over the car, Stutz continued to lose money. High performance with a high price tag had lost its appeal, or its market — or both. Stutz tried — slashing prices $1000, substituting a simple three-speed gearbox for the more sporty Warner four-speed that had been used since 1929. It didn't help. By 1935 manufacture had ceased. In 1937 Stutz petitioned for bankruptcy.

Production during the Thirties had totalled less than 700 cars. It was not enough — certainly not then and certainly not today, for all of us who would give a king's ransom to own one. Stutz was with us for far too short a time.

Rooney won, at 86.247 mph, Corum placed seventh. Anderson, had crashed, but fortunately with only minor injuries. He was back for the 50-miler at Atlantic City on September 5th, placing third in that event. Corum was second, and resoundingly victorious was Tom Rooney who drove his Black Hawk at a race-winning average of 93.308 mph. At Charlotte, North Carolina, on September 26th, Black Hawks finished one-two-three in another seventy-five-miler, Rooney again first, followed by Anderson and Corum.

It had been a very good year — that maiden year of the Stutz Black Hawk. The speedster had trampled everything before it to win every major stock car event, excepting one — and that only because they didn't enter it. When Stutz claimed that theirs was the fastest stock car in the country, no one stood up to challenge them.

Nineteen twenty-eight promised to be just as good. But, as it turned out, it was a year of one triumph and two disasters for Moskovics. Though not factory-sponsored either technically or financially, the second-place finish of a Stutz

MISTER TAYLOR'S BUGGY

*Forgotten
for decades,
this whimsical
steam carriage
was Canada's
first automobile.*

Stanstead, Quebec, was unimpressed. Even the local paper relegated the news to one paragraph at the bottom of its second page. Under a caption reading "steam pleasure carriage," *The Stanstead Journal* announced that Henry Seth Taylor's "mechanical curiosity" had been completed and that it would be exhibited at the local fair.

The year was 1867, and the mechanical curiosity was Canada's first horseless carriage. Its debut performance was less than momentous. After a breakdown the vehicle had to be pushed off the fair grounds —"contretemps detracting somewhat from the interest of the occasion," according to the newspaper report. But Stanstead reacted no more enthusiastically the following year when Taylor returned to the fair. His buggy performed flawlessly, a fact duly reported by *The Stanstead Journal*, although the trotting of a local horse named Canwell received equal newspaper attention.

But if Taylor's achievement received only token recognition during his lifetime, it was virtually ignored thereafter. In an 1897 issue *The Horseless Age* called an electric three-wheeler built that year Canada's first automobile. Later chroniclers would claim that honor for other

Canadian cars from the same decade. By the 1890's, however, Taylor's car was already a quarter of a century old.

One wonders today why the Taylor buggy did not attract more attention, if, perhaps, for no other reason than that it was attractive. The entire vehicle — carriage, engine and boiler — weighed but 500 pounds, and every pound and part of it was of Henry Seth Taylor's invention. The water tank was attached to the front axle, two rubber tubes leading from it to the rear-positioned boiler. Fashioned of steel, the boiler measured thirty inches high with a sixteen-inch diameter; it contained 207 five-eighths-inch flues of nine-inch length and was operated at a sixty-pound pressure. The iron braces and body fittings were designed specifically to handle the weight of the boiler. Taylor required the assistance of the local blacksmith, Joseph Mosher, for forging, but the rest of the work on the carriage was entirely his own. When finished, the buggy was a delightfully trim and graceful vehicle, the beautifully turned brass cylinders and drive shafts reflecting a jeweler's artisanship.

But, then, Henry Seth Taylor *was* a jeweler. He had been born April 9th, 1831, on a farm near Stanstead Plain, as Stanstead was then known.

As a lad, he was apprenticed to a skilled watchmaker, became a master of his trade and later opened a shop of his own. But the routine affairs of a jeweler's shop were not sufficient to spark his imagination. In the early 1860's he began planning a steam buggy, and in 1865 set to work building it.

Taylor was indeed an inventor. A promoter, unfortunately, he was not. He tinkered for the sake of tinkering; patenting his ideas didn't interest him. Surviving friends would speak of him as a "perfectly normal man, warm-hearted, genial, companionable, a kindly neighbor and good citizen"—noble virtues all, but hardly the characteristics that mark the vigorous innovator. And so, Henry Seth Taylor, the quiet inventor from Stanstead who built the first known Canadian automobile, is all but forgotten today.

Taylor was, of course, not the only steam car tinkerer of that era. With the close of the Civil War in the United States, various Yankee inventors had begun dabbling in harnessing steam to buggy or wagon — James F. Hill of Fleetwood, Pennsylvania, in the late 1860's, Enos Merrill Clough of Sunapee, New Hampshire, in 1869. Earlier, Richard Dudgeon had used

the streets of New York City as a test track for his experimental steam vehicles. And the prolific Sylvester H. Roper of Massachusetts built no less than ten steam-powered vehicles between the 1860's and 1894.

Whether Taylor ever met any of his Yankee steam compatriots is extremely doubtful. There is, however, a curious similarity between Taylor's buggy and the Roper steam car which was then being exhibited at fairs and carnivals in the United States. The arrangement of cylinders, connecting rods, rear axle and steering gear is identical, as is the ratchet mechanism of the rear wheels. The major difference is the location of the boiler. While Taylor's was behind the passengers, Roper placed his *under* them, an arrangement no doubt providing a toasty ride on a warm summer day. A further similarity may be seen in the September 12th, 1867, edition of *The Stanstead Journal*. In it, Taylor announced that his buggy would "run with any trotting horse that can be produced," a close paraphrase of the challenge printed in the Roper exhibition handbills.

There is, of course, the possibility that Taylor might have seen a demonstration of the Roper in New England. But that is a moot point.

What cannot be debated is that Taylor's vehicle was ready to make its debut in September, 1867. And further it was "intended to run without noise or smoke," and would "probably show some fast time." Irrefutable, too, is the fact that the steam buggy did indeed debut — but that was about all it did. Stanstead folk were more amused than awestruck as Taylor's vehicle propelled itself across the fair grounds. And when its steam hose burst and both Taylor and buggy were lost in a cloud of smoke, the crowd became uproarious. There were no offers of assistance as the embarrassed inventor pushed his invention off the field.

No doubt embarrassment continued to plague the gentle jeweler from Stanstead, for in the ensuing years when his steam buggy performed successfully at numerous fairs and carnivals in the area, Stanstead remained loath to admire; it preferred, instead, to be merely amused. To most of Taylor's neighbors, his steam buggy was a big toy, nothing more than

Cast brass rear axle bearing and housing.

Above, lubricator and throttle valve. Below, water ta

that. It was, perhaps, this lack of encouragement that drained from the inventor his enthusiasm for his invention. He continued tinkering with his buggy, but it became more a labor of loyalty than of love.

A hill just outside Stanstead Plain provided the coup de grace for the Taylor steam buggy. Halfway down, one summer morning, the inventor realized he couldn't hold his invention back. Taylor had never considered brakes for his vehicle; muddy ruts in unpaved roads had seemed sufficient stopping power. But on that morning the road was dry, and Taylor found himself speeding down the slope with a boiler full of scalding water directly behind him. The vehicle's steering apparatus — a tiller affair — was not particularly appropriate for moments of emergency, nor was Mr. Taylor. He instinctively jumped from the car and the buggy landed on its side at the foot of the hill. At dusk the following evening Taylor returned, discarded the buggy's shattered wheels, and toted the remains to his barn, hoisting it into the loft. Later he removed the boiler to use with a new engine in a small steam-powered boat he built.

On January 7th, 1887, Henry Seth Taylor died, and for a long while it appeared that his inventions had died with him. Then in 1931 an article appeared in a Canadian magazine attributing the Dominion's first automobile to the Stanstead inventor. Still, the buggy remained in its loft, gathering only dust and rust, sinking further and further into oblivion. During World War II, a junk dealer concluded that, even as scrap, the buggy was not worth the dismantling.

Finally in 1960, the Taylor property was sold and the buggy rediscovered. Richard M. Stewart, an automobile collector, purchased its remains and, using the only photograph ever taken of it, proceeded with the restoration. A new boiler and wheels were made to match the originals. Except for the addition of brakes — a change Stewart deemed advisable — the Taylor steam buggy looks today exactly as it did the day of its debut, a moving tribute — literally — to Taylor and indeed to all those farsighted men of a century ago who tinkered with the idea of replacing the horse.

Storage bin for firewood.　　　　　　　　*Rack and pinion steering mechanism, steam cylinder in background.*

HISPANO-SUIZA
The Legendary
Tulipwood-Bodied Roadster by Nieuport

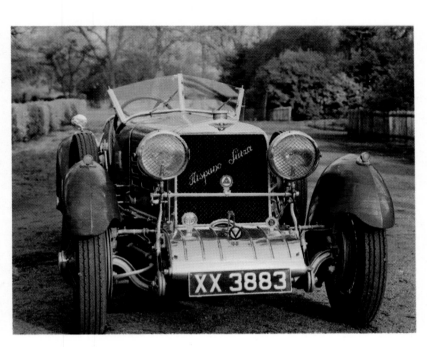

By its own admission the Hispano-Suiza was "Queen of the Road." It is a claim which scarcely anyone will dispute; if one were to cavil, perhaps, it would be on the choice of gender rather than the lack of modesty. For Hispano-Suizas were masculine cars: robust, vigorous machines with clean lines and strong hearts. Regal in breeding, they were honored members of that glorious company, the goodly fellowship of Rolls-Royce, Bentley, Bugatti, Isotta-Fraschini and Mercedes. More expensive than their fellows and usually swifter as well, Hispanos were indeed the motorcars of kings.

It was a king in fact who helped launch Hispano-Suiza's journey to fame. Alfonso XIII, "His Most Catholic Majesty," monarch of Spain, bought a twenty-horsepower Hispano-Suiza chassis at a 1905 automobile exhibition in Madrid. From then on the royal garages received the first production car of every model. In 1909 the factory wished to honor their royal

client and obtained permission to call Type T15 the "Alfonso XIII." Fifty years later an Alfonso XIII Hispano-Suiza could appear at a concours or at the start of a rally without arousing the least comment of "vintage" or "antique." By the same token the Hispano-Suizas of the Twenties and Thirties could appear anywhere today without seeming old hat. Hispano had style, but was not a slave of fashion. It is no more old-fashioned today than the music of Mozart or the craftsmanship of Cellini. Good design is classic and manages to stay aloof on the sidelines when fashion fades.

Coachwork for the Hispano-Suiza was created by the great masters of the art. With the exception of a Van Vooren design, which was unabashedly ugly, all Hispano-Suiza bodies were masterpieces. Park Ward built a boat-like body — complete with cowl ventilators — for Lord Ivor Churchill, a son of the seventh Duke of Marlborough and Consuelo Vanderbilt. Most of the Hispano coachwork was done in Paris, by such houses as Saoutchik, Henry Binder, Kellner, Alin et Liautard, Belvalette, Duvivier, Million-Guiet, Chapron, and Letourneur et Marchand — as well as Hibbard and Darrin, those two Americans in Paris. Weymann, famed for fabric bodies, was prominent on the list. Vanden Plas, in the mid-Twenties, distributed photographs showing two of his creations: one for a "Madame X," the other for General Mario

G. Menocal, President of Cuba during the years from 1913 until 1921.

The Barcelona factory had facilities for sheet-metal work and supplied bodies for many of its cars. As a general rule, however, the chassis were supplied with mudguards, running boards and engine hood only. Naturally many of the bodies were made by Spanish coachbuilders, and while their names do not have the familiar ring of Hooper, James Young or Mulliner — all of whom built Hispano bodies — their workmanship and design were superb. Among the best were Fiol and Solá, both of Barcelona; Labourdette and Ortega of Madrid; Internacional of San Sebastian; Pareja of Granada; Barros of Jaen; and Norte of Oviedo.

If the purchaser of an Hispano-Suiza felt so inclined, he could order his new car with not just one, but two bodies, one for winter driving and a sportier type for the summer. Much of the coachwork was done in wood rather than metal, making the cars take on something of the air of a speedboat or yacht tender.

A student of high-school Spanish might wonder at the mixed genders of "Hispano" and "Suiza." By all the rules the two should agree and read "Hispana" if the factory is meant, or "Suizo" if the name refers to the automobile. But an Hispano-Suiza was privileged to make its own rules.

The company, La Fábrica de Automoviles La

Hispano-Suiza, was incorporated in Barcelona in 1904. (By 1911 the Hispano-Suiza would be produced in France as well.) It was the outgrowth of a firm formed in 1899 by Emilio La Cuadra, a Spanish army captain, and its successor, Castro y Cia. La Cuadra's enterprise had had financial difficulties and five years later so did the Castro firm. At the time of reorganization one of the Castro executives was a twenty-six-year-old Swiss-born engineer, Marc Birkigt, who had moved to Catalonia to work on the Barcelona Water Towers and later on electrical equipment. Birkigt had cut his teeth on the twenty-horsepower Castro, but it was only a prelude to what was to come. At Barcelona he was made factory manager of the reorganized corporation, and thus began his rise to fame. Decades since, whenever the names of great automobile engineers are mentioned, Marc Birkigt's is either at the top of the list, or near it.

In an interesting parallel to the experience of Henry Royce, Birkigt had bought at about the same time — 1903 — a Decauville automobile, a two-cylinder car which was probably the first to have a unitary engine-clutch-gearbox. Driven by a desire for something better, Royce went on to build the car that became the Rolls-Royce, and Birkigt, once arrived in Barcelona, created the Hispano-Suiza. Another parallel with Royce, as well as with Ferdinand Porsche, is that Birkigt's first interest was in electricity, although he was

not so preoccupied with electric cars as Porsche was. The spiritual link with Rolls-Royce continued for some years; both recognized the value of quick-demountable wire wheels of Rudge-Whitworth design and used them on their motorcars, and at the time of World War I both Rolls-Royce and Hispano-Suiza built aircraft engines.

It is an economic fact of life that it is difficult — one might say impossible — to make money by building an expensive, limited-production car. Hispanos were expensive, and there is no question that production was extremely limited. For its commercial health, therefore, Hispano-Suiza built buses, trucks, industrial engines, aviation engines and specialized equipment for other industries. In today's business parlance, they "diversified." Transportation and transit companies — those that appeared to have a success potential at least — were offered the opportunity to purchase their Hispano-Suiza trucks or buses by an exchange of stock in their own operation. It made for good customer relations, although its effect on the cash flow can easily be imagined.

In 1910 the company had their first great racing success, the Coupe de L'Auto in the voiturette class at Boulogne, but it was the First World War that fully established the character of Hispano-Suiza, not through the automobile but rather the airplane. And here, too, was the first association of Hispano with Nieuport, builders of the magnificent tulipwood body on the 1924 roadster shown on these pages.

By the middle of the war, the airplane had become a new and terrible weapon, and airplanes needed reliable engines. Almost all of the leading automobile manufacturers turned their hands toward producing aircraft engines, among them Rolls-Royce, Packard, Isotta-Fraschini and Sunbeam.

The French government, recognizing a formidable adversary in the Mercedes engine, began a search for a motor of a fixed type that could match it. (Nearly all other Allied aviation engines were of the rotary variety.) A perfect score in fifty-hour tests on two Hispano-Suiza engines convinced the French that this machine was the answer, and orders for 800 were placed with Hispano-Suiza's French plants in December of 1915 and January of 1916. Subcontracts were soon needed to hasten the French production, and Italy, England and Japan — allies all then — supplied components.

Powering the Nieuport 28 two-seater fighter planes, Hispano quickly established superiority over their vaunted rivals of the German air force. Their engine had 500 less parts and — in its raw state — weighed one-third less than the Mercedes, two factors that made for volume production at low cost.

Among the most enthusiastic of Hispano admirers was the French ace, Georges Guynemer, who flew his plane *Vieux Charles* ("Old Charley") to countless victories in dogfights against his black-crossed adversaries.

28 The list of Allied aviators who attained the rank of "ace" in H-S-powered aircraft reads like a roster of the great: Guynemer, René Fonck, Nungesser, Madon, Guerin, Dorme, Heurteaux, Pinsard, Deullin for the French; Eddie Rickenbacker, Raoul Lufbery, Frank Luke (the "Balloon Buster"), Elliott Springs, Vaughn, Landis, Kindley, Putnam, Swaab among the Americans; Canadian Billy Bishop, Albert Ball, the one-eyed Mannock, McCudden, Fullard, Brunwin-Hales, McCubbin, Thompson, Wollett, Malone for the British; and the Italians Baracca, Scaroni, Piccio, di Calabria, Baracchini, Ranza — all attained their conquests in planes powered by Marc Birkigt's engines. Of all the aviation engines used by the Allies anywhere during the war, over fifty percent were Hispano-Suizas.

The Hispano-Suiza was regarded so well that it figures in a folk legend still current in France. The tubercular ace, Georges Guynemer, flew off on a mission one day and never returned. According to popular belief, he did not crash, nor was he downed by the enemy: He simply flew higher and higher and higher until he disappeared into space. Those who subscribe to this theory to account for Guynemer's mysterious disappearance never question its plausibility. After all, his plane's engine was an Hispano-Suiza.

So steeped in tradition is the aircraft-motorcar relationship that it is perfectly fitting that this roadster, a supreme example of the Hispano-Suiza automotive art, was crafted by the famous airplane builders of Nieuport, whose products were so well mated with the great H-S fighter engines of years gone by.

Certainly this Nieuport-bodied bolide is as impressive as their aircraft; it was engineered with the same virtues in mind — power, speed and durability — but added a new one, one which Nieuport proved themselves eminently qualified to provide: timeless grace of form to blend with beauty of function. Perfectly matched and mitred tulipwood made up the bulk of the coachwork; intended to lighten the car for competition, it succeeded more in creating an elegance that remained long after its last appearance on the circuits.

An eight-liter, six-cylinder, forty-five (tax-rated) horsepower car, the roadster was originally built for André Dubonnet, and entered by him in the 1924 Targa Florio. Its 110 x 140 mm 7979 cc displacement was the largest by far in the Targa that year.

The Autocar, in describing the race, was at the same time impressed and nonplussed by Dubonnet's new roadster. It had, said the British weekly, "a most beautiful boat-type body built by the Nieuport Aviation Company," but though first to be sent away, "was not very impressive in speed, for [the] engine did not run properly until warmed up." One may glean from this attitude just how much people expected of an Hispano, for despite its "improper" running, Dubonnet held a strong second place during the first sixty-seven-mile lap, trailing only Count Masetti in one of the six-cylinder Alfa Romeos.

A fast pace on poor roads forced frequent tire changes for all, but the Hispano's 3968 pounds particularly aggravated the tires and a seized clutch caused additional layover. Dubonnet dropped to eleventh on the second round with Mercedes' fabled Christian Werner taking the lead, but the stamina of his Hispano-Suiza mount was to assert itself in the end. He was ninth on the third round, seventh on the fourth, and eighteen minutes after Werner crossed the finish line Dubonnet arrived in fifth place, having halved his numerical position and matched Werner's hot pace for the last 150 miles of the 335-mile ordeal — a distinguished performance for any car and driver, but typical of the granitic staying power of an Hispano-Suiza.

The car has had a mixed history, its original long flared mudguards being replaced later by a pair of ugly cycle-type wings, which were discarded after its acquisition by Gerald Albertini, who designed the mudguards seen here and had them made by a boat builder on the Thames in keeping with the body lines.

A thoroughbred such as this deserves particular care and reverence, and the car's present owner, Mr. Richard E. Riegel, Jr., of Wilmington, Delaware, has maintained it without alteration. Excepting the mudguards, which admittedly add to its impressive beauty, it is as it was in 1924, when it carried André Dubonnet in that thrilling Targa Florio.

Marc Birkigt died in 1953 at the age of seventy-five, having lived through two world conflicts and the shattering Spanish Civil War. By then he had long since given up making automobiles and was devoting his genius to designing landing gear for large transport planes, to artillery, to railway engines. Pegaso acquired one of the Hispano-Suiza plants, but for some reason chose to name its car after the legendary flying horse rather than the flying stork; and agreeably so, for that proud symbol would look awry on anything but the "Queen of the Road."

Popular belief in Europe has it that the visit of a stork is good luck for the house that is its host, but though the stork resided at the Hispano-Suiza house for most of its existence, luck didn't hold for the marque. Changing times, the passing of royalty, the shifting of large incomes — all worked in unrehearsed concert to mark the end of an era for this large, highly expensive automobile. Hispano-Suiza did not survive the Second World War. Perhaps it was better that death came when it did. In an era when so many motorcars still in production have become mere shadows of their classic past, it is altogether pleasant to reflect that the Hispano-Suiza shall always be represented by uncompromised elegance combined with unequaled strength, attributes which have, for the most part, gone out of style. But the artistry of such models as this Nieuport masterpiece is ample attestation that such character did once exist.

W. H. Auden holds the belief that Mozart did his life's work in even his brief span of years. Surely he would feel the same way about the Hispano-Suiza.

HISPANO-SUIZA BY NIEUPORT

Built in France in 1924.
Hispano-Suiza Type H6b
six-cylinder in-line single overhead camshaft
bore and stroke, mm: 110 x 140
displacement: 7979.8 cc
horsepower, taxable: forty-five
brake horsepower: approximately two hundred
curb weight, unladen: 3968 pounds
top speed: one-hundred-fifteen-plus miles an hour

CHRYSLER: A HISTORY OF MIXED BLESSINGS

Product of an inspired genius, Chrysler travelled a rocky road to become a cherished marque, and became one of the world's great automotive enterprises.

When Walter Chrysler slammed the door — and slam it he did — on his way out of General Motors in 1919, he found several others invitingly ajar. They might have been labeled "opportunity." Walter Chrysler had never been foolhardy enough to wait for a second knock. He had already come a long way — from farm hand to calling card salesman to silverware drummer to grocery boy to railroad shop janitor and from thence up the scale to manager of the Pittsburgh works of the American Locomotive Company, plant manager of Buick, then president and general manager of that GM division. He knew all about opportunity, and he probably knew, too, that his retirement from the automotive business — predicated by policy disputes with Will Durant — would be merely a sabbatical.

Within five years he was heading a company that bore his name. On paper the transition seems easy enough, perhaps even inevitable. In reality it was just a lot of hard work. The first step was a reorganization of the automotive affairs of the failing Willys-Overland company, and from that Chrysler slid handily into a similar salvage job for Maxwell-Chalmers. The renovated car he marketed for the latter — the generic "Good Maxwell" — became the basis for the lesser-powered early Chryslers. But the Chrysler automobile that started it all was quite something else.

Its genesis was due to a brilliant engineering triumvirate — Fred M. Zeder, Owen R. Skelton and Carl Breer, known to Walter Chrysler as "The Three Musketeers." They had been busily and secretly at work for Chrysler for nearly a year on a car which, according to his vision, should possess "the power of a super-dreadnaught, but with the endurance and speed of a fleet scout cruiser." Chrysler's vision was sketchy — and perhaps a bit hyperbolic — at best, but apparently the triumvirate knew exactly what he meant. While Chrysler was busy reorganizing Maxwell-Chalmers, Zeder, Breer and Skelton were cacheted in a vacant Chalmers plant. Finally, in mid-1923, they invited Chrysler to see the fruits of their labor, a six-cylinder high compression engine. Chrysler was ecstatic. If the legend be true, he spent hours gazing at the powerplant, puttering with it, fondling it — all without a word, until finally, he looked at Zeder and shouted, "Fred, I'm with you."

A test car was thrown together — literally. The new engine was placed in a nondescript heap that had once been some sort of automobile — history doesn't record the make — and both Chrysler and the Z-S-B triumvirate spent months of joyous test driving on open roads, always on the watch for any high-powered vehicle they might gleefully embarrass. And they embarrassed quite a few.

About the historical significance of that first Chrysler there can be no contention. Whether one can call it the first truly modern American car, as some have, is subject to some question, but the basic fact of the car is not. It was the first medium-priced American production car

The 1925 Model Six roadster.

The 1926 Imperial E80 sedan.

with a high compression engine — and as such its place in automotive history is unshakable.

Its six-cylinder, L-head side-valve engine (76 x 120 mm) displaced a mere 3.2 liters but developed 68 bhp at 3200 rpm or 20 bhp per liter, practically unheard of in the industry in the early Twenties. Depending on body style, it was capable of a smooth 70 to 75 mph — just five mph slower than the new 5.9-liter Packard Eight. The standard compression ratio in use then was 4:1, but the Z-S-B triumvirate, after studying the "free breathing" cylinder head development of Harry Ricardo in England, among others, modified the so-called "Ricardo head" and produced an engine using a 4.7:1 ratio. It was smooth, well-mannered and fussless — and it featured a fully machined and counterbalanced crankshaft with seven main bearings.

Nor was this all. Featured as well were four-wheel hydraulic brakes, aluminum pistons, full pressure lubrication, air cleaner, oil filter and tubular front axle — among other inviting accessories never before combined on a volume-produced car. Many of these were, of course, scarcely innovative in themselves. Four-wheel brakes had been pioneered on the Model A Duesenberg — although their elaborate system was unsuitable for quantity production — and

The 1928 Model 72 roadster.

31

had also been presented on the Chalmers in the fall of 1923. But it was the Chrysler — with its volume production — that was to make them famous and the name Lockheed (for Scotsman Malcolm Loughead) a household word.

The styling of the first Chrysler, according to Oliver Clark, the junior member of the Z-S-B concern in charge, was perhaps haphazardly conceived. "It just kind of happened," as he later noted. If that be the case, it was no doubt the most successful Happening of the year. The car was rakishly low (ground clearance, nine inches) and light (2705 pounds in touring trim) and nicely proportioned on a 112¾-inch wheelbase. Wheels were varnished wood-spoked, trim was nickel, headlamps barrel-type and interior appointments tidy and dignified.

And it performed as well as it looked. With four-wheel brakes, steering light to the touch, and an engine quick to respond, its handling qualities could only be described in the superlative. Add to this a fuel consumption of better than 20 mpg and a price tag as low as $1395. Chrysler had himself quite a car. It was introduced to the public in January, 1924, at the Commodore Hotel in New York City, and by year's end, 32,000 Chryslers had been sold.

Midway through the following year the inevitable and justifiable name change became official — Chrysler Corporation succeeding Maxwell Motor Corporation — and the Maxwell automobile was dropped, being replaced by a four-cylinder Chrysler 58. The Chalmers had quietly left the scene the year previous.

Why the Chrysler succeeded is no mystery. It was a car suited to its age — it appeared, as a contemporary business magazine noted, "in a period when desires had supplanted needs, in an era when a car which could give for $1,500 the 'thrills' of a car of $5,000 was precisely what the people who could buy it would most wish to buy." Walter Chrysler was paternally proud of his new product, and he was anxious to prove that its sporting pretensions were not illusory. Ralph De Palma gave him an able assist on July 16th, 1924. He took a Chrysler Six touring car to Los Angeles for the 9.5-mile Mt. Wilson Hill Climb with its rise of 4636 feet and hard corners numbering 144. Not only did he win the event, but his time was two minutes faster than any previous stock car's and better than a minute less than the racing car record.

Then there was Chrysler's rather subdued assault on Le Mans. Of more import perhaps than their initial performance there was the fact of their very appearance. Chrysler was the first American manufacturer with confidence — or perhaps gall — enough to challenge the self-sure Europeans. This they did in 1925 with a completely stock Chrysler Six. The first American car at Le Mans drove the full twenty-four hours, performed with what journalists noted as "remarkable regularity," finished seventh and was then disqualified for failure to cover the minimum distance.

Chrysler fared rather better at home. In 1925

Ralph De Palma won the 1000-mile Stock Car Speed Trial at the Culver City (Los Angeles) Board Speedway at a 76.3 mph average. The following year Floyd Clymer drove an Imperial E80 the 702 miles from Kansas City to Denver in a cross-country speed run at an average of 51.8 mph. Even more formidable was the San Francisco-New York-Los Angeles transcontinental round-trip speed run undertaken by L. B. Miller and J. E. Weiber in 1927, the Chrysler completing the 6726 miles at a 40.2 mph average. And for a dash of the foolhardy, in 1928 Emil Millin, a South African journalist, headed an intrepid group in a Chrysler 70 for a three-odd month trek from Capetown to Cairo.

But these undertakings were child's play compared with the Chrysler effort at Le Mans in 1928 — a full team of four 4-liter Chrysler 72's to be driven by Stoffel/Rossignol, Ghica/Ghica, Zehender/Ledur and Chiron/de Vere. Louis Chiron recalls that the cars were basically stock, but with much of the comfort removed — the exhaust silence was gone, leaving considerable noise in its wake, suspension was stiffened and the engine was mildly souped. The Chiron car, as the Zehender/Ledur Chrysler, retired during the race, but the Stoffel-Rossignol car placed third, averaging 64.56 mph, and it was

followed in fourth place by the Ghica Chrysler. The race was won by a 4½-liter Bentley, but narrowly; second was taken by an ohc straight eight Stutz. The Stutz/Chrysler performance proved a genuine surprise — few thought the Chryslers, at least, would even finish the race — and until recently marked America's best effort in the Twenty-Four Hours at Le Mans.

Encouraged by their Le Mans performance, Chrysler sent five cars to the Belgian Twenty-Four Hour Grand Prix at Spa several weeks later. And again they finished commendably — an Imperial L80 placing second, and two 72's placing third and sixth. The event was won by an Alfa Romeo. Subsequent appearances at Le Mans were less successful; in 1928, the two Chryslers entered finished sixth and seventh; in 1931, they both retired. But on the credit side, in 1929 a Chrysler 65 set up an endurance record of 53,170 miles for stock cars on the German Avus track, and early in 1931 an Imperial Eight captured six official AAA Contest Board stock car records at Daytona Beach.

Chrysler Corporation's racing program was, however, ephemeral at best. Walter Chrysler was more interested in production and proliferation, and as the foregoing indicates, a steady stream of new Chrysler models had followed the in-

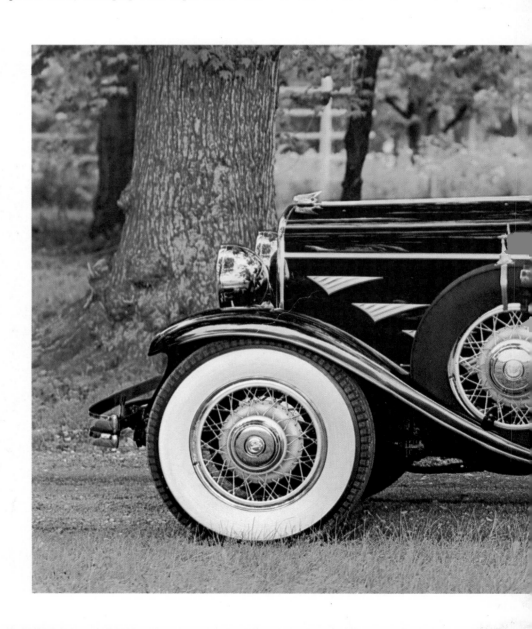

The 1929 Model 75 roadster.

The 1930 Model 77 dual cowl phaeton.

troduction of the first Six in 1924. So had new assembly plants. In 1926, Société Anonyme Chrysler was founded in Antwerp, Belgium, and in 1927 a similar operation was established in London. By 1928 there were Chrysler manufacturing and assembly plants in eight locations.

This growth could have been predicted in 1925, for in that year sales more than tripled the figure of Chrysler's 1924 maiden season. Whether sales were 107,000 or 119,000 is impossible to determine — even Chrysler Corporation figures contradict themselves on this point — but either figure is a remarkably healthy one for a new company and a new car. Nine body styles of the Chrysler Six Model B — there never was a Chrysler Model A — were offered that year, ranging in price from $1395 to $3725 and including styles called the "Imperial Sedan" and the "Crown Imperial."

Meanwhile Chrysler's Three Musketeers were busy at work. Late in December, 1925, the Imperial 80 was announced, to accompany the Model 58 (an uplifted Maxwell four), Model 60 (an inexpensive six) and Model 70 (an updated version of the original Six). The Imperial was a step above the rest — designed to dwell in the august company of Packard, Cadillac, Lincoln and Pierce-Arrow. Its design was really a luxurious extension of an already proven pattern — an uncomplicated side-valve L-head six of 3½ x 5 inches displacing 288.7 cubic inches and developing 92 bhp at 3000 rpm. For a car with a not unusually large engine, it was a lusty performer. *The Autocar*, in its road test, recorded a smooth and relatively quiet 74 mph, and noted with satisfaction acceleration from 10 to 30 mph in nine seconds for top gear and six seconds for second. Available in three wheelbase sizes — 120, 127 and 133 inches — and in eight body styles, the Imperial E80 ranged in price from $2494 to $3595, a relatively modest range for a car of such elegant appointments.

In 1927 the Model 58 became the 50, ostensibly for simplification; this made the Chrysler line read 50, 60, 70 (a "Finer 70" was thrown in that year) and Imperial 80. Prices were cut about fifteen percent; sales increased a commensurate amount, and Walter Chrysler took fourth place in the automotive industry. He had started in thirty-second.

Although laurels were certainly deserved, Walter Chrysler had no intention of resting on them. The following year — 1928 — he purchased Dodge, introduced the Plymouth and the DeSoto and took a firm grip on the industry's third position. Not that the Chrysler automobile was neglected — for certainly it was not. The E80 Imperial was replaced by the L80 — a bigger, more powerful and more expensive automobile. The six-cylinder engine was bored out to 3⅝ inches, increasing displacement to 309.3 cubic inches. But most dramatic was the new compression ratio — raised from the former 4.7:1 to 6:1 and resulting in a power increase to 112 bhp at 3200 rpm. It was designated the "Red Head" engine — but it was not

temperamental, rather as smooth and silent running as its predecessor. Wheelbase of the L80 was increased to 136 inches minimum, three inches longer than the E80's maximum. Factory bodies were reduced to five and remained much the same as before, retaining even the rounded radiator with its Vauxhall-style fluting — a design that pleased everyone except Vauxhall.

Chrysler entered the custom field with this lengthened L80 chassis. Designs from Le Baron, Locke and Dietrich were now offered in limited production. Walter Chrysler was especially enthused about these; Ray Dietrich later recalled the many "Saturday afternoons in the two-bit lunch room where Walter and I ate frankfurters washed down with beer and discussed new design programs."

Nor were the other Chrysler model lines neglected. The 50 was improved to the 52, the 60 to the 62 and the 70 to the 72. The Model 72 had a bore and stroke of 3¼ x 5 for 248.9 cubic inches, developing 75 hp at 3200 rpm. This was the car that competed at Le Mans, and it is significant indeed to note that a replica of it was easily available to anyone with $1600 to spare.

The years following saw a steady, albeit modest, increase in horsepower, and the expected change in model designation with recognizable styling alterations to effectively date the preceding model. The 1929 line was longer, lower and sported a thin-profile radiator. Downdraft carburetion was introduced that year. The addition of a four-speed gearbox the following year was one of the rare mistakes Chrysler made during its first corporative decade. It simply wasn't necessary or practical and was dropped soon thereafter.

The top of the Chrysler line — the Imperial — had not been conceived as a big moneymaker. Nonetheless, even with his prestige model, Walter Chrysler never succumbed to the popular extravagance of a V-12 or V-16. Eight cylinders were quite enough for him, and only after extensive development by the Z-S-B combine was the first eight-cylinder Chrysler introduced. It was the 1931 model year — a year that also saw the introduction of floating power engine mountings, rust-proofed bodies (Chrysler had pioneered rust-proofed fenders and sheet metal parts in 1929), vacuum ignition control and 14 millimeter spark plugs. The new 384.8-cubic-inch engine developed 125 hp at 3200 rpm. The chassis was of all-welded steel construction, a fact in which Chrysler took such promotional pride that they offered a demonstration to prove its strength at New York's Coney Island — with the help of a five-ton elephant. The A.S.P.C.A. was reportedly aghast, but neither elephant nor car was dented.

More important perhaps than the sturdy body, the extra power (for a top speed of 96 mph), the acceleration (0-60 in 20 seconds), riding qualities and road handling, for which Chrysler were already highly regarded, was the styling. The CG Series of Custom Imperials, introduced in 1931, presented a low and gracefully curved

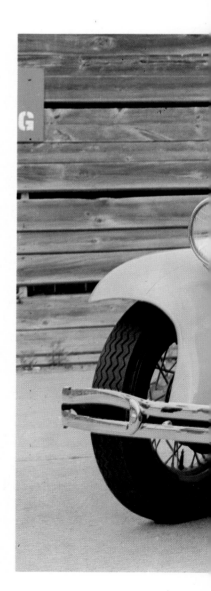

Chryslers that carried the company into the Thirties. At top left is the 1930 Model 66 five-passenger sport touring. At center left is the perky Model 6 roadster from 1931. Below is the Model 70 roadster from that same year. Above right is a Model 66 phaeton built in 1930.

The 1932 Model 8 convertible sedan.

The 1933 Imperial Eight convertible sedan.

silhouette that was the envy of the industry. Unabashedly derived from the L-29 Cord, the deeply set-back radiator grille was a styling coup that prompted GM executives to order Harley Earl back to the drawing boards. It was undoubtedly Chrysler's most pacesetting styling treatment up to that date — and since.

In 1934 Chrysler again made news with a totally new automobile. It was a Chrysler, to be sure, though it bore little resemblance to anything that preceded it. Most people con-

curred that with this car, the Airflow, Walter P. Chrysler had made a very large mistake.

If so, it was his first. And reason indicates that the Airflow should not have been a *lapsus calami*. It was a car of utility and logic, virtues certainly to recommend themselves to a nation of people thrown headlong into a depression a half decade earlier. Further, prosperity, while not just around the corner, was at least in the neighborhood, a factor that should also have been in the Airflow's favor. What better time to

The 1931 Custom Imperial roadster by Le Baron.

promote the delights of comfort and the excitement of something new? But the Airflow had a problem, a whole passel of them really.

The Airflow's origins go back to the autumn of 1927, and what might be called the Avian Legend. As the story goes, Carl Breer, while driving from Detroit to Port Huron, noticed a flock of geese in silken, effortless flight over the horizon. But as it neared and after noting neither a honk nor flap of wing, he discovered that the flock was, instead, a squadron of Army planes en route to Selfridge Field. That set him to thinking about the utter naturalness of aircraft design. Why shouldn't the automobile, too, take functional advantage of that element called air through which it also moved?

Back in Highland Park he pulled his compatriots Zeder and Skelton into a huddle — and what resulted from the tête-à-tête was six years of work transferring idea to reality. Walter Chrysler was enthusiastic; even when the Depression forced massive cuts in other areas, he told Breer, "You do whatever you want. Just don't tell anyone about it." Chrysler's engineering triumvirate proceeded to do just that.

Research at first began in a small wind tunnel, constructed for that purpose, in Dayton, Ohio, early tests there indicating that, of all things, to make maximum advantageous use of air currents a conventional car should preferably be driven in reverse! Half whimsically that was tried — the steering and drive mechanism on a standard sedan were reversed, and the car was driven around Detroit and on Fifth Avenue in New York backwards. This provoked a lot of stares, but no requests for duplicates.

From further tests — many miniature vehicles were made and examined in the wind tunnel — the basic shape of the Airflow suggested itself: zeppelin-like, or an oval tapering to the rear. This in itself — locating the bulk of the car at the front, contrary to usual practice — suggested a plethora of fresh design ideas. The engine was moved forward, over the front axle, not behind it. This in turn pulled the rest of the body forward, the rear seat being placed ahead of the rear axle, not over it. Resulting from all this was lower seating and a lower center of gravity. It all added up to what Chrysler called scientific weight distribution.

Automobile design must of necessity take into account those for whom the automobile is intended, but probably never before had the automobile driver and passengers been so fully the focus of attention as during the development of the Chrysler Airflow. With the engine forward, the strength of the front leaf springs was increased, while their actual rate was reduced, thus eliminating pitching and creating a bounce-rebound motion closely approximating natural walking frequencies. Initially considering unit-body construction, Chrysler engineers finally settled on a structure girded, beamed and trussed — almost bridgelike.

The exterior design of the Airflow was the

preserve of Oliver Clark, head of Chrysler body design. Clark, who had said of the first Chrysler that it just "kind of happened," found the Airflow happening all around him. Designing its body contours was really doin' what came naturally. The hood cascaded into a waterfall grille; the headlamps, devised by Breer and C. Harold Wills, were flush mounted; the fenders flowed smoothly downward, as did the roof line.

Sometime late in 1933 — after nearly six years of development — the Airflow production prototype was ready. Ready too were Breer, Zeder, Skelton and A. Griswold Herreshoff, scion of the famous yacht-building family and a Chrysler chassis engineer instrumental in the Airflow's suspension design. They took the car on its first test drive at Strubles Farm about 200 miles north of Detroit, then invited Walter Chrysler to do the same. He did. All of them were delighted. Here, they decided, was the "first real motorcar since the invention of the automobile," a catch phrase that would be widely publicized. Now all they had to do, ostensibly, was prepare for pro-

duction and wait until the New York Automobile Show in January to find out what everyone else thought.

But they were not to twiddle their corporate thumbs in the interim. With evangelic fervor, they advertised and promoted and plugged the Airflow. Generally Chrysler concentrated on its engineering advancements, acknowledging its design as not radical but natural, and its beauty as "the beauty of nature itself." Further effusions on style were left to others, and more than a few complied. "I would say that it is splendid just from its appearance," commented Prof. Alexander Klemin, who as the director of the Daniel Guggenheim School of Aeronautics, presented the academic approach. For those enamored of thé chic, there was the view of Carolyn Edmundson, fashion artist of *Harper's Bazaar*, who found the Airflow "breathlessly different-looking." From across the water quoth *Autocar* that "the more one sees of [them] the more they are apt to grow on one." The American *MoToR* was even more forthright:

Look at the Airflows for two or three days, the[y] contended, and suddenly they will look right an[d] conventional cars will look strange.

The people? Well, that was another story. Most of them who filed past the Chrysler exhibit at the show remained unconvinced that these were indeed production and not dream cars. Bu[t] production cars they were — available in three models, the Airflow Eight, Airflow Imperial and Airflow Custom Imperial, with three engines, the 298.66, 323.54 and 384.84-cubic-inch straight eights, the latter developing 150 hp and available on the long wheelbase (146½ inches) Custom Imperial. That model also featured a curved one-piece windshield, another innovation.

The Airflows were real cars all right, and, once auto show visitors realized that, they started placing orders in record numbers. Chrysler breathed easier, but not easily enough to stop plugging the Airflow. Later that year they sent a stock Imperial coupé out to Utah with the avowed purpose of establishing a few speed records. They captured seventy-two, in-

luding 95.7 mph for one mile, 90.04 for 500 miles and 84.43 for twenty-four hours. Another Airflow was driven off a 110-foot cliff in Pennsylvania, falling end over end, landing at the bottom on all four wheels, and then being driven away under its own power. That, too, was probably a record of some sort.

Unfortunately, however, no records would be run up on sales charts. Part of the problem was production: Retooling delayed models coming off the line as scheduled. And this created another problem: distrust. Rumors spread — and in effect they said the cars were no good. The American public decided to buy neither the Airflow idea, nor the car. In 1934 only 11,292 Airflows were sold. The sole conventional car in the Chrysler line, an economy six, outsold them by more than two and one-half times.

It would be 1937 before Chrysler would admit to making what amounted to a financial mistake; in the interim they devoted every effort, as *MoToR* pointed out, to making the Airflow "more appealing." The waterfall grille became a more conventional vee; the hood louvers, previously functional, became more simply decorative; roof contours were smoothed out — and sales continued to drop, to 7751 in 1935, 6275 in 1936, 4600 in 1937. The Airflow phaseout began in 1936 and was completed by August of 1937.

Numerous changes had been wrought, even during the Airflow's short, unhappy life. In 1935 a weary Walter Chrysler passed on the corporation presidency to his right-hand man, Kaufman Thuma Keller, like Chrysler an erstwhile railroad man and as hearty, two-fisted and go-getting an automotive executive as well. Earlier Oliver Clark had been promoted to executive body engineer, bringing in as chief body designer Ray Dietrich of Le Baron renown.

In the years before World War II Dietrich delivered Chryslers that were conventionally styled, pleasantly for the most part, if not memorably. There were new names, too, to evince a variety of images: the princely Royal, Windsor and Crown Imperial, the sporty Saratoga, the cosmopolitan New Yorker, the businesslike Traveler.

Two "idea" Chryslers — six examples of each were built in 1940-41 — deserve mention here too: the Thunderbolt and the Newport, designed by Ralph Roberts of Le Baron, each as natural and logical a car, Chrysler said, as "the birds of the air and the fish in the sea." The Thunderbolt was a retractable hardtop coupé, the Newport a dual cowl phaeton, and though neither was intended for production, they did provide viable proof that Chrysler had not forgotten nor were they embarrassed by the Airflow. Three cheers for corporate conviction.

On August 18th, 1940, Walter Chrysler died, having accomplished in one lifetime what most men couldn't have accomplished in three. A year and a half later Chrysler Corporation became deeply involved in military production.

It cannot be said that from 1946 to date Chrysler has been a success story — it's been about three. It is singularly amusing to leaf through business periodicals of the two-plus decades since the war, and find, at about five year intervals, new and different Chrysler "come back" articles. Where had they been? In Chrysler's case it seems that old truism can be reversed. What goes down must come up.

The end of the war found Chrysler in ascendance. They were, as they had been since the mid-Thirties, in the number two position in the industry. Like their competition Chrysler carried

". . . the more one sees of [them] the more they are apt to grow on one." So said a distinguished British motoring journal of the Chrysler Airflow. That didn't happen, unfortunately, and the Airflow, introduced in 1934, was discontinued by 1937. It has been only in retrospect that the car has again been looked upon with some appreciation. On the facing page is a 1936 Eight four-door sedan. Left is a 1934 Imperial coupé, below a 1935 Imperial sedan.

on initially with what was pretty much carryover design and engineering.

Few American cars of the 1946-48 period are fondly recalled today. But there is one Chrysler deserving of especial mention: the Town and Country convertible. It might have been overlarge and overweight with a broad chromium smile from fender to fender. The wood and steel body might have been maddeningly difficult to maintain. But it was beautiful, probably the smartest car on American roads following the war. It became the darling of the Hollywood set, appearing in numerous movies of the period, generally in the hands of the gambler or the "other man," this possibly because it was considered too rakish for forthright, upstanding heroes. The Town and Country sold well, as did all Chryslers.

Early in 1948 K. T. Keller was asked if Chrysler planned any design changes that year. At the time he said no, he saw no reason to. But Ford provided one that summer with the introduction of an all-new car. Just what Chrysler would do about it remained a deep dark secret.

Keller was not about to tell anyone — and he wasn't particularly worried, not about his competitors anyway. "How flattering to be considered one of the Big Three," he mocked to a reporter. But an idea of what the new Chryslers would look like could be gleaned from an address Keller made to the Stanford University School of Business later that summer. "Many of you Californians may have outgrown the habit," he said, "but there are parts of the country, containing millions of people, where both the men and the ladies are in the habit of getting behind the wheel, or on the back seat, wearing hats." This led one writer to prophesy that the new Chryslers probably wouldn't knock your eye out, but they certainly wouldn't knock your hat off either. He was right on both counts.

Henry King now headed Chrysler body design, but credit for the look of Chrysler's 1949 models has generally been awarded to "Old K.T." Engineering's *raison d'être* for the new cars was quite legitimate. Recognizing that there were seven million more cars on the road then than in 1941, and that stifling congestion was inevitable, Chrysler engineers saw the advantages of adding maneuverability to the already noted Chrysler comfort — "bigger on the inside, smaller on the outside," as the slogan went. And so went the Chryslers. All models in the line were shortened by four to five inches. But what Chrysler engineers took away in one dimension, K. T. Keller added in another: an inch and a half in height. He must have been the darling of the organized haberdashers.

But if those boxy Chryslers were sensible, they were scarcely fashionable — and it was becoming apparent that the American public might prefer to forego the former for the latter. Chrysler had their best year ever in 1949. They had a good year in 1950 too — but Ford had a better one and took over the number two spot in

the industry. The writing was on the wall.

Chrysler would remain oblivious to that fact, for a while. Engineers still held the cards, though the old triumvirate guard was changing for the new: and engineers James C. Zeder (Fred's brother), Paul C. Ackerman, Alan G. Loofbourrow, Robert M. Rodger, B. W. Bogan. The corporation's coup in 1951 was strictly an engineering one: a 331.06-cubic-inch hemi-head V-8, the biggest and most powerful in the industry. This was far and away the most advanced powerplant in the U.S., producing measures of sheer horsepower and torque that sent the rest of the industry scurrying back to their drawing boards.

But the new engine — despite notable competition successes — was not enough to compensate for ho-hum styling. Compulsory retirement had moved K. T. Keller to the board, his protégé, Lester G. "Tex" Colbert, taking over. It was Colbert who promoted one Virgil Exner from a dark corner in the advanced design studio to director of a newly-formed styling department. Exner's assignment: to update the styling image, not only on the Chrysler, but

right across the boards. Exner did his job well.

The "Forward Look" for 1955 — or the "100 Million Dollar Look," as it was known on the Chrysler — was a sensation. Here were New Yorkers and Windsors that were lower, longer, wider, with a look of performance and power. Most memorable, though, was the 300 series.

In January of 1955, in a letter to their dealers, Chrysler noted with disdain that "two of our competitors have seen fit to offer their customers cars with horsepower ratings slightly in excess of our 250 hp automobiles." Not about to be outdone, Chrysler already had a car waiting in the wings to put them back first "in the horsepower story." It turned out to be the massive, bellowing Chrysler 300. The American motoring press promptly dubbed it the "beautiful brute." And well they might. With a genuine 300 SAE horsepower now being extracted from their formidable hemi the 300 had the legs of all other U.S. production cars, and it soon began to dominate the young NASCAR circuits with the same relentless ferocity. If it was performance the American public hungered after, Chrysler had certainly served up a sizable bowl of it.

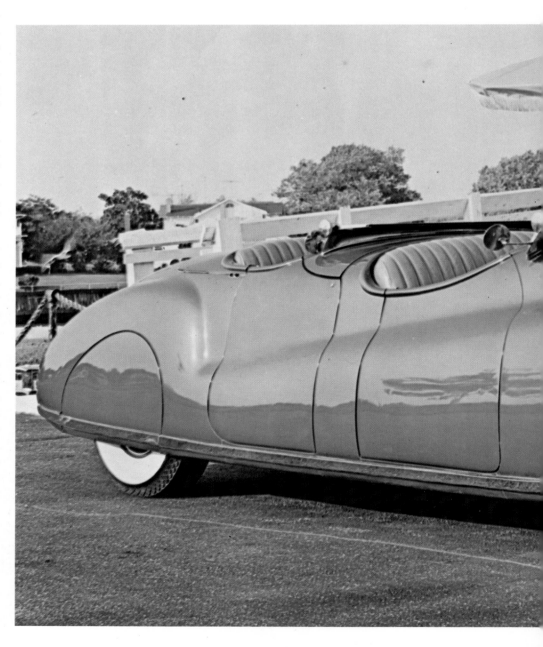

Above: The 1947 Imperial limousine. Below: The 1940 Newport phaeton designed by Ralph Roberts of Le Baron.

One of the most fondly remembered Chryslers of the Forties was the Town and Country. Above is a 1942 model, one of 999 built that year and priced at $1685. Below is the postwar variation—this one a 1948 model. The changes were minimal. On the right is an example of the fabulous 300 series Chryslers, also happily recalled today: this one a 1957 300C model.

No matter how one may view tailfins today — and admittedly it is usually with disdain — there can be no doubt that they were all the rage in the late Fifties. Chrysler Division served them up with a particular vengeance in 1957, with the "Flightsweep" look. And they helped carry the company from an unhealthy thirteen percent of the market in 1954 to a near twenty percent in 1957. The company had come back.

And comebacks, it seems, have been pretty much the story for Chrysler since, at least in the corporate sense. A series of crippling strikes amid the rush to be styling pacesetters resulted in lamentable quality control on their '57 line —

and the result was soon felt. Chrysler's share of the market plummeted drastically, a new executive regime picked up the pieces, and the corporation spent the Sixties — amid chortles from the competition about the "Big Two and a Half" — coming back again. While the De Soto met its end, and Dodge and Plymouth flirted with compacts, intermediates and sporty cars from time to time, the byword for the Chrysler car in both styling and engineering was evolution, not revolution — and that has remained pretty much the rule to this day. But now, inevitably, the future of the marque is an intrinsic part of the future of the company itself.

How solid Chrysler Corporation is today is the subject of considerable, sometimes pessimistic, comment. What the Seventies will bring from Chrysler we'll only know as it happens. From a company whose history has been replete with surprises, however, we might expect that there are a few more waiting in the wings.

DE TOMASO MANGUSTA

Mangusta (mon•goos•tə), n. Italian. (Eng. = mongoose) a small, ferretlike carnivore of India noted for its ability to hunt and kill the Cobra.

It's not very often these days that someone builds a racing machine that's disguised as a road car (though the reverse is too often true of late), but during the early part of the automobile's history there was hardly any difference between the two. The racing cars, if somewhat starker, were really only stripped down hotted-up touring cars, and it was still possible in the Thirties, and even into the Forties, to buy what was virtually a gussied-up Grand Prix car that was set up for use on public roads.

Not any more. Within the last fifteen years or so the racing car has become so highly developed, so esoteric, so *expensive*, that contemporary racing machinery set up for the road is almost unheard of. The mid-engine layout, which is the only way to go in a modern competition machine, is costly for more than one reason. A fully-synchronized five-speed plus reverse transaxle alone can cost as much as a small but well-fitted-out imported sedan. Added to this, the design and construction of a suitable chassis is a highly elaborate science, and such engineering talent as is required is very expensive. The same goes for the chaps who actually build it from the drawings. Then the same thing applies to the fabrication of the bodywork. When you've reached this point and are confronted with a completed car, your troubles are far from over, because you may now be faced

with development and redesign costs that may well exceed what the car has cost so far.

It's easy to see then why the boulevardier's racing car is a thing of the past nowadays — but for a few superlative exceptions, one of which has to be Alejandro de Tomaso's fabulous mid-engine coupé, the Mangusta.

The car was introduced — and stole the show — at Turin in late 1966. At the time it was powered by a five-liter, Weber-carburetored version of Ford's well-known 289, and though no one other than factory drivers had actually driven the car, there was little argument that it would be a stunning performer when someone finally did. It was. But what made it the splendid success that it became was, ironically, not its engineering but its glorious styling.

Giorgio Giugiaro, less than thirty at the time, probably the most exciting and gifted young

designer in Italy today, already had had a string of strikingly beautiful designs behind him — the Maserati Ghibli, the Iso Grifo, the Alfa Romeo Canguro, the Bizzarini GT, the recent Bizzarini Manta, and even AUTOMOBILE *Quarterly*'s own Bertone Mustang — when he developed the Mangusta for de Tomaso. His envelope for its superb chassis was a model of efficient space utilization and unrestrained flamboyance. There is no doubt that in ten or twenty years the car will be as striking and rakish as it appeared to all those who have viewed it — in Turin and ever since.

Styling, of course, is hardly the end of the tale. The way a Mangusta behaves is utterly beyond the ken of anyone who hasn't driven a modern racing automobile. Largely responsible for this is the chassis design, a sheet metal backbone type with fully independent

suspension through coil springs and control arms. It simply cannot be faulted. There is nothing missing, nor anything placed where it doesn't belong.

Then there are the specifications (as delivered in the United States). Engine: 230 bhp, 4.9-liter Ford V-8, mounted amidships behind the seats. Transmission: ZF fully-synchronized five-speed transaxle. Brakes: servo-assisted Girling 11.75-inch discs front and 11.00-inch rear. Steering: rack and pinion, 4.5 turns lock-to-lock. Wheels: Campagnolo 15-inch magnesium alloy. Tires: Dunlop SP radial 185x15 front and 225x15 rear. Cooling system: pressure-type, forward through the backbone chassis to aluminum cross-flow radiator and returned through the backbone. Electrical system: twelve-volt through Autolite alternator. Air conditioning was standard equipment. Curb weight unladen: about 3000 pounds.

These specifications, for the Mangustas delivered in America, are impressive enough,

yielding a top speed around 120 mph and zero-to-sixty times in the neighborhood of seven seconds. But even more astounding is the potential, as recorded by the 271 bhp Cobra-powered car on these pages, at Monza, in the summer of 1969.

Acceleration	0-60	5.9 seconds
"	0-100	13.7 seconds
Standing ¼ mile		14.25 seconds
Top Speed		152 mph

These times were recorded by this car after it had done some 200 flat-out shakedown laps around Monza. As a result they could doubtlessly be improved upon with a thorough tuneup. The factory told us that 250 kph (155 mph) had been attained often enough with the 289 to serve as a target during testing.

One of the many things that people have been saying to each other for so long that it's now ac-

cepted as Gospel is that if an automobile manufacturer goes racing then the products he sells to the public will be "better," which, of course, is so much patent nonsense. The manufacturers earnestly wish that you would believe this, otherwise they have been wasting all that money trying to get your attention. But you can bet your boots *they* don't believe it. The proper study of mankind is man, and the proper study of the sporty-compact-family car is precisely that and nothing else.

So, when an experienced manufacturer comes up with a chassis that looks like a racing car, one that literally goes, stops and handles like a racing car, you can be quite confident that it *is* a racing car, no matter how cozy and domesticated it might be.

De Tomaso will build other cars (and has in fact already created a successor), but however fine they may be, the Mangusta will remain a memorable milestone in automotive excitement.

DE TOMASO MANGUSTA
SPECIFICATIONS

ENGINE
Ford 289 cu. in. 271 bhp V-8
te: Cars delivered in the United States
ied the 302 cu. in. 230 bhp Ford V-8)

TRANSMISSION
fully-synchronized five-speed transaxle
ear Ratios: 1st 10.2:1; 2nd 6.18:1;
3rd 4.59:1; 4th 4.02:1; 5th 3.55:1.

SUSPENSION
nt: Unequal-length A-arms, with coil
brings, tubular shocks, anti-roll bar.
: Lower A-arms, upper transverse links,
r and lower trailing arms, coil springs,
tubular shocks, anti-roll bar.

DIMENSIONS
Wheelbase: 98.4 inches
ack front and rear: 55.2/57.4 inches
Overall length: 167.9 inches
Overall width: 72.6 inches
Overall height: 42.1 inches
Ground clearance: 6.3 inches

ADAMS-FARWELL

"Who wants to build a car like everybody else's?"
Fay Oliver Farwell must have reasoned.
"For starters, why not have the engine revolve
around the crankshaft?"

Probably few automotive gasoline engines built anywhere anytime are as much fun to watch as the charmer that appears on these pages. This, granted, is a rather whimsical recommendation for its appeal — and it's certainly not the only one: Of esoteric, technical and practical reasons, more on. But typical reciprocating internal combustion engines are more or less alike — once you've seen one you've seen them all. Normally there's not really much to see anyway — but in this revolving variation a whole performance awaits your pleasure: the crankshaft firmly and irrevocably locked, the cylinders poised, ready to do their stuff; a pull-up of the starting lever — and the entire engine's off on a demented merry go round. This little carousel of a car carries the delicious name of Adams-Farwell. It was built in Dubuque.

If there is a certain fancifulness to all this, it is not meant to diminish the seriousness of the Adams-Farwell. It wasn't a plaything or the ingenious caprice of a young blade with a few footloose ideas. It was instead a production car, created by a man in the bloom of middle age and built by a solidly established Iowa firm.

Fay Oliver Farwell, a self-taught mechanical genius from Pecatonia, Illinois, had joined the Adams Company of Dubuque in the mid to late 1880's. In 1895, he set to experimenting with the internal combustion engine. He had nurtured the rotary idea since early in his career; his desire to forego the ponderous weight of a flywheel led to this novel concept, and somewhere along the line he thought of air cooling.

By 1898 he had built several engines; then he decided to work up something to put one of them in. Between the front wheels of an iron-tired express wagon he placed his three-cylinder rotary engine, two-speed-and-reverse transmission and gas tank. It performed ably, but the following year he decided to forego his literal application of the "horseless carriage" idea — and moved the engine to the rear in his bicycle-wheeled Model 2 runabout. This had a larger engine than the first, 5x4 bore/stroke contrasted with the original's 4x4.

The 1901 Model 3 — with wooden artillery wheels — was bigger still, 4½ inches, and these dimensions carried Farwell through the Models 4 and 5. Only one each of these cars was built, although the Model 5, rated at 8 horsepower, served as a production prototype. It was shown at the Chicago Automobile Show in 1905, beneath a revolving electric sign made in the shape of the engine.

The company started taking orders. As manufacturers, they were obviously anxious to please. For those of stalwart heart and heavy foot, the Adams Company advised that their car could be operated with the body removed, and they were willing to provide a temporary seat for any customers anxious to enter the car "stripped" in competition. Not that the Adams people would care to take part in such nonsense themselves, however!

The only record of Adams-Farwell pitting their car against anything save the hills of Iowa was the Chicago-St. Paul race of July, 1905. And, if the legend be true, that was, in part, by accident. It seems that a Pierce-Arrow entered in that trek arrived in Dubuque in sorry condition, and its drivers asked the Adams Company for assistance, which was duly given. Their curiosity piqued by tales of the contest, the Adams-Farwell people followed along behind the Pierce in one of their cars for the remainder of the trek, until bored by the pace, they drove on ahead, to just outside the city of St. Paul. There they waited for the Pierce. It was, according to one of the Adams people, a long wait.

For 1906 the Adams-Farwell was available in either three- or five-cylinder variations, but the principles of their operation were identical. Many of the parts were duplicated while others were merely increased in size and strength. Each cylinder was complete with head, and part of the central

The Adams-Farwell five-cylinder engine at repose and at work. The company provided a pull-up lever on the floorboard of the car for starting: A lady or child could do it, so Adams-Farwell advertised. The car can be started just as well, however, by reaching in the back and simply grabbing hold of one of the cylinders and yanking on it— if it has been running recently, an asbestos glove is strongly recommended.

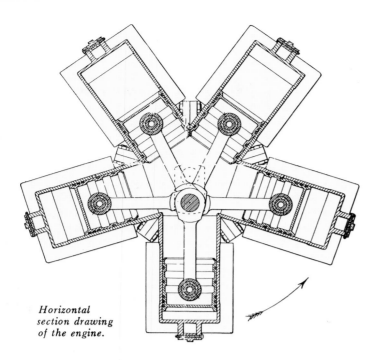

Horizontal
section drawing
of the engine.

Underside of
double clutch
sliding gear
transmission.

crankcase cast in one piece. As the case might require, either three or five of these cylinders were bolted together and sandwiched between an upper bronze flange and a lower cast steel flange, which carried bronze bushings, forming bearings around the vertical stationary crankshaft. The centrally-mounted carburetor was initially nourished by gravity feed, later a piston pump. Centrifugal force closed the valves. Heavy springing would have been superfluous; light piano wire sufficed for valve springs, and that was necessary only because in starting the slow speed might be insufficient to overcome the resistance of cold lubricating oil on the valve stems. Once started, valve springs weren't necessary at all.

Neither was a flywheel, of course — nor a fan for that matter. The revolving elements, cylinders and crankcase, were their own flywheel. Rotation provided the cooling, throwing off the hot air centrifugally and allowing nature to replace it with fresh. Variable compression also assisted in cold weather starting. Rumor had it that the engine could be turned around — one can hardly say turned over — with the thermometer below zero and the engine covered with frost.

The 1906 Model 8A Gentleman's Speed Roadster was frameless — one of the first examples of unit body construction — weighed but 1400 pounds and was capable of 75 mph. Thereafter Adams-Farwells got heavier and longer. By the 1909 Model 9's, the car was stretched as much as 128 inches between wheels, and its weight went ponderously over the ton. And the prices, which had originally started at around $2000, had since risen to $3000 and up. The Model 9's were the last of the Adams-Farwells — though contemporary sources reveal that they were produced until 1913. But by 1914 the marque was no more. In all, about fifty-two were built.

The Adams-Farwell car was forgotten for years. Finally in the mid-Forties this example was found in Florida, and after passing through the collections of D. Cameron Peck and Henry Austin Clark, Jr., it was purchased by Harrah's Automobile Collection in Reno, Nevada. The car is a five-cylinder 1906 Model 6A open convertible. Technically its 96-inch wheelbase is not that indicated in contemporary Adams-Farwell catalogues, but since the cars were generally built to order, there's no discrepancy here. Indeed there are some indications that the car was actually the 1903 prototype rebuilt to Model 6 specifications in 1911. But whatever the story behind it, the car is the only authentic Adams-Farwell known extant.

Why did the Adams-Farwell fail? No single answer readily suggests itself. It certainly wasn't the fault of the car. It may have been, as that sage observer of the automotive scene, James Rood Doolittle, said back then, "its territorial location." Yet Stephen Balzer hadn't found the rotary idea any more financially profitable in New York City. The rotary Bailey had rough going in Springfield, Massachusetts, and the Intrepid, built by the Rotary Motor Vehicle Company, failed to live up to its name in Boston.

But . . . what if they had all been built in Detroit?

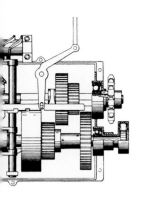

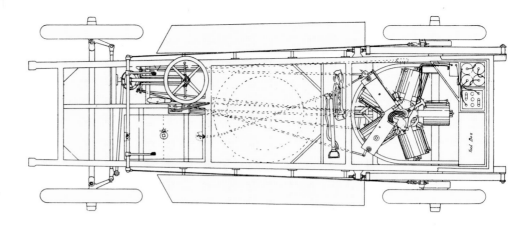

*Chassis drawing
of the
touring car.*

CORD L-29

A Magnificent and All But Forgotten Classic

Elsewhere in this book reference is made to Auburn as the bridesmaid of the Cord Corporation's automotive trilogy. The analogy may be taken one step further. In the procession of cars built under the aegis of Errett Lobban Cord, the L-29 could be called the flower girl. Mention the Cord today, and the reaction is almost invariable. "The 810 and 812 — those were the real Cords." All the L-29 did, apparently, was make ready the path for their arrival.

This is most distressing. To be unappreciated is an unhappy lot. And were the L-29 Cord capable of emotion, it would be feeling as low today as its chassis is to the ground — and rightly so. For the more we discovered about the Auburn the more fond of and impressed with the

car we became. In the same way we have becom□ enchanted with the L-29 Cord.

It must be pleasant being E. L. Cord, livin□ with the satisfaction of knowing you never bui□ an unexciting car. How many other manufa□ turers can make that claim? Of course, h□ should probably never be forgiven for allowin□ the Auburn, the Cord, the Duesenberg to s□ abruptly depart the automotive scene. But suc□ are the hazards of empire building. And Erre□ Lobban Cord was indeed an empire builder.

There can be no doubting the shrewdness □ the man. In 1927, while accelerating Aubur□ sales, he bought Duesenberg and got the Cor□ idea. In 1929 he introduced the fabulous Mode□ J Duesenberg, the show-stopping Auburn Cabi□ Speedster and the L-29 — and gathered all th□ companies he had been accumulating along th□ way into a holding corporation bearing hi□ name. Obviously the two years in between wer□ rife with activity, but probably of all the a□

endant corporate machinations, the project losest to E. L. Cord was the L-29. He revitalized ne Auburn and sold the Duesenberg — both eats probably few other men could have done – but the L-29 was his baby.

Not that Cord conceived the L-29 as his own ersonal whim — it wasn't a car he simply had build for its own sake. It was, as might be expected from Mr. Cord, a business proposition. first of all, he wanted a car to fill the price gap etween the Auburn and his newly acquired Duesenberg. Secondly, he wanted a car with instant sales appeal. What could be better than to ffer an attractively-priced car incorporating the rinciple that was the talk of motoring circles of he day — front wheel drive. The principle wasn't new, of course; it can even be whimsically taken back to the pre-automotive ra. Who ever saw a horse push a cart? But the lea of an automobile being pulled down a road nly began to enjoy popular vogue — with all

due respect to Walter Christie — in the Twenties. The reason was largely Harry Miller, the Locomobile Junior 8 — and Indianapolis. By coming up with America's first production front-drive automobile in thirty years, with built-in racing prestige to boot, E. L. Cord felt assured of a winner. It all seemed so simple.

But it wasn't.

In June of 1927 — after the Indianapolis race — Cord purchased, through the Auburn Automobile Company, the patent and manufacturing rights to the Miller design. Soon after he met with his friend Leon Duray in Chicago, and Duray informed him that the idea was pleasant but unfeasible — the Miller transmission design made it almost impossible to shift at speed, a decided handicap. But in addition to the Miller-designed Junior 8 which he had raced, Duray had also piloted another front-drive non-Miller car, the Detroit Special, in the recent Indy race. It had finished eighth, but neither shifting nor

front drive were the reasons, and Duray suggested that if Cord were still serious about the project he should contact that car's designer. Almost immediately Cornelius W. Van Ranst was on his way from Detroit to Chicago.

The subsequent meeting — attended by Cord, Van Ranst, Duray and Harry Miller — straightened matters out to Cord's satisfaction. The Miller gears, with their high inertia forces resulting from location on the high-torque side of the ring/pinion, could not feasibly be modified for commercial use; Cord rejected Van Ranst's idea of a gear layout putting the transmission in front of the axle, so finally the Detroit Special layout with its transmission between clutch and differential unit was agreed upon. Van Ranst was given the title of Project Engineer and trundled off to Miller's shop in Los Angeles to design and build the proposed front-drive car.

Five months later the group assembled again,

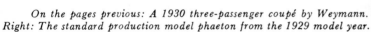

On the pages previous: A 1930 three-passenger coupé by Weymann.
Right: The standard production model phaeton from the 1929 model year.

this time in California to test the completed car. If ever an automobile could be called a pot-pourri, this was it. The engine was Auburn's Lycoming straight eight, reversed in the chassis to put the clutch forward and revised to get the water outlet up front. Front end design was courtesy of Leo Goossen. Front suspension with quarter-elliptic springs and inboard brakes was Miller-type, although the usual Miller Rzeppa constant-speed universal joints were replaced by a single Cardan joint in each drive shaft, machined to allow transmission of torque while at an angle of 40°. The body shell was Auburn's, as were the modified front and rear fenders. The radiator was strictly Miller, and the divided windshield was reminiscent of Brewster.

But it was all together, and with a great deal of delight the quartet — Cord, Van Ranst, Miller and Duray — took the car out on a tour of the hills and canyons of Beverly Hills, its first excursion outside the Miller shops. The only one

thoroughly pleased at the end of the tour was E. L. Cord. The others found the jerking and vibra-tions accompanying any sharp turn rather disagreeable. Cord didn't think anyone would mind. Van Ranst was convinced everyone would, and that the trouble was the single Cardan joint, remediable by replacement with a dual unit. That decided, Van Ranst was hired to design the production car. A few hours later he found himself on the Southern Pacific "Chief" headed for the Duesenberg plant in Indianapolis. Time, as Bulwer-Lytton noted about a century ago, is money — obviously Cord agreed.

Entrenched in Indianapolis, Van Ranst first turned to the universal joint task, producing, after considerable work, a compact joint capable of carrying the torque at a 42° shaft angle. This would enable the 137½-inch wheelbase Cord to have a turning radius of 21.5 feet, considerably better than that of a modern, rear-drive 122-inch wheelbase car.

By August of 1928, the design team had left Indianapolis for the larger facilities of the Auburn plant, and as chassis and drive train design progressed — Van Ranst was told to use as many Miller-patented features and available standard parts as possible — thoughts turned to body styling. Al Leamy was Auburn's chief of body design, and initially his ideas were greeted with feverish indifference. One Saturday between holes at the Auburn Country Club Cord approached another Auburn engineer, John Oswald. What Cord wanted was a racy-looking car, perhaps by using "tablespoon" fenders, perhaps by inducing Van Ranst to drop the chassis frame to sixteen inches above road level so the car would be the lowest on the road, perhaps by following the body moldings of a Hibbard & Darrin car shown at the last New York salon. He wasn't sure, but he directed Oswald to a blackboard and told him to come up with something. Oswald did, Cord liked it —

nd that was that. It was early October, 1928.

Oswald was a busy man for the next two months — not only was he the designer, but he was draftsman, metal worker, body builder, engineer and foreman for the prototype L-29. There were a few alterations to the original design: A Leamy-designed radiator shell was incorporated, and, because the drive train proved six inches longer than anticipated, there was of necessity a central bulge in the firewall ahead of the front seats.

The first L-29 was a sedan, shown before a group of Auburn personnel at the local town theatre near year's end. Their reaction was enthusiastic. It was back to the drawing boards for a cabriolet model and out onto the test track with the sedan. The latter excursion proved disastrous. One trip around the track — it was a plowed cornfield — and all the doors popped open. All and sundry were convinced something was needed for torsional rigidity, and Auburn's

chief engineer Herb Snow came up with the idea of an X-frame bracing, the first use of an X-frame in the American industry.

Meanwhile work had started on five prototypes for further testing and publicity purposes. The first one was rushed to completion by Cord, who then commandeered the car and a mechanic and drove nonstop, save refueling breaks for car and crew, from Auburn, Indiana, to Phoenix, Arizona. Arriving at the Phoenix airport, Cord immediately hopped a plane to New York where top Auburn executives were enjoying a leisurely sojourn at the automobile show, and astounded everyone with his casual reportage of the 2000-mile trek. The car was driven back to Auburn by the mechanic, encountering along the way just one slight mishap, courtesy of a tottering Dodge driver who apparently cared little that Prohibition was the law of the land. By this time it was January, 1929. The four other prototypes were driven to

California for promotional photography, production of the car and publicity commenced during the summer — and in September the new L-29 Cord was formally presented. "Years have been devoted to its development. Being the leader, we were unhurried" — thus, nudging the truth a bit, did Cord announce the debut of the L-29, a car which "requires no selling to those who can afford it."

The L-29 was priced at $3095 for sedan and brougham versions, $3295 for cabriolet and phaeton. This placed it in league with Chrysler, Packard and Cadillac — and in a market not noted for daring in automotive tastes.

The fact that the L-29 was out of the ordinary became more a source of delight for the automotive press than for prospective buyers. The European press particularly were enthusiastic about the car, representing as it did a vehicle "different in almost every possible way from the general run of American design." *The*

A 1931 standard production model cabriolet.

Autocar found the average transatlantic machine distressingly conventional. But the Cord, well, it was different.

Actually, except for drive train layout and other necessary deviations peculiar to front wheel drive, the L-29 Cord was conventionally put together and certainly not revolutionary. The engine was a 298.6-cubic-inch L-head eight, developing 115 hp at 3300 rpm, similar to the big Auburns of the day. Many historians still believe that the Cord engine was a turned-around Auburn, but noted Cord authority Robert Fabris has proved them substantially wrong. Externally the two looked like identical opposites — if that makes sense — the Cord's Lycoming eight reversed 180 degrees in the chassis with the clutch, flywheel and chain drive facing forward and the vibration damper at the rear. Cord had instructed that as many Auburn parts as possible be used, but internally it just couldn't be done: The head had to be revised to

get a water fitting up front; the crankcase was entirely redesigned to provide a rear engine mount and to affect the unique front attachment to the frame. The oil pan was reshaped to fit the new crankcase. The crank- and camshafts were unalike; the Cord crankshaft now turned counterclockwise, although an extra gear in the crankhandle drive train allowed one to hand crank the car in the normal clockwise direction. Statistically, more than seventy parts in the Cord engine could not be interchanged with their Auburn counterparts, which clearly adds up to an engine all Cord's own.

Driving the L-29 Cord under all ordinary conditions was, according to contemporary reports, much like driving a conventional rear-drive car, except that curves and corners could be taken comfortably at considerably faster speeds. The three-speed transmission was a noisy affair in the indirect gears, but they were necessary only to start from a halt. Noise again became a minor

problem at highway speeds of about 60 mph, but then few cars of the day were noted for excessive silence at speed. The only area in which the front drive was felt undesirable was on steep hills, where, as detractors thought in those days, because of the shift of weight to the rear, coupled with the L-29's engine location behind the front axle, the car lost some traction. In the later 810 and 812 Cords the engine was brought forward — and in the L-29's defense it might be added that the test driver for *The Autocar*, on a 1-in-6 gradient, stopped the L-29 and restarted it several times with ease and only a slight spinning of the front wheels.

It would be difficult to find anyone who has driven an L-29 who was not delighted with the experience. The European press accorded it almost sports car characteristics — and since the L-29 had a 137½-inch wheelbase and 4710 weighty pounds, that's saying quite a bit.

All this should not be taken to mean that the

-29 was a hot performer. It was not. Rather it had a pleasant tepidity — as if it didn't really care about such ephemerae as acceleration curves and standing quarter miles. The top speed recorded for the car was only 76.92 mph. Traveling from 0 to 50 took about 26 seconds, which meant that if you chanced to see an L-29 at a stoplight, you'd have ample time for a nice long look before it got away. And the car most certainly deserved that.

It was in the area of body style that the L-29 shone most brilliantly. What a beautiful car it was, long, low and sleek, standing just sixty-four inches high — the industry average was seventy-two — and stretching nearly 200 inches, nearly half of that hood, with broad sweeping front fenders and a sharply-veed grille. It was a big car, every line of it exuding power with grace. And because of its flat frame rails and low silhouette height, the L-29 proved particularly attractive to the talents of master coachbuilders, among those known to have applied coachwork to it being Murphy, Weymann, Rollston, Freestone and Webb, Fuller, Proux and, of course, Cord's own Union City Body Company under its more fashionable coachbuilding name of Legrand.

Alexis de Sakhnoffsky, too, created a memorable one. The Russian-born designer had been in the United States about a year, in the employ of the Hayes Body Company — and he saw the L-29 as his *modus operandi* for winning a fifth straight Grand Prix de Monaco. He was right. The mountain-mist blue coupé he fashioned took the Concours by storm, and its winning of the prestigious Grand Prix was the first for an entirely custom-built American entry. A week later the car captured the Grand Prix d'Honneur at the Beaulieu Concours.

Probably the most dashing of all bodies designed for the L-29 was Phil Wright's speedster. That it was ever built was the result of a fortuitous, albeit at the time unfortunate, set of circumstances. Wright was a free-lance designer for Murphy in Los Angeles when he conceived the L-29 speedster idea, but Murphy's general manager, Frank Spring, was conservative in persuasion and pooh-poohed the suggestion. Soon after, in 1930, Wright packed his portfolio and a few other things, left Murphy, and drove off for the hopefully more receptive design pastures of Detroit, stopping off at Chicago en route. His car was stolen there, and being but twenty-three years old, of modest means and free spirit, he decided to scout out a job. He stopped first at the Cord sales agency on Michigan Boulevard, showed his speedster design to the floor salesman, and by early afternoon was in the offices of Roy Faulkner, who was then presiding over E. L. Cord's corporate affairs. So enthused was Faulkner with the speedster that he wanted one ready for the next auto show and hired Wright to supervise its building. The car was the hit of the show and was subsequently purchased by Paul Bern, a director remembered most notably for his short and tragic marriage to film star Jean Harlow.

CORD L-29 SPECIFICATIONS

ENGINE — *Eight cylinders in line. Bore and stroke: 1929-31 FD, 3¼ x 4½ (82.5 x 114.2 mm), 298.6 cu. in. (4934 cc); 1932 FF, 3⅜ x 4½ (85.6 x 114.2 mm), 321.9 cu. in. (5270 cc). Side valve with detachable head. 2 valves per cylinder. Standard compression ratio: 5.25:1, optional 6.5. Aluminum pistons. Separate block and crankcase. 5 bearing crankshaft with vibration damper.*

Engine, transmission and differential in unit and rigidly mounted in frame. Ignition: Delco Remy six-volt, positive ground. Carburetion: Updraft twin-throat Schebler, 1½" dia. per throat. Mechanical fuel pump 20 (U.S.) gallon tank at rear.

TRANSMISSION

Clutch: Single dry plate by Long. 11" diameter. Gearbox: Sliding pinion, three speeds and reverse. Ratios: 3.11, 1.69 and 1.00:1. Final drive: Hypoid spiral bevel. Ratios: 4.18, 4.42, 4.82:1.

CHASSIS — *Frame: Channel section steel 7" deep x 3" flange x 7/32" thickness, with four cross members and X-member.*
Wheelbase: 11'1½".
Track: 58" front, 60" rear.
Suspension: Dual quarter elliptics in front, half elliptics in rear. Houdaille-Hershey shock absorbers.

The car's whereabouts today remains a mystery.

Whether special bodied or factory built, the L-29 Cord was a thing of beauty. And conceivably it should have had a better than average chance for survival. True, there were mechanical teething problems, but these could have been solved; dealers of conventionally driven cars did start a whisper campaign of some proportion regarding the risks of front wheel drive in climbing slippery hills, but that could have been gradually countered by word of mouth from satisfied owners — and there is little to indicate that L-29 owners were anything but satisfied. True, the price was rather high, but in the Twenties cost was generally no deterrent to success, provided the product was appealing enough — and that the L-29 assuredly was. But less than three months after the Cord was introduced, the Wall Street straw broke the country's back, and the L-29, like just about everything else of value, limped into the Thirties. In 1931 the L-29's prices were dropped to the $2395-$2595 range, but that helped little. Thinking that perhaps more power would, Cord had the engine bored out in 1932 from 3¼ to 3⅜ inches, raising output to 125 hp at 3600 rpm. But that didn't help either. Later that year, after little more than two years in production, the L-29 quietly bowed out of the automotive scene. According to engine serial numbers, a few over fifty-three hundred cars had been built.

The L-29 Cord was neither ruefully mourned then, nor would it be well remembered later. The tenor of the times was responsible for the former, and, of course, the fantastic 810 and 812 for the latter. Without the L-29, there no doubt would have been no 810 or 812. There's some glory in that. But not enough — certainly not enough for as fine a car as the L-29. It can stand on its own four wheels — a car worthy of being revered and remembered for simply being, beautifully, itself.

M.G. TC

A Sports Car Institution

The less fortunate of you ought to be warned that if you never owned a TC, or never even wanted one, you'll probably wonder what all this fuss is about. But if you were one of those lucky ones who were first seduced by this irresistible and utterly irreplaceable little siren, this may stir your memory.

The M.G. TC is responsible for several thousand fellows like you being whatever you are today. (It is also responsible for your not being a lot of things too.) The reason is that, back around 1948 or so, you chanced to see a new TC sitting in some dealer's lot. You went over and looked at it with the same easy familiarity you might give a visitor from Alpha Centauri, and then . . . you sat in it.

Had you listened carefully at that moment you might have heard the scuffle as your innocent guardian angel was summarily elbowed aside by a demented pixie who took control of your destiny and with whom each of you still commune in the darkness of your room.

You had become a car nut.

It took varying amounts of time, work, begging, borrowing, etc. for some of you to achieve your prize, but you eventually did, and in most cases the consummation was far sweeter than the ultimate possession of a more conventional young man's target. For you and the car were about to Learn About Life together.

One of the first things you noticed after you had driven your M.G. home was that it didn't *sound* like all those other TC's around. A brief phone call to the fellow down the street, whom you had bitterly envied until that afternoon, determined the cure. By the time the necessary tools were assembled it was dark, but you rigged some makeshift lights as best you could, jacked the car up, unbuttoned the exhaust system, and got to hooking out the wads of spun glass from the muffler with a bent coathanger and sawing off the long, perforated cone that went through its middle. It took only half an hour or so to transform your pristine Midget Two-Seater, as Lord Nuffield's torpid flacks insisted it b

alled, into a roaring, fire-breathing, asphalt-shredding TC M.G. Well, that's how it seemed . . Then you drove the car all night.

Nearly every town eventually had a small group of TC owners who would gather of an evening at the local bug house, or maybe at a drive-in. In the past you had seen them and hated them frequently, but now you were welcomed as though you had been with them for years, and one supposes, in spirit, you had.

By today's standards most TC pushers were uncommonly fussy about their cars, and you might remember how woe would instantly betide anyone who drove up with a dirty one, or even a dirty engine. His brethren would offer to donate a few coins each so he could go and get himself steam cleaned or something, until he couldn't take it any longer and would sulk off to the nearest u-serve car wash. Then the rest of you

would usually pitch in and help. When one of the crowd was laid up the others would dutifully visit with the sick, and then you'd try to steal his girl friend.

Once in a while you'd get involved in a miniature midnight Grand Prix along one of the six lane boulevards that headed toward town. A "grid" of maybe six or eight cars would form up, someone would give the signal and the air would be rich with burning clutches and crunching gears. The thing would last until traffic was encountered — or the fuzz. Nobody was ever really hurt during this foolishness. The public didn't seem to mind much, probably assuming that, like the Mafia, you were only trying to kill each other and didn't constitute much of a threat to anyone else. The police had a vastly different attitude.

Some of you got brave and took your TC's

racing with a vengeance later on, only to discover that the real thing resulted in about a fifty percent increase in thrills for about a thousand percent increase in cost. There's a moral there somewhere.

Owning a TC automatically made one a nature lover. You had to be, because whatever it was doing outside — raining, freezing, scorching or sandstorming — it was also doing it inside. Pretty soon, after an early period during which you would fitfully struggle with the sidescreens and top, you would finally pack both away, fold down the windshield, lie back and enjoy it. This way you also found out pretty fast if she really loved you.

No car built before or since has been as utterly indestructible as the TC. Strong words? Consider, for instance, the indignities that were imposed upon that spindly little three-bearing

crank. As long as you ensured that a modicum of oil was getting to it there was apparently no limit to what it could stand. Even "Stage Three" — which could mean, among other things, a twelve-to-one compression ratio, pure methanol for fuel and as much as 105 hp at 7000 rpm. Not bad for 1250 cc's that normally generated around 54 hp at 5200.

The TC's brakes, Lockheed hydraulic, were extraordinarily good, particularly in view of the incredibly narrow 4.50x19 tires. The car had its flaws too, but nothing really to be concerned about — except for that maddening curiosity that lurked down at the end of the steering column. The service manual called it the steering

box. You called it lots of other things too.

Everyone had his own pet names for it; some of the printable ones were "Enever's Folly" and "Pandora." Comes the problem. After your car had travelled some six to eight thousand miles a little slack would begin to appear in the steering. Right on the ball, those visionary engineers at Abingdon had prepared you for such a contingency. All you had to do was undo three bolts retaining the cover plate and lift it right off. It doesn't matter what was inside. Around the edge of the box you would find that there were stacked lots of thin brass shims. All you needed to do was peel one off (of the right thickness) and then put the cover plate back on. Then you'd

find that not only was the slack gone but you couldn't turn the steering wheel. So you took the cover plate off, replaced the shim and took off a thinner one. Then you had slack in your steering again, so you . . . after a while you got used to the slack.

Then Abingdon introduced the TD. It looked awful in the photographs, but when the first batch arrived from across the pond it looked even worse. The TC's perfect proportions were gone, replaced by an expedient, easy-to-build blandness that had all the character of an enormous toy. Some of you ended up buying TD's, and for a while the rest of them gave you a bad time about its disc wheels and Erector Set lines, but in their hearts they knew Abingdon had been right — it really was a better car.

So the TC became merely another outdated sports car, its market value eventually sank to something below zero and no one seemed to care anymore — until some twenty years later. Now people everywhere are digging up TC's, lavishing unconscionable amounts of money on them, adding them to collections, or flogging them, unrestored, for more than they cost when new — a situation that can bring to even the most dour and forbidding countenance the faintest trace of a smile.

Care to regain your youth . . . for about $1250?

THE UBIQUITOUS
CHEVROLET

The 1913 Classic Six Series C touring.

Named after a Swiss-born mechanic to whom it brought little financial gain, it grew to become the foundation of the industry's mightiest empire.

For more people today than any other car, Chevrolet equals success. Chevrolet Motor Division is at its historic corporate peak right now, this minute. And all indications point to the situation continuing indefinitely.

Chevrolet's current range of cars spans the entire gamut of the marketplace; they are handsome, appealing, and in some cases exciting, but most of all — perhaps proof positive of the Division's standing — they are the most diverse in its history.

Yet history has many glories for Chevrolet. Today's challenging automobile industry demands the best from a producer, and to say the least, Chevrolet's record on this count has been a good one.

The automobile business is incredibly, impossibly demanding. It gathers miles of computer tape etched with market facts to guide its decisions, then makes them on the basis of the gut-hunches that pay off in success for the more talented men in the industry. The tapestry that is Chevrolet's history is knotted with hundreds of thousands of these decisions, each one marking the beginning of a new thread in the company's affairs. Some companies have watched helplessly as the threads ran out, short of the goals they'd set. But Chevrolet has chosen well, fantastically well. The essence of their story is found in the record of the key decisions down through the years that made a car, and a company, so great.

Decision Number One was that of William Crapo Durant to hire Louis Chevrolet. Neither of these men shaped the important later fate of the Chevrolet car, but both were indispensable to its creation. Durant was the older of the two, born in Boston in 1861, while Louis Chevrolet's birth was in Switzerland in 1878. At thirty years of age Chevrolet was recognized as a talented mechanic and an outstanding racing driver in 1908 when he and his brother Arthur were hired into Buick by Durant, then busy assembling the elements of General Motors.

At first the Chevrolets served Durant and his enterprises as chauffeurs and as racing drivers for the successful Buick team. But in 1910 Durant lost control of Buick and of General Motors. Durant's incomparable promotional genius was not frustrated for long by this massive setback. He put several schemes in motion. In October of 1910 Louis Chevrolet retired from racing and set to work in a small garage on Detroit's Grand River Avenue to create a new automobile bearing his name. Durant backed him, relying on his mechanical ability and on the name "Chevrolet," which was eminently famous.

To help him Louis invited Etienne Planche to come west from New York. Chevrolet and Planche had probably met when the two were working for the Walter Motor Company in New York. Planche was free in late 1909 after plans fell through to build the Roebling-Planche car he had designed, a machine that was a predecessor of the Mercer. Working together they prepared designs for four-cylinder and six-cylinder engines. Durant okayed their proceeding with the latter.

On May 30th, 1911, a press release uncovered the joint project: "W. C. Durant of the General Motors company and racer Louis Chevrolet, one of the speed wonders of the day and a co-worker with Mr. Durant in the manufacture of exploitation of fast cars, will establish a factory in Detroit for the manufacture of a new high-priced car whose chief distinctive feature will be an engine perfected during the last winter by Chevrolet assisted financially by Durant." The story went on to refer to the forthcoming new car as a "Durant-Chevrolet."

For Durant, 1911 was another year for decisions. He followed through on his Chevrolet commitment on November 3rd when he organized the Chevrolet Motor Company of Michigan, with Louis Chevrolet, William H. Little and Edwin R. Campbell as incorporators. By that time Chevrolet and Planche had completed their first prototype cars, and a large, open garage was rented on West Grand Boulevard to begin assembly of the 1912 Chevrolet Classic 6, or Type C, from purchased parts.

At $2150, this first Chevrolet was indeed a high-priced car for its day. In fact not until 1955 was Chevrolet destined to make so expensive a passenger car (excluding the Corvette) again. Its engine was a T-head six with twin camshafts alongside two blocks of three cylin-

The 1916 Baby Grand Series H-4 touring.

ders. Dimensions were 3 9/16 by 5 inches, for 299 cubic inches. With a cone clutch, three-speed box and leaf springs, the chassis was conventional, on a 120-inch wheelbase. The car was big and handsome for the day, with a distinctive vee-fronted and vee-topped radiator. And, the records show, the small shop managed to build and sell 2999 of these cars in 1912.

Durant, adding to his empire, bought the Flint Wagon Works in late 1911, and installed William H. Little, former Buick manager, in charge. Little's obligation was to build and sell a lot of wagons as well as cars. As Durant explained his plan to a potential investor, "The company [Little] has obtained a contract and license from the Chevrolet Motor Company . . . which enables it to manufacture an attractive line of motorcars without experimental or engineering expense (the heaviest expense items

connected with the motorcar business) and by reason of this arrangement will be able to turn out a finished product in ample time for the 1912 trade."

Achieving this became the responsibility of A.B.C. Hardy, who succeeded Little as head of Little in early 1912. Hardy took a small motor, had it revamped and improved and put it into a small roadster for sale at $650, which was somewhere near Ford's latest price. The Little was underpowered but had good lines, and Hardy sold 3500 during his first year.

The efficiency of production in Flint under Hardy convinced Durant to make another key decision in Chevrolet history: to give up the idea of a big Ford-type plant in Detroit and instead to base Chevrolet manufacture in Flint, with assembly operations around the country. For 1913 the price of the Detroit-built Chevrolet

Classic 6 was upped to $2500 to improve th[e] profit picture, and production was maintained fo[r] some months, but then in August of 1913 th[e] move was made to Flint, initially to a form[er] Imperial Wheel Company building, with A.B.C. Hardy in charge of both Little and Chevrol[et] production.

Louis Chevrolet, who foresaw with dislike t[he] merging of Little and Chevrolet products, le[ft] the Durant empire in 1913 to pursue his ow[n] racing and high performance projects. Eviden[ce] suggests that this was entirely as he wanted i[t.] As described by a later associate, "Chevrolet w[as] one of the most highly competitive individua[ls] ever connected with auto racing — a terrif[ic] fighter, with great drive. He had natura[l] mechanical ability, with no technical trainin[g.] Although he was a fairly good promoter, he w[as] not a good businessman."

Businessmen created the 1914 Little-Chevrolet line of cars. In the $1300-$1500 price class there were closely related L-head sixes, the Little Six and the Chevrolet Type L, 220 and 271 cubic inches respectively. Chevrolet was still the more costly line of the two and became the dominant one as production of Littles was phased out during 1915. The Little roadster left its mark on the design of the appealing Chevrolet Royal Mail, a roadster body style on the new Model H chassis with a new overhead valve four-cylinder engine late 1913.

This four was destined to be the first of three basic engines, each outstanding in its way, that have powered Chevrolets to marketing success. was close to square in its dimensions, at 3 /16 by 4 inches, for a 170.9-cubic-inch displacement. There were 1.5-inch valves, a ated rocker cover, a three-bearing crankshaft

and cylinders cast integrally with the crankcase. In 1918 a stroke one and a quarter inches longer was added, bringing displacement to 224.3 cubic inches for FA and later FB series Chevrolets. The last such big four, in 1922, had a new cylinder head with three exhaust ports instead of the usual single outlet. That year also marked the last production of the famous Royal Mail roadsters and Baby Grand touring cars, models which had been priced in the $800-$1200 range.

Nineteen-fifteen was a year of bold decisions by Durant. In September he organized the Chevrolet Motor Company of Delaware. Through the promotion of this new entity he developed a market for an exchange of its promising shares for those of General Motors, which since 1910 had not been paying dividends to its stockholders, and in this way Durant once again gained a controlling interest in GM — through

Chevrolet. The latter was finally merged into GM on May 2nd, 1918. Chevrolet did control General Motors then and to a certain extent does so today, accounting consistently for more than half of the huge firm's output. The modern-day anti-agglomerationists want to see the act of 1915 nullified, and while it is very easy to imagine Chevrolet existing without General Motors, the survival of GM without its mass-volume basis is by no means assured.

Durant's other bold move during 1915 was the preparation of the first Chevrolet designed to meet the Model T head-on, the 490, named appropriately for its price. That had been the price of the "T," but Ford replied by dropping the latter to $440 for 1916. And so it was to go through the Chevrolet 490 era, through 1922, Ford always holding an advantage in both vehicle quality and cost.

Displacement of the Model H four-cylinder engine was maintained, though simplifications in bottom-end design and equipment occurred. The 1890-pound 490 was suspended by quarter-elliptic springs on a 102-inch wheelbase. Among its distinctive characteristics (until 1922) was a bevel gear rear axle which emitted a loud grinding noise euphemistically referred to as "the Chevrolet hum." It probably harmonized well with the chatter of the exposed rocker gear!

While Chevrolet were now active in the battle against Ford, they were also building cars in the $1100-$1400 price bracket, directly competing with GM's Oakland and Oldsmobile. One of the most interesting of these was the Type D V-8 introduced in January, 1917, atop the first great wave of V-8 enthusiasm. The pushrod, overhead-valve engine had three main bearings, and measured 3⅜ by 4 inches for 286.3 cid. The D-Type Chevrolet had handsome touring and

roadster bodies on the 120-inch wheelbase of a 3200 pound car.

During the 1915 battle for GM control Durant moved his base of operations, the Chevrolet headquarters, to New York City. Then he made purchases around the country to enable Chevrolet to assemble the popular 490 at many points in North America. Thus 490's were produced at Flint, St. Louis, Tarrytown (New York), Oshawa (Canada), Oakland (California) and Fort Worth (Texas). Factory sales leaped to 70,701 in 1916, then to 125,882 in 1917. They dropped, then bounced back to 150,226 in 1920, accounting for a healthy share of General Motors' North American sales of 393,075 vehicles.

As president of General Motors Durant had expanded the firm's operations spectacularly between 1915 and 1920. His personal fortunes were heavily overcommitted to the support of GM shares on Wall Street, and when business

slackened in September of 1920 Durant and GM were in major trouble. Both would be rescued from ruin though Durant had to retire from the presidency on November 30th, 1920, being succeeded by Pierre S. du Pont, whose family fortune had been keeping the GM ship afloat.

At this time Alfred P. Sloan, Jr., became, as he has written, "a sort of executive vice-president in charge of all operations, reporting to Mr. du Pont," who in the interim had also made himself general manager of Chevrolet. In a survey of GM's prospects by a staff of talented engineers, Mr. du Pont was advised to liquidate the entire Chevrolet operation, since there was "no chance that it could be made a profitable business." Sloan went to du Pont and told him what he thought Chevrolet might accomplish if they built a good product and sold it aggressively. The general manager "listened most patiently, and finally said, 'Forget the report. We will go ahead

Left: The 1921 touring model of the 490, the car designed to challenge the Model T Ford. Above: The Superior utility coach of 1923, featuring copper cooling. Below: The 1925 Superior Series K touring.

Below: The 1928 National Series AB touring. "Bigger and Better" was Chevrolet's advertising slogan that year. Wheelbase was increased four inches to 107, the hood was longer, the radiator taller. The "better" half was the addition of four-wheel brakes and some refinements to the four-cylinder engine. A look under the hood would have confirmed that a six could have fit there nicely, but Chevrolet was to keep the new engine under wraps until Ford announced their new four-cylinder Model A. The six-cylinder Chevrolet was introduced in late December of 1928. Left: The 1930 Universal Series AD roadster. A companion car to this one was the sport roadster, the first model in which Chevrolet provided a rumble seat. Right: The 1932 Confederate Series BA special sedan. Design changes this year included the substitution of an interior sun visor for the previous exterior type. Four small side doors also appeared, in place of the previous hood louvers.

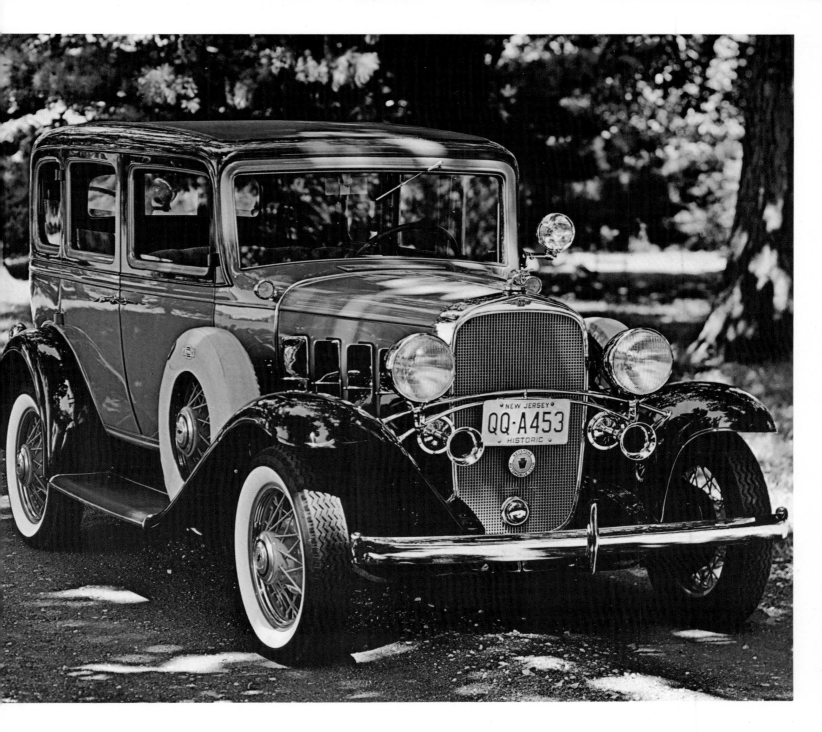

and see what we can do.' So Chevrolet was saved and General Motors avoided what would have been a catastrophe."

In 1921 Chevrolet's headquarters were returned to Detroit, where du Pont and Sloan set up an advisory committee on GM's future car alignment. In what was permanently to influence the future, this committee suggested that Chevrolet remain GM's lowest-priced car and that it concentrate on that market. It was audacious to consider then that Chevrolet, a money-losing operation to the tune of $5 million, would present a serious challenge to Ford, holding sixty percent of the vehicle market against Chevrolet's mere four percent. But, as Sloan recalled, "We did not propose to compete head on, but to produce a car that would be superior to the Ford, yet so near the Ford price that demand would be drawn from the Ford grade and lifted to the slightly higher price in preference to Ford's utility design." With complete candor

Chevrolet put this policy to work in 1923 with a new version of the 490 called, literally, the "Superior." Since October of 1921 Chevrolet had a very capable new engineer, Ormond E. Hunt, and from March of 1922 an equally competent chief executive, William S. Knudsen. The combination of this talent with the new Superior had its effect, as Chevrolet sales for 1923 zoomed to 480,737 units.

Through 1928 Chevrolet continued to rely on the 170.9-cubic-inch four for power. A new body and chassis were rushed through for 1925, appearing very late, just at the turn of the year. This Series K Chevrolet was much improved, with a disc clutch, semi-elliptic springs and the much improved rear axle developed for the air cooled cars.

Meanwhile Henry M. Crane, a consultant to Alfred P. Sloan, developed a light L-head six-cylinder engine. It became the job of Chevrolet's engineering department to build a low-priced

car around it, which in turn went into production at the Oakland Division in 1926 as the Pontiac. This gave O. E. Hunt and his team valuable experiences with sixes which they began to apply to an all-new powerplant for Chevrolet in 1925.

Chevy's new six had to continue to uphold the company's established slogan, "Valves in head, ahead in value." Hunt chose the same 3¾-inch stroke as the Pontiac but used a larger bore, 3 5/16 inches instead of 3¼ inches. He kept weight and cost down with the unusual one-piece sheet metal cover for the pushrod side of the block and cylinder head. Three main bearings were supplied with oil by gravity, the rod bearings being oiled by splash. At its unveiling, at the end of December, 1928, the six developed 46 bhp at 2600 rpm. It would give rise to two nicknames: the "Cast Iron Wonder," because of the use of cast iron pistons destined to be a feature of all six-cylinder Chevrolets for a

Above: The 1929 International Series AC coach. This was the first model year of the Chevrolet six-cylinder engine, which would become affectionately known as the "Cast Iron Wonder." Left: The 1931 Independence Series AE convertible cabriolet. Styling for this model year was completely new, with chromed headlamps, the tie bar between them now chromed, too, and curved as well—replacing the previous straight, black enamel tie-bar design. Wheelbase had been increased to 109 inches, and three additional deluxe body styles had been added, including the convertible cabriolet. Right: The 1933 Master Series CA sport roadster. Wheelbase was further increased this year—to 110 inches. Styling changes included a vee-shaped radiator grille, the shell of which was painted to match the body, with a thin chrome molding around the grille itself.

quarter of a century, and the "Stove Bolt Six," because of its use of ¼"-20 slotted head bolts or "stove bolts" as they came to be called. Neither appellation was particularly appreciated by Chevrolet at the time. But antiquity has a way of adding charm to a nickname — and the "Cast Iron Wonder," particularly today, has the same nostalgic appeal as the "Tin Lizzie."

The 1928 Chevrolet National had already been rated to accept the six, but the new engine was quietly held in reserve for introduction only after Mr. Ford had announced his new four-cylinder Model A. When Ford shut down in May of 1927 for retooling, Chevy bounded into first place, and while Dearborn took the lead again in 1929 and 1930, Chevy bounced back in the tough 1931 year. With the exceptions of 1935, 1957 and 1959, Chevrolet has been Number One in the auto industry ever since.

Following the all-important move to the six, another pivotal decision in Chevrolet history was that of Knudsen and Hunt to engage GM's brand new Art and Colour Section to help style the longer 1928 model. This was the first task of Harley Earl's new group outside its initial work for Cadillac and La Salle. In 1929 a choice of colors became available on the new Chevy International six. Earl and his men made radical changes for the 1933 Chevrolet, introducing the A-body concept for the first time. That year marked the first alignment of the Master and Standard lines, the latter being a shorter, lighter version with, in '33 and '34, a shorter-stroke engine. At $445 this Depression-era Standard was the lowest-priced Chevrolet ever.

Before he handed the division over to Marvin E. Coyle in October, 1933, Bill Knudsen made another key decision — giving the Chevrolet independent front suspension, and "knee action" duly made its debut on the 1934 Chevrolet, in the form of the system developed in France by André Dubonnet. A selective regression took place in 1935 with the reintroduction of a model with solid front axle, the "Master without knees." Such an alternate was available right up through 1940. In '39 a conventional coil and wishbone front suspension had replaced the Dubonnet arrangement, and only the most markedly obstinate conservatives chose the cart-sprung option.

Nineteen-thirty-five marked the end of a Chevrolet tradition: the open four-door touring car. In that year only 1160 phaetons left the lines. But 1935 also marked a new era in dealer relations. William E. Holler, who had become sales manager in 1933, developed the Quality Dealer Program, extending policies initiated by Richard H. Grant during the previous decade. Through this program Chevrolet strongly supported its dealers, instead of weakening their position through factory-owned dealerships as other automakers often did. Chevrolet, as Grant and Holler knew, would only be as strong as its dealers. To this day Chevy maintains an almost reverent attitude toward the sovereignty of its more than 6000 agencies.

Like all GM cars Chevrolets metamorphosed rapidly in shape during the Thirties. An extensive redesign was carried out in 1937, when a single 112¼-inch wheelbase chassis was standardized in place of the previous differentiation between Master and Standard models. By 1937, the "Cast Iron Wonder," now officially called the "Blue Flame" six, had undergone substantial re-engineering, and had nearly square proportions, 3½ by 3¾ inches, for 216.5 cid and 85 bhp at 3200 rpm. It had four main bearings instead of three, improved oil and water pumps, as well as a shorter overall length in spite of the enlarged bore.

One of these engines in a 1939 Master 85 coupé played an important role in Chevrolet history. It was in that year that a twenty-eight-year-old driver raced for the first time a Chevrolet, a used car his friends had bought him when they couldn't find the Ford he really wanted. He didn't win with it, but Juan Mañuel Fangio did well enough to gain some help from General Motors of Argentina, and for 1940 he had a fully-prepared '39 solid-axled coupé, with which he won the incredible 5900-mile Buenos Aires-Lima road race at an average of 53.6 mph over some of the worst roads in the world. In the next two years Fangio won four major races in a row with his coupé, and he continued to race it after the war, collecting three more overall wins with it. In his last race with a Chevrolet, the Grand Prix of the Republic on November 11th, 1949, Fangio found his opponents had stolen a march on him in engine power, but he still placed second behind his rival Juan Galvez. Then he sold the most famous Chevrolet in all of South America.

Record sales were attained in 1941, when 1,339,952 cars and trucks were marketed by Chevrolet. But war requirements were already intruding, and Chevrolet halted production late that year. It was not until October 3rd, 1945, that the next Chevrolet passenger car was assembled, at the plant in Kansas City, Missouri.

Maurice Olley and a team of designers had readied a new smaller Chevy, the Cadet, for possible postwar production. In fact several millions of dollars were spent on tooling at the Cleveland plant before it became evident that no radically new models would be needed to satisfy the postwar demand. This time there was no repetition of the post-Armistice slump that GM executives still vividly recalled from the First World War. Instead it was decided in 1946 to plan the next major model change for 1949.

As part of an overall GM changeover the '49 Chevrolet had flush front fenders, a curved windshield and lower hood for vastly improved vision. The car was 2½ inches lower on a new front suspension and its wheelbase had been shortened by one inch to 115 inches. It was a good-looking, clean car, especially in the Fleetline fastback version. Tom McCahill noted that the '49 was "by far the best handling car in its class," perhaps going off the deep end a wee bit when he wrote that it "held tough curves like an English M.G. and that's tops." He cited only one limitation, attributable to the engine's continued use of splash lubrication and cast iron pistons: "The Chevy doesn't stand up well under excessive, high-speed driving." But then again, perhaps he'd never heard of Fangio.

In 1949 Chevrolet set another all-time sales record at 1.5 million units, and GM decided to make the 1950 Chevrolet the first car in its class with a fully automatic transmission with the Powerglide torque converter box. That led to another record: 2.1 million cars and trucks, some 300,000 of them with Powerglide. These came with a larger 235-cubic-inch engine. Tom McCahill found it, "thanks to its extra power, considerably faster in pickup than any former Chevrolet."

Nineteen-fifty-two brought two changes at Chevrolet: five teeth on the center bar of the grille and the appointment in May of Edward N. Cole to the post of chief engineer. For '53 the Powerglide engine was given aluminum pistons — farewell to the Cast Iron Wonder — and modern oiling system, and power steering became an option. These were practical but unexciting cars; thanks to Wayne Horning special cylinder heads were available that could make the Chevy six into a short-track stormer. A lot of hot-rodders knew how to extract more power from it. But until Ed Cole came along Chevrolet couldn't have cared less.

Cole's arrival, from Cadillac, was another brilliant and pivotal Chevrolet decision. He contributed to the design of the Corvette and made some changes in the new V-8 engine design of his predecessor, E. H. Kelley. Instead of the rocker shafts and split-level combustion chambers the V-8 was to have inherited from the six, Cole brought in wedge-type chambers and the startling stamped steel rocker arms on individual studs. Cole upped displacement of the engine to 265 from 231 cubic inches, but kept it as compact as possible at 516 pounds, thirty-seven pounds less than the six, with 16

Left: The 1935 Master Series EA sport coupé. Below: The 1936 Master Series FA coach. The major styling change between these two model years was the hinging of the doors, at the rear for 1935, then returned to the front the following year.

horsepower in the manual shift version.

The 1955 Chevrolet was a terrific package, and it sold well in the industry's great year of the Fifties, with a new sales peak for Chevy of 1,821,695 cars and well over 2.2 million cars and trucks combined. On September 9th, to underline the new engine's ability, Zora Arkus-Duntov drove a pre-production 1956 Chevrolet to the top of Pikes Peak in 17 minutes 24.05 seconds, beating by two minutes a record set by Ford in 1934.

By mid-1956 Ed Cole had boosted his new engine's output by stages to 225 bhp at 5200 rpm. He had also been boosted to the general managership of Chevrolet. For 1957 he celebrated with the 283-cubic-inch version of the V-8 and the fuel injection that allowed it to produce one horsepower per cubic inch in the Corvette — at the time an amazing achievement.

Along with its GM brethren, Chevrolet went slightly berserk in 1958, buoyed by the optimistic decisions made in the boom year of 1955. The cars were all new with an X-type frame, dramatically bigger and up to five inches longer than the '57 Chevy. In 1955 Chevrolet had abandoned torque tube drive, and now they went all the way with rear axle locating arms and coil springs, plus an optional air suspension system. "Impala," from a 1956 Motorama show car, became a new top-of-the-line designation that was destined for fame. Yet 1958 was Chevy's poorest postwar sales year — "only" 1,543,992 cars and trucks left the factories.

Those who were startled by the '58 Chevy were stunned by the '59, a flamboyant carriage conceived in the frenzy of overtime at Styling that followed the announcement of Virgil Exner's "Forward Look" Chrysler line. Grotesque in retrospect, with its flared rear fenders that led to wild rumors of levitation at speed, the '59 was the swan song of retiring chief stylist Harley Earl. Under his able successor, William Mitchell, some of GM's best designers headed the Chevrolet studio.

A design team led by veteran Ned Nickels did the painstaking exploration that finally led to the immaculate outline of the first Corvair, introduced in October of 1959 — the Division's first car with integral construction and a rear engine. The Corvair sold leisurely compared to Ford's Falcon and work began at once on a "Fisher Falcon," to become the 1962 Chevy II.

Late in 1961 Semon E. "Bunkie" Knudsen became general manager of Chevrolet, following in the footsteps of his late father. He took part in the decision to launch, for 1964, a new range of intermediate-sized GM cars, Chevrolet's being the Chevelle. At first a wishy-washy kind of car, the Chevelle has since gained enormously in gusto and style to become the industry's best selling intermediate.

This was a period of responding, not leading, for Chevrolet. The Chevy II was a response to the Falcon, the Chevelle a parallel development to the earlier Fairlane, the deluxe Caprice a response to the Ford LTD, and the Camaro a

...mpletely new body design was
...duced by Chevrolet on the Special
...xe series of 1940. The radiator
...now stretched from front fender
...nt fender, sealed-beam headlamps
...red for the first time, and
...illamps were set in the body panels.
...red at left is the 1940 Special
...e Series KA coupé. For 1941
...ars had stretched three inches—to a
...nch wheelbase. Concealed safety
...replaced running boards, and the
...was, again, completely new.
...headlamps were now set into the front
...rs, above which appeared a chrome
...ng. The grille was modified only
...gh to render obsolete the previous
...l year design. Pictured above
...1941 Special DeLuxe Series AH coupé.
...ebruary 1, 1942, automobile production
...suspended, and Chevrolet spent
...war years in military manufacture.
...first postwar Chevrolets were
...ally the same as the prewar cars,
...the only noticeable changes being
...design, emblem, nameplate
...bumpers. Pictured at right
...e 1947 Fleetmaster Series EK coupé.

75

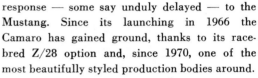

In 1949 Chevrolet introduced their all-new postwar car. Available in two series—the Fleetline and the Styleline—the cars were two and a half inches lower than their predecessors, with lower hoods for increased visibility, as well as flush front fenders and a curved windshield. Pictured at left is the 1949 Styleline DeLuxe Series GK coupé. In 1950 was introduced the Bel Air, the first hard-top coupé in the low-priced field. Pictured below is a Bel Air Series KK from 1952, distinguished by the five teeth on the center of its grille. Grille design had been the major point of departure for Chevrolets from 1949 to 1952. In 1953 the Division brought out their second completely new postwar car, available in three series: the One Fifty, the Two Ten and the Bel Air. Pictured above is a One Fifty sedan from 1954.

response — some say unduly delayed — to the Mustang. Since its launching in 1966 the Camaro has gained ground, thanks to its race-bred Z/28 option and, since 1970, one of the most beautifully styled production bodies around.

After the A.M.A. racing ban in June, 1957, which ended a string of Chevrolet victories on the short stock car tracks, Ed Cole lay low for a while. Then in the early Sixties he decided to put his engineers to work on a new seven-liter V-8. It appeared at Daytona in February, 1963, just after GM management had rapped its divisions' knuckles for being bad boys in racing, and set blisteringly fast qualifying times. This ingenious V-8 went underground for a while, then emerged on 1965½ Chevrolet models with 396 cid.

To the Chevrolet's sales department, the new engine was the "Turbo-Jet 396," but to hot-rodders it was the "porcupine," with its valve stems canted every which way, providing excellent breathing. For 1966, with Pete Estes as its new general manager, Chevrolet expanded it to 427 cubic inches.

In 1965 Chevrolet set a new record with factory sales of 2,585,014 cars and a total of 3,203,958 units. That solid achievement stretched even Chevrolet's mighty production facilities to the limit.

Pete Este's successor, John Z. DeLorean, looks forward, with reason, to new records in years to come. In 1969 he dropped the by-then-moribund Corvair, and later that year he produced the Monte Carlo, which marked Chevrolet's first entrance into the luxury personal car field. In 1971 came Vega, an ambitious re-beginning for the American small car. It is likely that DeLorean and his team have made several more key decisions, and like the other choices which have shaped Chevrolet's dramatic growth over the years, they are probably good ones.

Their average hasn't been too bad.

THE CARABO: BY CARROZZERIA BERTONE

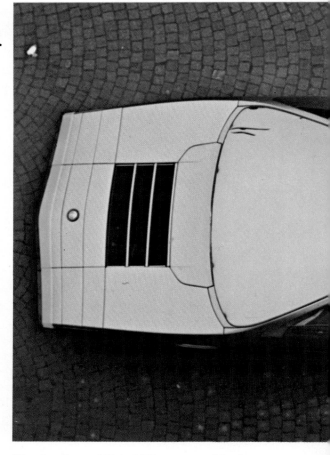

Up until 1968 the word "carabo" to an Italian brought to mind, if anything, the small, green-gold beetle after which the Egyptians fashioned their scarab amulets. The Paris automobile show changed all that. Suddenly Italians who had never heard of Nefertiti knew what a carabo was. It was one of the most exciting automobiles to come along in years, and it was built by a Turinese coachbuilding firm headed by a likeable and talented gentleman by the name of Nuccio Bertone.

Ask Nuccio Bertone a straightforward question — why he builds cars — and his reply is equally direct: He wants to. And his desire is an intense one, or as the Italians say, it is *la passione*. A beautiful automobile, according to Bertone, who has built many, is most often realized by a passionate approach. And that is an approach not casually come by. It is as inherent as heredity; environment is its school. Or as Bertone says, "I just happened to have the right father."

His father, Giovanni Bertone, was born into a large farming family in 1884. He began learning his trade — wood and metal working for horse-drawn carriages — at the age of twelve. In 1907 he left his rural community for the city of Turin, married and went to work. By 1912 he had a shop — actually just a small canopied courtyard — and three employees. Then followed the rather natural transition from horse-drawn to horseless carriages. Those were the pioneering days when the manufacturer built only the mechanical components for the car, the body being fitted by independent coachbuilders on special order from each client. Thus, every car was a problem in itself, and the coachmaker's hands were generally tied to the whim of each individual patron.

Giovanni Bertone wanted to design and build a complete car on his own, and in 1920 he asked S.P.A. of Turin to let him try. It was a rather daring proposal, but S.P.A. agreed — rather reluctantly perhaps, for Giovanni's courtyard "shop" seemed hardly adequate to the task. But it worked.

The chassis, an S.P.A. 9000, was towed by horse every morning from the factory to the shop and back at day's end. It completion brought a steady stream of orders from factory clients — Ceirano, Chiribiri, F.A.S.T., Fiat, S.C.A.T., Itala — into the shop of Giovanni Bertone. He expanded his facilities to twice their original size and his work force to twenty employees. Then followed a close collaboration with Vincenzo Lancia and the Lancia automobile factory and, ultimately, prosperity.

But the prosperous Twenties turned into the Thirties and depression. It was during that time, chroniclers have stated, that Bertone's twenty-year-old son Nuccio left college to sell his father's cars and virtually saved the enterprise. This may be somewhat exaggerated, but there can be no doubt that Nuccio did help in the family business, and even before he reached his teens.

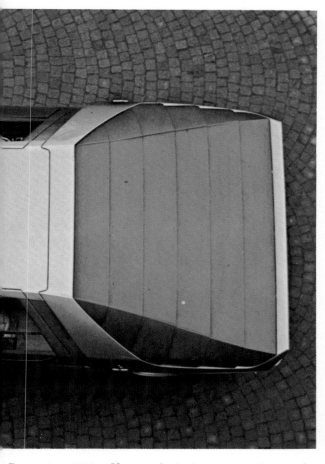

Born in 1914, Nuccio had been reared in the coachbuilder's world; he and Carrozzeria Bertone grew up together. From the first day the lad could guide a pencil, his father had dedicated himself to teaching his son all the tools of an accomplished artisan-artist, from the way iron should be wrought to the right lines for a body panel. And Nuccio learned quickly.

If the father was correct in the first postwar period in his decision to build independently, the son was right in the post-World War II era with his concept of building in series. By 1950 Nuccio had become manager of Carrozzeria Bertone. Those early postwar years were scarcely favorable to the making of long-range plans by Italian coachmakers. The coachbuilding era was finished — or so most people said — the days of customized luxury in automobiles would be relived only in history books. Nuccio Bertone didn't agree. The

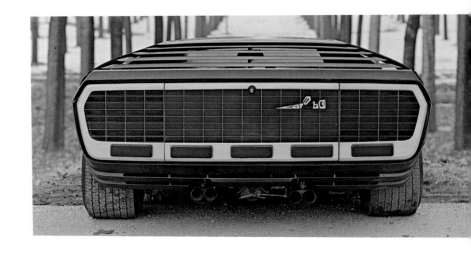

aftermath of war, he believed, could not forever quash the appeal of distinctive and beautiful automobiles. It was a tenuous belief at best in those years, but Bertone stolidly clung to it. With Italian factory chassis persistently difficult to come by, the demise of the Italian coachbuilding business seemed imminent. The only solution appeared to be the courting of new outlets on the international market.

Bertone has said that part of his success is due to being the right man in the right place at the right time. There is truth in this, although Bertone seems somehow to prepare himself for such fortuitous moments. Such was the case at the 1952 Turin show where he exhibited two M.G. chassis with original coupé and cabriolet bodies. It led to a contract with a Mr. S. H. Arnolt from Chicago resulting in nearly five

hundred Bertone bodies on M.G. and Bristol chassis. But the real turning point in the Bertone success story was 1953, when the prototype of the Giulietta Sprint was completed for the Alfa Romeo factory. Some 40,000 copies followed.

In the five years preceding 1960, the work force in Carrozzeria Bertone more than doubled and unit production increased more than six times. By 1961, 800 workers were producing better than 10,000 units annually. Although relocation of the factory in 1958 had provided for three times more working space, by 1963 Carrozzeria Bertone had outgrown even this, and a new factory was needed.

Thus, today Carrozzeria Bertone reaps the benefits of having conceived of mass producing specials before many other coachbuilders and of having prepared itself accordingly. (It is an advantage they share with Pininfarina.) The firm is supported, of course, by these series productions.

But more exciting surely — to any coachbuilder — must be the idea cars, those one-off models built to test new ideas, new design approaches, where the stylist's imagination is not fettered by production limitations or cost. Carrozzeria Bertone has built some memorable cars in this line. Such experimental assignments as the BAT series for Alfa Romeo and the Corvair Testudo exemplified his daring with ultra streamlining. And the one-off Alfa Romeo Canguro gave testimony to his delight in finding use for new materials. In the Canguro he used a cement common to the aeronautical

industry to attach the glass panels to the metal frames, thus giving a durable bond while at the same time avoiding the bulky rubber molding usually employed in the automobile industry. The secret, according to Bertone, is to know how to use the materials industry has prepared, regardless of whether they were originally made for use on motorcars. "Nobody forbids it," he says.

Although design exercises like these are not intended for production, their value should not be viewed as merely ephemeral. Good ideas have a way of coming back. Thus many of the ideas incorporated in Bertone's Testudo idea car later found their way into his design of the production Fiat 850 Spyder. This is most encouraging, particularly when one reflects upon Carrozzeria Bertone's more recent design exercise, the Carabo.

Bertone's approach to the design of the Carabo was for a car best suited to the high-speed superhighways of Europe. He succeeded brilliantly. The car represents a fine amalgam

between interior space and comfort, between aerodynamics and aesthetics.

Based on the Alfa Romeo P 33 Strada chassis, with Alfa's 1995 cc 230 hp V-8 engine, it is capable of an effortless 160 miles an hour. Its frame is unique, being of H shape, made of fabricated round members some twelve inches in diameter, which are joined forward and aft by light alloy castings to carry the suspension, the engine and transmission assembly. Inside the frame there is a rubber bag for the fuel. Suspension is of the standard racing type, all independent with transverse arms and reaction members, coil springs and telescopic shock absorbers. Steering is by rack and pinion.

The Carabo was developed rather rapidly in Bertone's experimental and styling studio. Indeed it was constructed and completed in just ten weeks from the day the Alfa chassis was received from the factory. And then Nuccio Bertone stood back and looked at it.

Bertone's definition of an automobile is interesting. To

him, an automobile is a sensation, "or better still a group of sensations, the first one being the shape, the surprise of the shape. This is a feeling I have, this surprise: If a new car fails to surprise me, then I am sure it will not go well."

Assuredly, the Carabo must have been a pleasant surprise to him. It certainly was to spectators at all the automobile shows it visited in 1968 and 1969. Barely forty inches high, it was a breathtakingly striking sight, with not a misplaced line anywhere. From the tip of its nose to the top of the windscreen, the line is taut — almost darting — smoothly, yet powerfully, making its way to the finned rear quarter. It looks fast, just standing still.

Good ideas abound in the Carabo. Particularly noteworthy was Bertone's use of a new type of glass manufactured in Belgium by Glaverbel. Called VHR (*verre à haute résistance*), it is comparatively thin and therefore light, possessing a high resistance to impact and great flexibility. Apart from this practical value, VHR adds immeasurably to the overall sculptured feel of the car, revealing its lines in a full unbroken manner impossible with conventional glazing. In addition, VHR's thermo-reflective properties insure a much more comfortable interior. Moreover, this type of glass changes color from green to gold in response to changes in exterior light, thus protecting passengers from excessive

glare. Visibility into the car from outside is reduced measurably. From inside, however, visibility is simply fantastic—indeed, it could not be better.

Innovative on the Carabo, too, were the two fluorescent rings, orange around the nose, green around the tail, which would remain clearly visible even in the poorest of weather. Their purpose, of course, is to make it possible to see at once whether a car in the distance is coming or going — a considerable aid to improved driver safety.

The mounting and operating of an automobile's doors have been a traditional problem. Doors hinged on a vertical axis, whether at the front or at the rear, seem always to get in the way — or into the road, which is worse. Sliding doors, on the other hand, have their aesthetic as well as practical limitations, as do those hinged in some manner along the roof. The Carabo solved the problem nicely, its doors offering no impediment whatsoever to ingress/egress, or to nearby traffic, and being completely free of stylistic limitations. They open forward, swinging upward and are balanced by a hydropneumatic device much like a shock absorber. They do not use space alongside the car, so one can park eight inches from another car, or a wall, and still easily get inside and out. A certainly practical feature, which just happens to look great too.

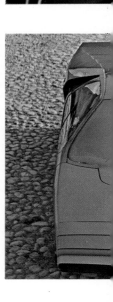

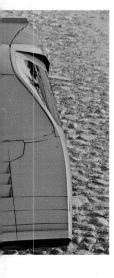

The Carabo was a sensation wherever it was shown. And although H.R.H. the Prince Faisal and other connoisseurs lined up for it, the car was not sold. Alfa Romeo wanted it, and following show appearances, it was returned to Milan for further study. But maybe, someday, if we're lucky, we may be able to buy a car very much like it.

"To build smart and beautiful cars one must remain an artist but without losing sight of the commercial realities," Nuccio Bertone has said. And, although today the reality of being able to go into one's neighborhood foreign car dealer and drive out with the likes of the Carabo may seem remote, who's to say that tomorrow that pleasure might not be very real indeed?

To Nuccio Bertone the essence of a car is a sensual thing, even sexual. Cars are masculine or feminine in appeal, and although the differences are obvious to Bertone, he slyly refrains from giving examples to avoid damages in sales from either side. "For if a person likes a car, let's not bother him or her with notions that it is not meant for his or her type." One wonders how he views the Carabo. To our view, it would look good on anyone — nay, even more than that, it would make anyone look good.

In the meantime Nuccio Bertone will continue doing that which he likes best — designing cars, and encouraging others to do the same. Part of the appeal of a Bertone design is youth. Nuccio Bertone is in his late fifties now, but he looks and acts younger. And it is significant that the average age of his assistants is about twenty-five. Bertone likes young people because of the fresh and daring approach they can bring to a coachmaking problem. Generally the assistants he brings to his studios do not have wide experience in designing, because he feels the advantages of this background might be offset by preconceived ideas that a man of design experience may feel obliged to defend. A young man can be molded, and if this is done delicately, he will not lose the personal approach that Bertone so highly values. Like his father, Nuccio Bertone relishes his role as a teacher.

Bertone is a man of surprisingly few interests outside of his work. And like most Italians, he is a man of sentiment. On the site of the canopied courtyard that was the original Carrozzeria Bertone, he has built a large apartment house, and he himself lives in the ninth and tenth floor penthouse. The decor is modern with such luxurious details as a spiral staircase and an overhanging garden. But his most prized possession is the anvil on which his father forged the ornate ironwork for the coaches he built even before Nuccio was born. Today the son produces some of the most sensational looking cars in the world. As witness the Carabo.

1894 BALZER

An American Pioneer That Lacked Everything But Ingenuity

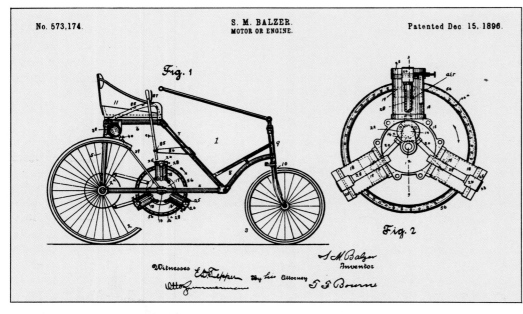

By 1894 the horseless carriage had hardly frightened its first hundred horses, but it was certainly upon us in strength — if one counts strength in terms of sheer numbers. Hundreds of inventors and semi-inventors had been paving its way for six-score years, ever since Oliver Evans first conceived of the notion of "steam waggons moving without the aid of animal fource" in 1772. Still, the motorcar, or "motocycle" as it was popularly called in those days, had hardly evolved into the fairly uniform creature it was to become, and the internal combustion engine — its ultimate power source — was still in its infancy.

It took many forms, this strange new powerplant, relying, as one quaint observer put it, "on a remarkable series of hopefully controllable explosions," and one of the most peculiar among a passel of oddities was certainly S. M. Balzer's little carriage.

Stephen Balzer had been building gasoline engines prior to this first complete automobile, so one must assume its various features had received some trial by fire, but records extant unfortunately do not reveal the exact workings of every component. Yet, in whatever sense one applies the word "unconventional," even in this early stage in the history of the American automobile, the voiturette on these pages qualified, especially when one takes a look at the engine.

Firstly, the engine revolved — all of it — around a fixed crankshaft. It was a three-cylinder affair, air cooled, with cylinders and crankcase orbiting merrily around the crankshaft in a vertical plane, accompanied by a stub shaft which housed the driving gears. The gears in turn were hooked to a three-step, constant-mesh transmission with three speeds but no reverse, which translated power by a clutch on the left side of a divided rear axle, providing power only to the left rear wheel.

Gear ratios were selected by the driver's manipulation of a lever keying the appropriate gear to its shaft, the clutch also being controlled by the same lever.

Ignition was make-and-break, provided by a brush-wiped commutator on the driveshaft and operated by a cam on the crank. There were two poppet valves per cylinder, the inlet being automatic and opened by atmospheric pressure, the exhaust positively actuated by the same cam on this stationary crankshaft.

Fuel in the form of gasoline vapor was routed from the tank underneath the floorboard

rough a fitting that was apparently a kind of ixing valve. After leaving the valve the mixture as piped through a hollow duct to a junction ith three pipes leading to the inlet valves, the pes themselves mounted within a heating amber built on the revolving crankcase. After mbustion the exhaust gases were emitted rough three more pipes leading into a ankcase chamber which appears to have served a combination muffler and fuel pre-heater, nce it contains numerous tiny holes drilled rough its outer wall.

The engine having been completed in New ork City in 1894, Balzer framed it in a spartan tle vehicle less than six feet long and three et wide, rolling on spindly wire wheels twenty- x inches in diameter in the rear, seventeen in- es in the front. The car was steered by a tiller - at least that much was conventional.

That Stephen Balzer never progressed beyond the one-off stage should in no way discredit his efforts; he was not alone, and in good company besides. He provided but one more step in the progress of the automobile, and his con- tributions, like those of so many others, would add to its development into the mighty agent of transport and industry it was destined to become.

The Balzer may be viewed in the Smithsonian Institution's exhibit of automobiles and motorcycles, which spans a century of American auto history from the circa 1869 Roper Steam Velocipede to one of the fifty Chrysler gas turbine cars of 1964. When the ingenious little horseless carriage was first restored by the Smithsonian in 1959, its severely aged tires were replaced with single-tube pneumatic types, but this appears to have been in keeping with the

original concept. The front tires found on the Balzer had spaces into which a double-ended in- ner tube had been inserted; the tube container was then laced closed with the outside cover. The rear tires found on the vehicle closely resembled typical open casings, but employed a wire inside each bead which was tightened by means of a turnbuckle.

The Smithsonian Collection houses over forty automobiles, self-powered cycles and motor trucks, which are rotated in and out of the Vehi- cle Hall of the Museum of History and Technology, assuring that all of them are ex- hibited to the public during the course of a few years. The Institution has a comprehensively equipped restoration shop and research library, and its contributions to the preservation of automotive history are in keeping with its reputation in all areas of Americana.

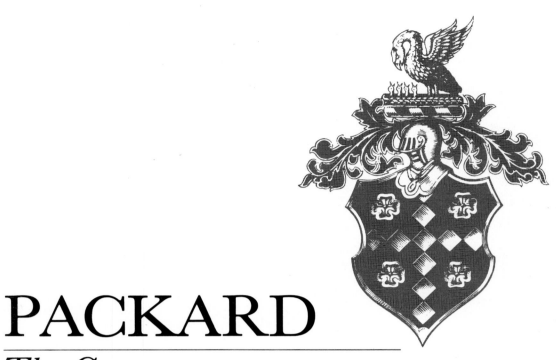

PACKARD
The Car
We Couldn't Afford to Lose

The 1910 Model 30 gentleman's roadster

The name Packard immediately brings to mind dignity, permanence, quality, élan. It is no trick of letters, created by the chance way they're combined to form the noun, but rather one of psychology, because motorcars bearing the proud name of Packard dominated the highest echelons of the American automobile industry for six decades, and presided over the era marking that industry's finest hours. Even today, many years after its final departure, Packard's heritage remains, and few rivals match the reverence with which it is held by connoisseurs of America's grand marques.

While others might boast of producing the "Standard of the World," Packard was surely the Standard of America. In the midst of great events, days that shaped the Twentieth Century course of the Republic, Packard was there. The Lincoln Highway was pioneered by Packard executives. When presidents began to forsake the carriage for the motorcar, they did so most often for a Packard. When the ticker tape rained down on Charles A. Lindbergh, as he rode triumphantly through New York after his epic flight, it rained down also on the Packard which carried him. And as long as there are men who admire that fabulous creation called the automobile, there will be Packards for them to own and enjoy. And to love.

The story of how James Ward Packard, an engineer from Warren, Ohio, came to build the

Above: The 1903 Model F touring.

first Packard car is almost as well-known as that of Paul Revere. Both these legends involve rides. Mr. Packard's was in a Winton, for which he had travelled out to Cleveland, intending to drive it the fifty miles back to Warren. He arrived home only after successive breakdowns, constant overheating, failure of several major components, and accumulation of considerable grease and dirt on the person of the driver. When Packard took the car back to Winton, proposing a number of improvements, the mustachioed proprietor of that Cleveland factory told him to build a car himself, if he was so smart. Packard did.

On November 6, 1899, the first Packard automobile was born. It rolled forth under its own power onto the tree-shaded streets of Warren, frightening horses and attracting cheers and jeers from the townspeople. A month later the Automobile Division of The New York and Ohio Company was formed for the manufacture of Packard automobiles. Later the firm was reorganized as the Ohio Automobile Company. Not until 1903, as the result of another reorganization, did it become the Packard Motor Car Company. Though the company had several names, the cars were always known as Packards.

Model A, as the initial Packard car was called, was a single-seat buggy-type machine with wire wheels. Steering was by a tiller. Power

Below left: The 1911 Model 30 touring car.
Pictured above are two examples of the
popular Model 18—similar in design to the
famous 30, save for its smaller size
and its wider range of body style. On
the left is pictured the runabout from 1909;
on the right the limousine model from 1910.

came from a single cylinder operating horizontally under the seat and developing 12 bhp. A chain drive transmitted this to the wheels. There was an automatic spark advance, patented by Packard, something not common until many years later. In 1900 and 1901 the Models B and C followed, still of only one-cylinder configuration, but the C was equipped with a steering wheel instead of a tiller, and was capable of at least 40 mph. Packard had insisted on one-cylinder machines, demanding reliable, uncomplicated design, but in 1902 he sold out to a wealthy industrialist, Henry B. Joy, who felt rather otherwise.

Joy had become entranced with Packards after seeing two early models start instantly and roar away in pursuit of a New York fire apparatus. When Warren's city fathers hesitated in giving Packard permission to expand, Mr. Joy was able to persuade him to move his manufacturing operations to Detroit. Later, after a series of disagreements with Joy interests and his courtship of a Warren girl who liked her hometown enough to want to stay, Packard announced that he would be unable to follow the

car company to Detroit. He remained in Warren, serving as Packard president until 1909 and continued as chairman of the board for three years longer. Philanthropy occupied his last years. He presented $1 million to the Seamen's Church Institute of New York and $1.2 million to his alma mater, Lehigh University, for an engineering building which now bears his name. In it is displayed the 1899 Model A, the first Packard ever built.

The Packard Motor Car Company now came to Detroit and here, on the edge of town, a young architect named Albert Kahn built for the firm a reinforced concrete factory — the world's first. This building, on East Grand Boulevard, was the most modern of its day and a model for many to come, including Ford's huge Highland Park plant.

In 1903 the four-cylinder Model K appeared, designed by Charles Schmidt, formerly with Mors. Next came the famous Model L, bearing the first of the ox-yoke radiators whose shape was to be continued in one form or another right on down to the Studebaker-styled Packard Hawk of 1958, the marque's final year.

Henry B. Joy, who took over as Packard president in 1909, was a hard-driving, spontaneous and dynamic executive who in moments of impatience would say: "Let's do something, even if it's wrong!" He believed in research and invention. He was among the incorporators of the Detroit Automobile Club. In 1903 he was arrested for speeding in Detroit and learned that

the speed limits were six mph on main thoroughfares and eight mph on boulevards. He wrote letters of complaint to the newspapers and eventually the limits were raised. He had a role in the Selden Patent controversy. The holders of this patent demanded a five percent royalty on all cars sold, but Joy and nine others formed an organization to negotiate or fight. They negotiated the royalty down to one-and-a-fourth percent and paid until the patent was ruled invalid. The group today is the Automobile Manufacturers Association.

Equally colorful were some of the men who sold the early Packards. Alvin T. Fuller, a young Boston bicycle dealer, obtained the Packard distributorship for New England in 1903. He also sold Cadillacs and other cars. Incredibly successful at these — and other — enterprises, he amassed a fortune of more than twenty million dollars. A Republican, he served in Congress and also as Lieutenant Governor and Governor of Massachusetts, but never cashed any of the $80,646 he received in paychecks. He refused to stay the executions of Sacco and Vanzetti and vetoed more bills than any Governor of Massachusetts up to that time. He lived until 1958.

Earle C. Anthony, who had made a car of his own when he was only twelve years old and who founded the *Pelican*, the University of California humor magazine, began to sell Packards in Los Angeles in 1905 and sold them as long as they were made, once buying a mile-long train of them worth $815,000 in a single shipment. He also built the first filling stations in the West, started Radio Station KFI, introduced neon signs and started a stage line with Packards from Los Angeles to Bakersfield which was a

Above: The 1912 Model 6-48 special victoria. Below right: The 1930 Model 733 roadster. One of ten bodies offered on the 733 chassis, the roadster sold for $2425. Below left: The 1928 Model 443 custom phaeton. The colorful chassis was a no-extra-cost factory option; total price of the car was $3875.

forerunner of Greyhound. He died in 1961.

Through its first and second decades, Packard became associated with reliability and speed. In 1913, when the murderer Harry K. Thaw clocked 80 mph in a Packard, escaping from the Matteawan Asylum for the Criminal Insane, the Packard magazine reproduced accounts of the chase. They added that "when high speed is necessary, when a fast getaway is absolutely imperative, ask the man who owns one."

The Man Who Owned One, as Packard never tired of reminding us, usually was an enthusiastic salesman. He was given still more to crow over in late 1915, when the twelve-cylinder Twin-Six was announced for the 1916 model year. Besides being the world's first series-production twelve, the Twin-Six was one of the first U.S. cars to use aluminum pistons. To the public it was stark fascination. Police had to keep crowds in line when it was first exhibited: Resultant orders sent Packard production soaring to the then-impressive total of 10,000-plus cars a year — fantastic for a luxury car in those days, even one priced as low as $2600.

Although the Twin-Six was finally phased out by more efficient eight-cylinder models in 1923, it continued to be revised and issued in small quantities through the years. In addition to Packard automobiles, it inspired the World War I Liberty motor and powered several championship motorboats, including Gar Wood's water speed record breaker, which ran that figure up to 124.91 mph in 1922. Motor racing in the same period saw Ralph De Palma attain a new land speed record of 149.87 mph, using a special aircraft version of the Twin-Six engine in his famous Packard 905 racing car.

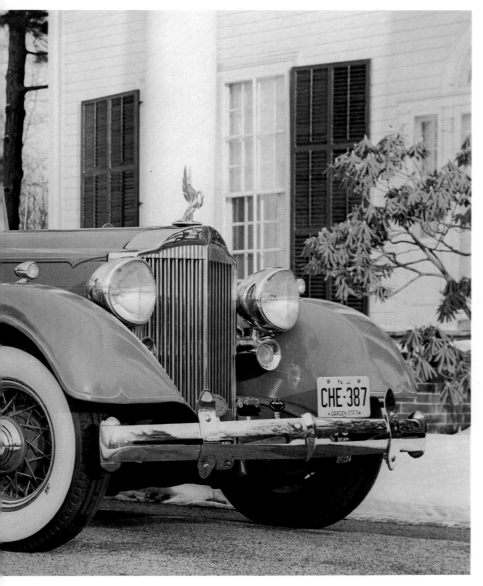

Above left: The 1930 Model 740 dual cowl phaeton. Above right: The 1930 Model 734 boattail speedster. Priced at $5210, 150 of these cars were sold in the short-lived Speedster Series. Below left: The 1934 Model 1104 convertible victoria by Dietrich.

A significant managerial change occurred in 1916, when Henry B. Joy resigned from Packard in protest over the board's failure to ratify his proposed merger with Charles W. Nash. The command shifted to Alvan Macauley, who had been vice-president since 1913, and again Packard's fortunes surged.

Macauley's motto for his product was "a gentleman's car, built by gentlemen." He meant every word. No detail of manufacture, service or advertising escaped his watchful eyes, and he ran Packard with assurance. It was appropriate, for the company was on the verge of an era which would see the marque at the heights of fame, fortune and excellence.

This golden Packard age would see the marque's reputation span the globe, and its name enmeshed with the bluest bloods in every nation on earth. Eccentricity and Packard were one. A Chinese in the Dutch East Indies bought a Packard to drive once a year to the grave of his grandfather. An Indian Maharani sent her pink bedroom slipper to Detroit and ordered a custom car with upholstery to match. An Indian Rajah once bought a limousine with amber glass permitting occupants to see out but preventing those outside from seeing in.

King Alfonso of Spain was a Packard owner. King Alexander of Yugoslavia owned forty-eight Packards and had them equipped with gun holsters, radiator ornaments in the shape of his

own, and flickering green and white lights for rearing traffic. The Belgian royal house owned many Packards. Queen Astrid was killed in one then King Leopold, who was driving, took his eyes from the Swiss highway they were following to look at a map in her lap. Prince Eugene de Ligne of Belgium drove another across the Sahara Desert.

Russians have been fascinated by Packards. Czar Nicholas owned a Twin-Six on which the front wheels were replaced by skis for snow travel. His brother, Grand Duke Michael, also had a Packard in which he attempted to escape during the Revolution. He was murdered but his

Left: A convertible coupé from 1936. Below right: The Fifteenth Series Twelve Model 1507 club sedan from 1937. Below left: The 1937 110 convertible coupé. This model would later be designated the Six.

Twin-Six survived and later won a Soviet road race from Leningrad to Moscow. As a result of this test, Russia imported many Packards for Stalin and other leaders. Early models of the Russian Zis were almost identical copies of the 1940 Packard, as Stalin had persuaded Roosevelt to give him the old dies for the classic-styled 160-180 series during the Second World War.

The 84 bhp straight eight which replaced the Twin-Six in 1923 heralded the advent of the classic Packards. It was joined by an outstanding 420-cubic-inch V-12 in 1933, by which time all Packards offered vacuum-servo brakes and synchromesh transmission as standard equipment. The exciting styling that immediately identified these cars as Packards was continued throughout the Thirties.

The classic Packard outnumbered cars of its age as surely as it still does today on the roster of the Classic Car Club of America. All its illustrious rivals — Pierce-Arrow, Lincoln, Cadillac and Chrysler Imperial — were outsold by Packard. Coachwork was by the finest houses of Europe and America. The list of firms contributing to Packard during those years reads like a roll call from coachbuilding's hall of fame: Dietrich, Waterhouse, Fernandez and Darrin, Murphy, Brewster, Le Baron, Holbrook, Derham, Judkins. Only the finest were worthy of the Packard chassis and its mighty super eights or V-12's. Despite the Depression, Packard continued to build these cars for the wealthy who survived, but as more and more luxury makes declined, it became obvious that something more salesworthy would have to be offered if the com-

pany was to prosper. The answer was entrusted to George T. Christopher, a former General Motors executive, who came out of retirement in 1934 to head up Packard manufacturing, and who succeeded Macauley as president in 1942. Christopher's solution was the medium-priced Packard "120," a smaller, mass-produced model that buoyed sales and set Packard's all-time record of 109,518 units in 1937. Christopher certainly saved the company. The argument that he contributed thereby to Packard's loss of reputation as a luxury car is moot. Without the 120, there would have been no luxury cars at all; thanks to it, Packard continued to turn them out up to and after the Second World War.

The company switched to war production in late 1941. Their engines powered British and American ships and planes, making one of the most significant contributions of any automobile manufacturer to the Allied victory. They emerged from the war free of debt, and braced for battle in the subsequent sellers' market.

Though the classic age had long departed, Christopher continued aiming at Packard's traditional market, with the Custom Super Clip-

per, a smooth-lined holdover from before the war, and the "free-flow" Custom Eight sedans, limousines and convertible victorias of 1948-50. Though controversial in styling, the latter were among the highest-priced cars of their day, and were built accordingly.

Hugh J. Ferry, a lifetime Packard man, relieved Christopher in 1949, and skippered the design-change which produced the Patrician, boasting new standards of silent, dignified, comfortable motoring. Ferry, himself up in years, almost immediately began seeking a successor, and in 1952 the Packard board elected James Nance, Ferry's hand-picked man, as Packard's new chief executive.

Nance, a high-powered salesman who had resurrected Hotpoint from the appliance industry graveyard, took over with a vengeance. He decreed a comeback for Packard, who had lost the luxury car sales race to Cadillac in 1950, and embarked on several questionable programs

Right: The Packard Model 120 four-door sedan. Below: The 1940 Darrin Packard Super 8 victoria, designed by Howard "Dutch" Darrin in Hollywood and built in Connersville, Indiana.

Above: One of the 90,525 cars sold in the 1948 Packard Twenty-Second Series, this one a Custom Eight limousine. Below: The 1951 Patrician, Packard's only total postwar redesign.

without regard to finances. In the process of sweeping clean, this New Broom destroyed Packard's entire archives and historical records. To autophiles, it was akin to the burning of the Library at Alexandria by the ferocious Turks. And in the wake of Nance's onslaught against the past, virtually all of Packard's history was destroyed, save for a few bits and scraps here and there rescued by loyal and ardently devoted Packard staffers.

The company had saved everything from the very beginning — tons of material had been stored. Every painting, photograph, design, drawing and blueprint was put to the torch. There were many unforgettable cloak and dagger attempts to rescue what many historians consider were the most complete records of any corporation. One executive in the design department risked his career and bribed a truck driver to bring a giant truckload of literature to his lawn. Unfortunately, the driver took sick the following morning and his relief was unaware of the plans. On this truck was a complete fifty-year file of advertising amassed by advertising director Hugh Hitchcock, including the two chosen by Julian Watkins in his book, *The 100 Greatest Advertisements.* Young and Rubicam, who had produced these advertisements, had been dropped in 1951 after nineteen years as

Packard's agency and had been replaced by Maxon, Inc. Nance dropped Maxon in favor of first Ruthrauff and Ryan and then D'Arcy.

Instead of buying a large percentage of parts from sub-suppliers — thirty-four percent had come from General Motors — Nance undertook to make virtually everything and spent millions on new manufacturing facilities. American Motors had been buying engines from Packard but quit doing so when Nance failed to reciprocate. A fine new Packard engine assembly line eventually was sold for scrap metal. While Packard operated profitably and paid dividends in 1952 and 1953, with 80,341 cars sold that year, much trouble was ahead.

In 1954 the firm began to lose money, and despite the vigor of Nance's onslaught, failed to catch up to, or even close on Cadillac, which would have at least been a moral victory. Despite innovations like torsion-bar, self-leveling suspension, pushbutton ultramatic, a potent new V-8 and high standards of luxury, recovery still eluded the Packard Motor Car Company.

Late in 1954 Nance merged with Studebaker. Packard sales rallied in 1955, but that was a

*The Caribbean convertible—with the Eldorado
Cadillac—was the pinnacle of ultra-expensive,
luxury open air motoring of the Fifties.
Above left, a 1953 model. Above right,
one from 1955. Below: The 1956 Patrician
four-door sedan, the last of the big
Packards, and the end of a great tradition.*

record year for the industry at large, and did not
forecast a trend. Despite an elegant Patrician
and a massively beautiful and fast Caribbean,
the 1956 model year witnessed another
downturn, this time for good.

The 1957 model Packard was a glorified
Studebaker; S-P had realized that two distinctly
different lines of cars were beyond their minimal
resources. The marque reappeared in 1958, but
was now irrefutably ugly and hardly represen-
tative of what had gone before. By mid-1958, the
name of Packard officially passed into history.

In 1962 the company dropped Packard from
the corporate title. They said it was
"anachronistic, a hindrance to the development
of a new and more vital corporate image." But if
that was so, what could one say for Studebaker?

It was all pointless, of course. Packard had
died long before, in 1958, or in 1956. Every now
and then one hears of some entrepreneurial
scheme to revive the marque, on a fiberglass
contraption powered by a production V-8 —
something a few people with too much money
think a "modern Packard" ought to be. It won't
work. Let it rest. Automotive enthusiasts all over
the world have been proving, far better than any
would-be revivalist, that, as the company themselves so often told us: "only Packard can build
a Packard."

THE DOBLE STEAM CAR

On the road, the utterly silent, effortless and majestic flight of this greatest of all steamers bears out its famous claim "The Ultimate Car."

The Doble had a mystique entirely its own – the clinical cleanliness of its steam generato the array of totally unfamiliar gadgets and co trols, the simplicity of driving techniqu everything about the Doble was different. The can be no doubting that the Doble was the fine steam car ever built anywhere. Indeed it w much more than that. Historians have placed t Doble among the first rank of all automobiles all time. And rightly so.

Abner Doble, the eldest of four brothers, w born in San Francisco in 1895. He and h brothers William, John and Warren grew u with an engineering background, all serving a prenticeships in the family industry. A half ce tury earlier Abner's grandfather had set up forge for making miner's tools, this busine naturally prospering in the California of t mid-Nineteenth Century. The Abner Doble Co pany was passed to Abner's father, W. A. Dob who with his brother invented and developed t Doble Water Wheel. The business flourished.

Young Abner had built his first steam car, u ing a salvaged chassis and Locomobile fire tu

boiler, while a high school student. In 1910, while studying engineering at the Massachusetts Institute of Technology, he began a second, this time a completely original design. During the course of this experimentation he visited the Stanley plant in Newton, Massachusetts. The meeting was less than cordial, the Stanley brothers — F. E. and F. O. — being completely unimpressed with his ideas for better condensers and rapid cold starting. Abner — aged sixteen — went away determined to show the Stanleys a thing or two. This he did. Completing his first Model A in 1912, Abner drove it to the Stanley plant. Upon examination, the brothers grudgingly admitted that Abner had made his point. The Model A had a water tube boiler, which was a fast steam raiser, and a Harrison cellular radiator built to Doble's specifications, which efficiently condensed all exhaust steam. This was a marked advance over the condensers used on other steam cars up to that time — they had had an exhaust steam outlet since their tubular condensers could handle only part of the steam used. Three years later, incidentally, steamers from the Stanleys were installed with condensers.

Abner built five Model A's in all, selling four and retaining the fifth for further experimentation. By now he had left M.I.T. and gone into business. Patents were applied for, the Model B was produced and the Abner Doble Motor Vehicle Company was formed on October 30th, 1914, with a capitalization of half a million dollars. Abner was nineteen years old.

The Model B was an improved Model A, using the same twin-cylinder double-acting single expansion engine mounted on the rear axle. During thousands of miles of test driving over a period of two years, the Doble brothers made repeated performance checks, and found the car capable of accelerating from 0 to 60 mph in fifteen seconds, with a top speed of 75 mph.

Despite Doble's ambitious plans he found that to introduce a new car — and a steamer at that — required more financing than he had, and after a tour of industrial towns with the Model B during 1915 he interested one C. L. Lewis. The General Engineering Company was formed in 1916 to produce the Doble, Lewis being awarded

the presidency. The Model B was not put into production but lessons from it were built into the Model C, or G.E.C. Doble. This utilized a horizontal single expansion twin-cylinder unit, but employed the "uniflow" principle, in which steam admission was by the usual method (i.e., valve controlled) but the exhaust was through ports in the cylinder walls midway along the stroke and controlled by the piston like a two-stroke internal combustion engine.

But the most radical innovation on this Doble series lay in the combustion arrangements. Until then, all steamers had used a Bunsen-burner-type vaporizer, requiring a pilot light which had to be lit by the driver before turning on the burner, and involving two separate fuel systems, gasoline being used for the pilot light and kerosene for the main burner. A steam car start took anything up to twenty-five minutes. The 1916 Doble, however, used fuel atomization, electric ignition, one fuel only for both starting and running, eliminated the pilot light altogether, required no more starting preparation than its gasoline rivals, and could be

A 1925 Series E-23 phaeton by Murphy.

under way with a working head of steam in less than three minutes. Doble had achieved a breakthrough in steam technology comparable with the advent of reliable electric ignition, and later the electric starter, in gasoline car practice. The overall concept — a motor-blower, carburetor and spark plug controlled by steam pressure and temperature to give automatic operation — had originated with Abner's brilliant brother, John A. Doble, about 1911 or 1912. John, then a mere fifteen years old, had left San Francisco and joined Abner in Massachusetts to work on the Model A.

The General Engineering Company announced the new Doble at the New York show for 1917 models, concurrently with some modest national advertising. It was the greatest sensation the New York show had ever experienced. Less than three days later the volume of mail concerning the car became so great that the Post Office refused to deliver it, and cars had to be sent to collect it. Over fifty thousand letters were received and seven hundred telegrams arrived from prospective dealers and stockholders. More than 11,000 orders for cars were placed within three months. Production had already begun, and a few cars had been completed when Uncle Sam stepped on Abner Doble with both feet. Because of the demands for steel in vital wartime industries, said the National War Emergency Board, no steel could be allocated to Doble manufacture "for the duration." This put an end to the G.E.C. Doble; production stopped, and Abner Doble had to reorganize the firm.

A new concern, Doble-Detroit, emerged as its successor, and it seems that the U.S. Government must have had second thoughts about restrictions on steel supplies. The Doble-Detroit was announced in January, 1919, and in the succeeding ten months pilot models had been built and tested throughout the country. The "new" Doble-Detroit was actually an improved Model C, and it was probably just as well for Abner Doble's reputation that it did not get into quantity production. The uniflow engine, which had looked so good on paper, was found wanting in practice. In any case, wartime conditions and financial maneuvering seem to have throttled the project before the war's end — and Doble severed himself from the company and returned to California in 1919.

During his absence there had been built in San Francisco several "monotube" steam generators used for testing turbine fittings in the shipyards. Monotube boilers, having one main water tube in a continuous spiral coil, had been used on other steam cars as early as 1900, but without automatic burners and feed water controls. The San Francisco shipyard boilers, however, had automatic firing and the combustion chamber *above* the boiler tube coil. Abner decided to adapt the principle to his next automobile, but his first step was to get rid of the unreliable uniflow engine in his Doble-Detroit and replace it with a two-cylinder compound he had designed. Then a monotube boiler was designed and installed in the test chassis.

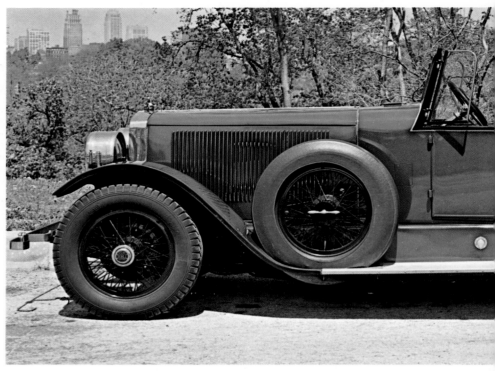

A roadster-bodied Series E-20 Doble from 1925. This car, a particularly fast model, has coachwork from the house of Murphy.

Hand in hand with these changes went a new condenser and bolt-on disc wheels. Then came an auxiliary unit, mounted at the front of the car and shaft-driven from the rear, embodying four feed pumps. Thus was evolved the next distinct design, the Doble Model D.

Meanwhile in 1920 the Doble brothers had organized Doble Steam Motors of California. They spent a hundred thousand dollars on Model D research, resulting in a design free from major weaknesses. However, it was still a twin-cylinder, and there were a few — very few — expensive gasoline cars which were slightly smoother and nominally more powerful. The Dobles were not introducing just another car, they intended to reassert the superiority of steam itself. And to do that they needed a car at least the equal of the best gasoline automobiles. They got it — the Series E Doble — in principle a four-cylinder Model D, with larger steam generator, lengthened wheelbase and additional refinements. What a car it was.

Early in 1924 the Automobile Club of America conducted an impartial test in New York. A Doble phaeton was left overnight in a garage, then rolled out by hand into the street, where it stood for an hour and a half with the ambient temperature at the freezing point. The ignition was then switched on, within 23.1 seconds operating pressure was reached, and after forty-one seconds the car was on the move with a load of four passengers, accelerating from standstill to 20 mph in 3.9 seconds and to 40 mph in 12.5 seconds. The engineers admitted to being "startled." Tests at the factory showed these figures could be bettered, one car reaching 40 in eight seconds, while a stripped chassis went from 0 to 75 mph in a mere ten seconds!

But the most intriguing demonstrations were the impromptu ones by Doble works drivers on the open road. The chassis as they came off the

dynamometer were capable of 108 mph, and i pre-delivery tests, there were many opportuniti for the Doble boys to exercise their immensel powerful charges, to the painful discomfort the "gasoline crowd."

Production had begun during 1923 with th factory offering eight body styles priced fro $8800 to $11,200. But price was no deterren Famous Hollywood figures, wealthy dowager bankers and industrialists — all ordered Dobl as companion cars to their Cadillacs, Packard Rolls-Royces, Mercedes, et al. "I know them a but I prefer the Doble," was the brief but swee ing comment by Howard Hughes. "The Doble the last word in automobile engineering, declared Italy's foremost motoring magazine *L Vie D'Italia*. "Steam will become the dominatin factory in the industry."

But it was not to be. Manipulation of Dob stock by certain stock traders and speculator killed the company and the car. The Dob brothers themselves were unaware of the double dealings until they reached serious proportions they tried to undo what had been done, bu unsuccessfully. In April of 1931 Doble Stea Motors went into liquidation. Abner Dob would continue to espouse his steam principle in the United States and abroad, until July 1961 when he died, defeated in his dream b circumstances beyond control — financial mi dealings, the Depression, and war.

Technically Abner Doble's achievements ca not be faulted. Whereas other steam engineer produced cars whose merits were at best dubiou in comparison with the gasoline car, th California genius took the steamer an transformed it into a vehicle more desirable tha its rival. As an entirely acceptable alternative t the gasoline car, the Doble is an essay in wha might have been. It also remains a precursor o what might yet be.

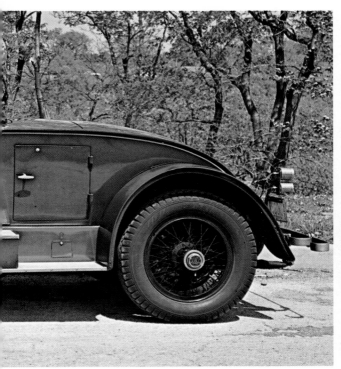
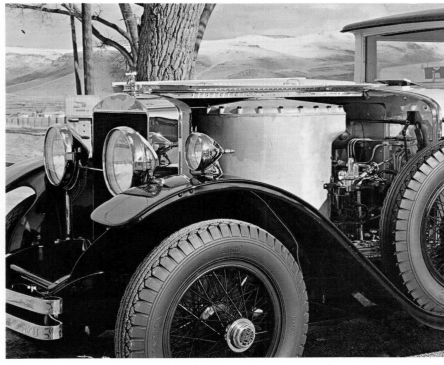

A coupé-bodied Series E-24 Doble from 1925. This particular vehicle, with coachwork by Murphy, was Abner Doble's personal car.

PLYMOUTH

*A success story built upon
a well chosen name,
some good timing
and a degree of luck.*

This is a story of the Plymouth. It's a frankly old-fashioned story. Today, of course, one doesn't drive a Plymouth; one drives a Satellite, a Road Runner, a Fury, a Barracuda — all models whose mention is guaranteed to evoke a host of scenic, heroic or pleasantly brutal emotions. But this is a story of the Plymouth, the car so designated because it typified "the endurance and strength, the rugged honesty, the enterprise, that determination of achievement and the freedom from old limitations of that Pilgrim band who were the first American colonists."

The Plymouth was appropriately named. It was hailed in 1933 as the product of the "number three corporation" and "number two personality" in the automotive world. The corporation was, of course, Chrysler, the personality, Walter Percy Chrysler, erstwhile Union Pacific roundhouse sweeper and one of those rare men whose achievements seemingly pale those of Horatio Alger. In Twentieth Century terms what he accomplished was no less spectacular than the Pilgrims making it to Plymouth Rock.

Chrysler's Plymouth was the rock on which much of his company's success was founded during the early years of the Depression. But to put the Plymouth story into perspective one must go back two decades before the 1928 date of its introduction. At that time Walter Chrysler was thirty-three years old. Born in Wamego, Kansas, son of a passenger train engineer on the old Kansas Pacific Railroad, he had worked his way up from a locomotive machinist's apprentice to become superintendent of motive power for the Chicago Great Western Railway at Oelwein, Iowa. It was at the seventh annual Chicago Automobile Show in December, 1907, so the now famous story goes, that Chrysler became enamored of an ivory-white Locomobile touring car. Its price, as he was repeatedly told, was $5000 cash — $800 more than his yearly salary.

He had $700 in the bank, for which he promptly wired. After borrowing better than a year's salary, he bought the car and asked that it be delivered to Oelwein. Why didn't he take it himself? As Chrysler explained, "The roads are bad at this time of year, and besides I don't know how to drive."

The car was duly delivered, and to the dismay of his wife, who not only thought the purchase folly but couldn't understand why the vehicle shouldn't be used for its intended purpose, Chrysler had a friend haul the car to his barn, whereupon he dismantled it completely, studied all the parts and soon knew as much about Locomobile as anyone in Bridgeport. It took Chrysler three years to repay his Locomobile loan, a period during which, he later noted, he "pulled [the car] to pieces about forty times." By that time he was convinced his future was with the automobile: "It knew no limits except a right-of-way."

Walter Chrysler was in the automobile business by 1911, as Buick plant manager for General Motors. Within four years he was president and general manager of the Buick division, commanding a salary of $500,000 a year. Four years later, after numerous policy disputes with William C. Durant, he resigned — and retired.

He was back at work a year later, having accepted a flat million-dollar-a-year salary to salvage the sinking Willys-Overland company. One of his first exercises of authority was to cut John North Willys' salary in half; as the cost-conscious Chrysler explained, "The majority of men pay too much attention to the way stations and not enough to the terminals." In the midst of the Willys mopping-up job came a call to aid Maxwell-Chalmers, whose problems included an indebted company — reputedly within twenty-four hours of bankruptcy — and a discredited product. Chrysler unhesitatingly accepted the challenge, at a $100,000-a-year salary plus stock

options. Upon his advice, an addition[al] $15,000,000 was invested in the company, th[e] cars were redesigned and their prices cut. Th[e] resulting car, hailed without embarrassment [as] "The Good Maxwell," sold well enough to enab[le] the company to begin paying its debts.

But what Chrysler wanted — and had wante[d] since first tearing the Locomobile apart — wa[s] his own car. While at Willys he had discovered [a] team of three consulting engineers, Fred [M.] Zeder, Carl Breer and Owen R. Skelton, whos[e] automotive design ideas he liked and whom h[e] hired to carry them out. The result was th[e] Chrysler automobile, and it was introduced a[t] the Hotel Commodore in New York City durin[g] the first week in January, 1924. Chrysler spe[nt] much of that week inside one of the close[d] models on display dickering with Edward [F.] Tinker of Chase Securities about the matter [of] the $5,000,000 needed to put the car into pr[o]duction. The deal was closed in Tinker's barbe[r] shop by B. E. Hutchinson, whom Chrysler ha[d] brought to Maxwell-Chalmers in 1921 a[s] treasurer, while Walter Chrysler paced th[e] sidewalks outside. One year later the Chrysle[r] Corporation was officially born.

There was little reason to believe that Walte[r] Chrysler's corporation would survive. Com[petition in the automobile industry had alway[s] been sharp; by 1925, however, it was fierce. In[deed, as *Fortune* magazine noted in the Thirti[es] "Had he not succeeded, every scrap of evidenc[e] would have proved that no one could."

But succeed he did. More than 32,00[0] Chryslers were sold during its debut year, an[d] by 1926 Chrysler Corporation had climbed fro[m] thirty-second place in the industry to fifth. Th[e] Chrysler was a car of its age, a car not so muc[h] needed as a car very much desired, a car style[d] and powered to give its driver the thrills of [a] $5000 machine at one-third the price.

Equally of its age was the Plymout[h]

A 1929 Model U rumble-seat roadster.

onically, Walter Chrysler completely failed to ~~foresee~~ the Depression. He was the ultimate optimist; to him, prosperity would go on forever. Instinctively, however, he prepared for the inevitable. He bought Dodge Brothers. It was a propitious move. Without Dodge, Chrysler Corporation might not have weathered the Depression. Without Dodge, there would have been no Plymouth.

Undoubtedly Walter Chrysler already had visions of a Big Three of automakers; he knew, in any case, that his corporation would be a minor and probably short-lived Detroit resident unless he could crack the mass market. His plant, however, was too small for that, and to

A 1931 Model PA business coupé.

build facilities on the scale he required was financially unfeasible. Thus the stage was set for the Dodge deal.

Numerous legends have grown up about that transaction. Most stories have it that Clarence Dillon, of the New York banking house that controlled Dodge, approached Chrysler in the spring of 1928. A contemporary account, however, noted that it was Chrysler who opened negotiations with an abortive offer in 1926. This is very likely true, since embryonic planning for the Plymouth automobile had begun as early as that year.

Dodge, in the middle Twenties, had been possibly the strongest of the independents, but by 1927, because of both bad styling and mismanagement, it had lost much of its luster.

Dillon, whose specialty was mergers, not automobiles, had had visions of a Dodge Packard-Hudson-Essex combination with Briggs Body, but that failed to materialize. Then he saw Chrysler. It was an interesting bargaining situation. Dillon wanted to sell; Chrysler wanted to buy. Both of them wanted it badly, but neither admitted it. It was the typical cat and mouse game. And it ended with the mouse swallowing the cat — Chrysler got Dodge Brothers, a firm several times his company's size. And what he got was not only a first-class plant and a well-known car, but a dealer network and sales organization considered to be one of the best in the country. Chrysler later admitted that he wanted the Dodge dealers as much as the Dodge manufacturing capacity.

A 1932 Model PB convertible sedan.

The deal was closed at 5:30 p.m. the evening of July 31st, 1928, in the Ritz-Carlton Hotel in New York City. In Detroit, K. T. Keller, whom Chrysler had met during his Buick days and who had left GM in 1926 to join Chrysler Corporation, sat at the end of an open telephone wire from New York. He waited a full hour before hearing Hutchinson exclaim, "We've bought Dodge." There was a pregnant pause; then Hutchinson began some jocular gibing about the lack of response from Detroit, only to discover that no one was on the other end of the line. Keller and his men were on their way to the Dodge Brothers plant while Hutchinson was still talking, taking with them previously prepared signs reading "Chrysler Corporation: Dodge Division," which they plastered all around the

Dodge facilities. The next morning when Dillon called Chrysler to advise that the Dodge plant was running smoothly and could run itself for three months sight unseen, Chrysler could dryly answer, "Hell, Clarence, our boys moved in yesterday."

Walter Chrysler had that rare ability of completing yesterday what no one expected him to begin until tomorrow. His introduction of the Plymouth offers ample evidence of that. Although his plans for entry into the low-priced field rested heavily on the Dodge deal, the first Plymouth came off the assembly line on June 11th. An anonymous announcement revealing its imminent entry into the mass market was made June 16th, and the debut showing of the new car took place early in July. Not only was the ink 109 not dry on the Dodge transaction, but the signatories hadn't even approached the paper!

The promotion that heralded the new Plymouth was of epic proportions; the mysterious pre-showing announcement, the well-engineered introduction, the Plymouth dealers in showrooms across the country neatly clad as Pilgrims, the presentation of Amelia Earhart debuting on the lecture platform in Plymouth's behalf at New York's Madison Square Garden. At *Time* put it, Chrysler had "gone into the low-priced field with the throttle wide open." Three months after the Plymouth's introduction, in fact, Chrysler erected a new plant for its manufacture in Detroit. Four crews of workmen — two working in from each of the ends, the other two working out from the middle — were assigned to the task. The building was completed in three months.

The first Plymouth — the Model Q — was advertised as "Chrysler-designed" and "Chrysler-built." Actually it was a redesigned four-cylinder Chrysler 52, which in turn had been the 58, which in turn had been redesigned from the old four-cylinder Maxwell. It produced 45 hp at 2800 rpm, weighed 2555 pounds and sold for $725 in sedan form, with roadster and coupé versions priced at $670. It featured four-wheel hydraulic brakes, full pressure engine lubrication, aluminum alloy pistons and an independent hand brake. Not until 1939 would its low-price competitors offer that complete combination.

Plymouth was not, however, a competitor of Ford or Chevrolet during its maiden year. Shipments totaled 58,000, a figure dwarfed by the more than half million of the former and near million of the latter. Nonetheless, before the year was out, rumors began circulating in Europe that the Ford Motor Company planned to unite with Chrysler to fight General Motors. The talk was unfounded; Walter Chrysler was far too busy trying to make the Plymouth itself competitive, and Henry Ford was having his own Model A problems.

In 1930 Walter Chrysler faced his problem squarely. On March 7th that year, Plymouth cut its prices to put it heartily in the lowest price market. Later that month the company announced that all Chrysler, Dodge and De Soto dealers would henceforth handle Plymouth sales and service as well. Overnight Plymouth obtained more than 7000 additional dealer outlets. Despite this action, however, and the added improvements to the new Model 30-U Plymouth, including the application of oil filters and the adoption of electric gasoline gauges for the first time in low-priced cars, the year 1930, like the two years preceding it, saw more Chryslers and Dodges sold than their low-priced companion.

The picture changed, however, in 1931 when Walter Chrysler introduced the all-new Plymouth, the day when *Fortune* noted, "The gentleman with the tireless brown eyes left the gentleman with the snappy blue eyes something to think about." In June the first Model PA —

the product of two and one-half million dollars

A 1931 PA two-door sedan, featuring "free wheeling" as well as "floating power."

The 1933 line of Plymouth cars included a redesigned radiator, two more cylinders, and the model designation of PC. The convertible coupé model featured a rumble seat and fold-down windshield.

in research and retooling — came off the assembly line. Walter Chrysler waited impatiently for the third car to roll by, climbed into its driver's seat and drove immediately to Henry Ford's office in Dearborn. After a leisurely hour or two with the Fords — both Henry and Edsel — at their Engineering Laboratory, he took his hosts outside, showed them Plymouth No. 3, gave them a demonstration ride, triumphantly presented them with the car, and went home by taxicab. It was later reported that Ford plans for a new and better Model A were rather disarranged by the advent of the new Plymouth.

And the Plymouth PA was indeed new. Its 110-inch wheelbase was 6.5 inches longer than the Ford. It boasted free-wheeling and pioneered "floating power," the patented method of suspending the engine in balance on rubber mountings credited to the genius of Fred Zeder. Its 196-cubic-inch engine delivered 56 hp at 2800 rpm, and its price range was $535 to $645.

Despite the Depression, Walter Chrysler had reason to be optimistic. In 1931, Plymouth sales reached 94,000, and by year's end Plymouth had replaced Buick in the number three spot in national sales volume. The new Plymouth was extensively promoted, through its oft-used "Ride in All Three" slogan and such gimmicks as a national contest offering prizes up to $25,000 for the best essay on floating power. In 1932 the "New Finer" Plymouth PB was introduced, its wheelbase lengthened to 112, its horsepower raised to sixty-five. Sales continued to climb. In newspaper and magazine ads that year, Walter Chrysler's earnest face looked out at readers while his hand affectionately patted the hood of his new Plymouth.

In 1932 Plymouth sales were 95,599 as compared to 232,125 Fords and 305,763 Chevrolets. In 1933, 218,491 Plymouths were sold compared to Ford's 271,994, and Chevrolet's 438,888. This was a rise from 9.50 to 16.29 percent of the market in one year. It was, as *Motor* called it, a "Three-Ring Battle." By the end of 1933, one out of every four cars sold was a Plymouth. And although a December, 1933, issue of *Fortune* headlined "Mr. Ford Doesn't Care," the industry wondered.

A redesigned radiator and two more cylinders were among the new features of the 1933 Plymouth line, the new L-head six-cylinder engines delivering 70 hp at 3600 rpm. Plymouth's first offering that year was a standard 107-inch-wheelbase model, which was not immediately as popular as had been hoped. The company countered this situation by stretching the wheelbase out to a 112-inch PD Deluxe model and offering a wide range of choice in color and gadgets which practically made Plymouth a custom job. Customers could elect to have one windshield wiper or two, safety glass in part or throughout, two spare wheels or one, plus, of course, a variety of exterior color and interior upholstery. The idea — incorporating a total of 258 different body combinations — was an immediate success, until the day its effect 111

A 1934 Model PE four-door sedan.

was felt. In Detroit production managers looked at the 5000 cars in their lot, the 5000 orders waiting to be filled, and quickly discovered there was no harmony between the first and the second. The solution was quickly discovered, a system by which the entire output of the plant could be made to order from dealers. And it worked beautifully. With thirty-five copies of an order made and sent to various points on the assembly line, a specific car ordered by a specific customer could be put together as quickly and smoothly as if it were a standard product.

Individual front-wheel suspension, a V-shaped radiator and an increase in horsepower to seventy-seven were among the inducements offered potential customers in the following year. The public was impressed. Plymouth sales reached 313,990, and on August 10th, the one-millionth Plymouth rolled off the assembly line. For the PJ model line for 1935, Plymouth increased its engine output to 85 hp and incorporated a water jacket extending the full length of the cylinder bores. Sales continued to climb.

Just before the Depression, Walter Chrysler had authorized construction of what was then the world's tallest skyscraper — the Chrysler Building in Manhattan. In the ensuing years he

divided his time between that office, to which he rushed via speedboat from weekends at his Great Neck, Long Island, home, and his Detroit plant, where his Number 1 time card was invariably the first one punched in each morning. His family was luxuriously comfortable, but as *The Business Week* noted in 1931, "Chrysler sleeps chez Pullman or in his own lofty garret above the Cloud Club, with forty men fighting to get to him." In 1935, weary from the fatiguing pace of Big Three competition, Walter Chrysler turned over the presidency to K. T. Keller. He died five years later.

Between Walter Chrysler's retirement and America's entry into World War II, Plymouth automobiles continued their yearly design and engineering evolution. Model designations now incorporated numbers, beginning in 1936 with the P-1. That year — during which Plymouth made over 500,000 cars — saw a vertically barred radiator grille design and horizontal louvers as new Plymouth design features. In 1937 Plymouth introduced a safety-styled interior, with all controls and knobs recessed. Cars in the 1938 P-6 line offered a four-inch longer hood, obtained through tilting the radiator grille forward until it was practically vertical. That was the tenth anniversary year for Plymouth —

A 1939 Model P-8 two-door deluxe sedan.

A 1941 Model P-12 special deluxe club coupé.

a good one, as its first ten-year sales record far surpassed that of any other automobile manufacturer in America.

The year 1939 saw the Plymouth gearshift lever move to the steering column and the introduction of a power-operated convertible model. Sealed-beam headlights made their debut in 1940 models; the year 1941 saw the battery move underneath the hood and 1942 saw the running boards disappear. Plymouth production, of course, came to an abrupt halt early in 1942.

The Plymouth idea, as conceived by Walter Chrysler, was to offer the public a good, reliable, low-priced car sold and serviced through a powerful dealership. Therein lay its success. After the war Plymouth decided to offer more — a barrage of new names: Concord, Cambridge and Cranbrook; Plaza, Savoy and Belvedere; Fury, Valiant and Barracuda. Today one rarely hears anyone admit he drives a Plymouth, though obviously many people do. Fortunately, however, a group of iconoclastic pre-1949 Plymouth owners have banded together in enthusiastic appreciation of the Plymouth that was a Plymouth. Through their efforts, the name lives on — not just as a company, but as a car — a car whose story sounded one of the happier chords of a depressed decade.

THE ECCENTRIC MASTERPIECES OF ETTORE BUGATTI

They were among the most remarkable automobiles of all time. Here excitement, beauty, engineering and art were gathered into one marque by a uniquely gifted creator.

Of the more than five thousand makes automobile that have come and gone, the Buga seems to be the most interesting. That is not say that it was the *best* automobile ever bu The Type 68 Hispano-Suiza was a better than the comparable Type 50 Bugatti; the two cylinder Lanchester was mechanically more teresting than any Bugatti; the Monza A Romeo was probably a better motorcar than contemporary Type 55 Bugatti. Of course, e in this narrow field of view, the Bugatti has superiorities, and many of them. For examp

The Bugatti "Black Bess," originally owned by famous aviator Roland Garros, sported a four-cylinder, five-liter overhead camshaft engine. Bugatti introduced his three-valve layout on this racing car, built in 1913, and it is noteworthy, too, as the only Bugatti ever built which had chain drive.

e Type 35 Grand Prix was one of the most ccessful racing cars that was ever built and most beautiful (the Type 29 "tank" was the liest!); in majesty of concept the Type 41, *La yale*, stands quite by itself; the Type 57SC is n today, more than thirty years after its ogee, strikingly good looking and comparable performance to all but the fastest Gran rismo motorcars that we have.

But in the large view, overall, the Bugatti is iquely fascinating. What other automobile nufacturer has produced such a range of models: a child's car, a car which was intended as a processional carriage for princes, a chain-drive racing car, a four-wheel-drive car, a ladies' touring car, Grand Prix cars of extraordinary capability, sports cars, GT cars? Ettore Bugatti himself is in the select company of Ford, Royce, Birkigt, Porsche, and Ferrari. Ford was far more successful commercially, Royce was more single-minded, Birkigt was a better engineer, Porsche was a sounder designer and Ferrari has had a much longer career; but these automotive giants somehow do not move one, individually, as

Bugatti does. It is a measure of the fascination of Bugatti and his cars that the literature is of remarkable volume: A number of major books on Bugatti have been published since World War II; the history and ownership of every surviving car has been catalogued; a magazine has been published steadily for more than forty years by The Bugatti Owners Club, which has its headquarters in England and is one of the oldest and strongest of all one-marque clubs.

Ettore Bugatti was an Italian who lived nearly all his life in France. He was, as the French say,

Above: The Type 13, the first to bear the name of its builder, had an eight-valve, four-cylinder engine. This 1910 model was one of five built that first production year.

Left and above left: The Type 30 "Toast Rack," an open, two-liter, eight-cylinder tourer of 1926. Introduced in 1922, this was Bugatti's first eight-cylinder production car, and the basis for several successful racing cars.

un type, a character, an exotic, one of a kind, greatly gifted, very proud, unswervingly independent, indifferent to any opinion but his own, amused, aristocratic, impractical, profligate, a connoisseur, a gourmet, a *bon vivant*. He died in 1947 at the age of sixty-six after a life full of creation and drama. In the many existing photographs of him his personality and vitality are clearly shown. In one he is in one of his racing cars in 1925, crowded into the cockpit with his two sons, Jean who was fourteen at the time and his younger brother Roland who was three year old. Bugatti is smiling at the photographer and waving, his hand gloved in what looks to be immaculate chamois. Another picture shows him sitting solemn and stiff in a car he built for the Paris-Madrid race of 1903. In another, he is wearing goggles and a helmet. The helmet is odd-looking. M. Bugatti has been amusing himself and taken a knife or a scissors to the brim of a bowler hat and made a helmet of it. He didn't cut all the brim off, he left a neat little bill in front to shade his eyes. In still another picture he is twenty or so, and apparently about to go riding. He is wearing a cap, a flared short coat, pipestem breeches he must have put on barefoot, a hard collar four inches high, and on his left wrist a bracelet and an inch and a half of cuff, altogether a figure of shattering elegance and *sang-froid*.

Bugatti was a moody man, imperious and egotistic. There was the strong drive of the artist in him. His father was a silversmith, a cabinet maker and a furniture designer, and Ettore Bugatti had intended to be an artist. But he began to believe, even before he was out of his teens, that his brother Rembrandt possessed a talent superior to his own, and it was not in his nature to be content with being second-best, so he chose another métier. He was right about Rembrandt, who was indeed remarkably gifted. He was a sculptor, with most of his work centered upon animals. In April, 1966, the Piccadilly Gallery in London gave an exhibition of twenty-one of his bronzes. They were delightful. There were two that are particularly memorable. One was a study of a running deer and the other was a seated nude; like nearly all the pieces in the show, they sold almost as soon as it opened, and for very high prices.

Ettore Bugatti began to concern himself with motor vehicles when he was sixteen or seventeen years old. He had been working for the Prinetti & Stucchi firm for just over a year when he bought a twin-engine tricycle from the company and modified it, then entered it in the Paris-Bordeaux road race in 1899, but retired halfway through after hitting a dog and damaging the tricar beyond repair. He ran in a number of other races after that and won at least three: Verona-Mantua, Pignerol-Turin, Padua-Treviso. In 1898 he had designed and built a small four-wheel, four-cylinder car. His third car, financed by the Count Gulinelli di Ferrari, won a gold medal in the International Sport Exhibition in Milan in 1901.

The Type 44 was an eight-cylinder, three-liter touring car introduced in 1927 and produced until 1930. During the latter year it was superseded by the 3.3-liter Type 49, which would be built for four years thereafter. Numerous coachbuilders built upon these two cars. The Type 44 above, from 1927, has a body by the English house of Harrington.

By 1902, when he was twenty-one, Bugatti had a reputation which was strong enough to attract some useful attention: He was hired as a designer by the de Diétrich company. He raced in a Frankfurt meeting, coming second to a Mercedes-Simplex in a machine identified in the program as a de Diétrich-Bugatti, apparently driving with notable skill and élan. He built a car for the 1903 Paris-Madrid race, but he wasn't allowed to start it on the ground that the driver's position was too far to the rear, and too low, for safety. In 1903 Bugatti was designing the Hermès car for Emile Mathis of Strasbourg. Later on he designed for Deutz, Isotta-Fraschini and Peugeot.

While in Strasbourg Bugatti met a banker, a M. de Viscaya, who suggested to him that an abandoned dye-works in Molsheim, which was then Alsace-Lorraine and is now Bas-Rhin, might make a good nucleus for a factory. Bugatti looked at the place, agreed with the suggestion, and de Viscaya financed him. Ernest Friderich, who had once worked for Emile Mathis, was not only a master-mechanic and Bugatti's lifelong friend, but his main associate. The original staff numbered three, and in 1910 they built five cars. Things went well, and by 1911 there was a work force of sixty-five people, and Friderich, doubling as race driver for the factory, won his class in the Grand Prix du

Mans in a car that is generally considered to

Above: The Type 46, built from 1929 to 1936, was a large car, and a fast one when fitted with close-coupled coachwork. A model such as the one above was capable of over 100 mph. Left: The Type 43 Grand Sport, built from 1927 to 1931, was powered by the 35B engine, and was grandly said to be the fastest sports car in the world.

have been the first all-Bugatti production: the eight-valve four-cylinder Type 13. The car was so small that there was no place to attach the spare wheel. Friderich was second to a high Fiat with an engine five times as big as the Bugatti's. It was a stunning surprise, and it made Bugatti famous overnight. In that one stroke he had doomed the huge, slow-turning engines that were then standard for all powerful cars, and he had demonstrated that roadholding, the ability to stick in fast corners, was more important than sheer power.

Every Bugatti ever built, from that day on, was notable for its superb roadholding. Other cars might be faster on a long straightaway, but European races, then as now, were run on courses full of bends and corners, and it was in the corners that the Bugatti was supreme. Bugatti cars began to set up a list of records for speed and reliability that was to run for years without challenge. In 1924, 1925, 1926 and 1927 alone, Bugattis won 1851 races, a number which was unapproached until the great Ferrari successes began in the Fifties.

Like most other successful men, Bugatti was very stubborn, and he was not quick to admit error, sometimes preferring to cover it with sarcastic wit. As an example of this, long after the hydraulic brake had shown what it was, Bugatti stuck with cables, and when one of his customers complained about them, he is said to 119

have replied, "I make my cars to go, not to stop." He may not have said it, but certainly it sounds like him.

He built around fifty different models of motorcar, from the Type 13 to the Type 64, and one that he particularly liked was the Type 46, which made its appearance in 1929. It was certainly not his best production, many owners complaining that it had a wicked driveshaft vibration among other things, but it was Bugatti's favorite. In fact he liked it so much that he would still build one to order in 1939. One Parisian client brought his 46 back to the factory for adjustment time after time. One day M. Bugatti came upon the fellow in a corridor.

"You, monsieur, I think," he said, "are the one who has brought his Type 46 back three times?"

The man admitted quite readily that it was true, full of hope that *Le Patron* himself would now see to things.

Bugatti stared at him. "Do not," he said, "let it happen again."

A reigning Balkan monarch who was visiting in France wanted to buy a Royale, the Type 41, of which only seven were built — at a chassis price of $20,000. In the beginning, when Bugatti first began to make the Type 41, and before the Great Depression of the Thirties forced a more realistic view, he had intended selling the car only to the most select clients. The Balkan ruler

The Type 57SC (left), built during 1937-38, was a very fast, low-chassis, supercharged version of the Type 57. The Type 35B of 1927 to 1930 (below left) was the winningest Grand Prix car of its era. The stunning Type 55 (below) had a Type 51 GP engine set in a Type 54 GP chassis. It was built from 1932-35.

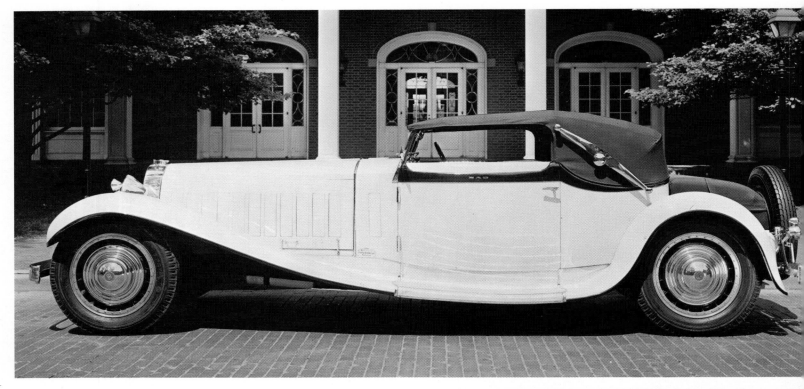

visited his chateau in Molsheim, and *Le Patron* covertly estimated his character. He was told after the visit that there was not, alas, a Royale available, nor could Bugatti say, unhappily, when the factory would be able to make one.

"Never!" Bugatti told one of his assistants after the encounter. "The man's table manners are beyond belief!"

"My dear fellow," Bugatti replied to a customer who was complaining that his Bugatti was difficult to start in cold weather, "if you can afford a Type 55 Bugatti, surely you can afford a heated garage!"

Ettore Bugatti had earned the right to be arrogant. The Type 55 Bugatti might not start first crack on a cold January morning, but it was among the fastest cars on the world market in 1932. Its one-hundred-fifteen miles an hour is not a great figure today, almost forty years later, but certainly no one could call it slow, either, and its fenderline is still the loveliest one ever to be put on an automobile. This triple-curved line was the work of Bugatti's son Jean, and it appeared on the roadster 41, too. It is only one example of Jean Bugatti's great talent in coach designing.

After World War I, Bugatti returned to racing and the spectacular success in the Grand Prix du Mans in 1920 (Friderich won the race with a lead of nearly twenty minutes) escalated him quickly into the top rank of European motorcar builders. Over the next few years he expanded his little factory until he was employing a thousand people. The factory was a complex of one-story buildings, all fitted with identical heavy brass-bound doors with locks made by Bugatti to which only *Le Patron* held the master key. Much more than just the factory was on these grounds. There were two museums built, one for his brother Rembrandt's sculpture, and the other for a collection of horse-drawn car-

With 4.9 supercharged liters to propel it, the Type 50, built from 1930-34, was a very impressive performer. This car, shown at right above, was also the first Bugatti to have twin overhead cams.

In 1929 M. Bugatti introduced the most grandiose, impressive, expensive, majestic automobile ever manufactured: the Type 41, La Royale. Seven cars were built. At right is the two-door sedan by Kellner. Above is the two-seater by Weinberger of Munich.

riages. Horses were his second passion and there was a covered riding hall and stables for fifteen of them. He was a man of many interests. He raised wire-haired fox terriers for a few years and even fancy pigeons. Besides this, he distilled his own liqueurs. He also maintained an inn, L'Hostellerie du Pur Sang, for the convenience of his clients. Bugatti's own chateau was a stone's throw away, set in a luxurious park. It was here, after an important race victory, of which there were many, that there might be a garden party, with Madame Bugatti and their two daughters and two sons in attendance, and perhaps the winning driver would receive from Bugatti the highest award of the firm, an elaborate wristwatch from a famous Swiss house, made to his own design in the horseshoe form of the Bugatti radiator. Only one of these wristwatches is known to exist today, and it is in England.

As might be expected, Bugatti presided over this domain as its absolute ruler. It was his habit every morning to tour the factory, either on a bicycle of his own design and make, or in the small open electric Type 56 runabout. On these tours he dressed colorfully and with much dash.

His word was law. One of his primary concerns, almost an obsession with him, was with cleanliness. He insisted that the offices, benches, and workshops be absolutely spotless and shining; even the brass doors and locks were immaculately polished. He was imperious. It is said that when the company which was supplying him with electricity asked for payment of an overdue bill (Bugatti's financial affairs tended to run on a feast-or-famine pattern) he paid it — and then ordered a power station to be built on the factory grounds. When the power station was finished, Bugatti called an officer of the power company, showed him through the spotless new plant, tiled throughout, and said, "I did not like the tone of your letter of some months past, and as you see, I shall have no further need for your company's services. Good day."

For Ettore Bugatti, as for so many others, the golden years probably ended in 1929. The Depression of the 1930's brought new power to the labor unions, and Bugatti, paternalistic to the bone, was never quite able to accept the fact that his workers, whom he considered part of his family, had indeed staged a sit-down strike.

Most of the years just before World War II [h]e spent away from Molsheim, in his Paris office[,] returning for very brief visits and then on[ly] rarely. He left the running of the factory to h[is] older son Jean, then twenty-six years old, an[d] the nucleus of old-time executives, Erne[st] Friderich, Pierre Marco and the others. Jea[n,] whom his father had always forbidden to rac[e,] was killed in August of 1939 while testing a c[ar] which was entered for the Grand Prix at [La] Baule. It was a great blow to his father.

During the war the Germans used Molshei[m] for torpedo manufacture. After the liberation [it] was occupied by the Canadians and t[he] Americans. The Canadians had an accident[al] fire which was very destructive and t[he] Americans, in their retreat before the last b[ig] German offensive of the war, removed all the r[e]maining machine tools and lost the identify[ing] papers. After that the French government seize[d] the plant as enemy property because Etto[re] Bugatti was still an Italian national. He foug[ht] the case in the courts and won, and after th[at] began to work hard again. He designed a chea[p] trawler to help the French fishing industry [to] recover from the effects of the war; a tiny ra[ce]

g car; a sailboat with steel tripods instead of regular masts, and many other things. (In his lifetime Bugatti registered over three hundred and fifty patents, ranging from safety razors to gasoline-powered railcars; the latter were for years the fastest in the world.) But Ettore Bugatti overworked. The death of his son Jean, the strain of the war years and the long court case to recover the plant had weakened him. He became ill in May, 1947, and died on the twenty-first of August at the American Hospital in Neuilly.

His memorial is built of the twelve hundred Bugatti automobiles that still survive today of the seventy-five hundred he made. This is an extraordinarily high percentage, particularly when one considers that France went through two terrible wars during the factory's existence. It is a remarkable indication of the value attached to Bugatti motorcars from the beginning.

Not only in variety, but in temperament, in performance, in actual personality, when they are all seen together, they do stand alone, and no one who has ever owned a Bugatti, or ever driven a Bugatti any considerable distance, is likely ever to quite forget it.

The last Grand Prix car to be successfully raced by the Bugatti factory was the Type 59.
Introduced in 1933 originally as a 2.6-liter car, its capacity was subsequently
raised to 3257 cc. In the capable hands of such drivers as René Dreyfus, Jean-Pierre Wimille and
Tazio Nuvolari, the Type 59 was capable of over 160 miles an hour.
The touring versions of the 59, the Type 57 and its variants, were the last production Bugattis.

AUBURN

Though modest in price in comparison with its sisters Duesenberg and Cord, the Auburn was a fleet and beautiful marque that is no less so four decades after motoring's golden age.

The Auburn was always a bridesmaid. It was a family problem really. Its qualities — beguiling good looks, spirited performance, complete reliability, unprecedented value-for-money — are clearly worthy of the most ardent acknowledgement. Yet the Auburn historically has never really come into its own: It seems forever destined to be driven in the shadow of Duesenberg and Cord. Of this injustice, more anon. For we are perhaps getting ahead of the story. The Auburns spoken of here are those of the E. L. Cord era, the cars those enthusiasts who so fondly remember Auburn remember so fondly. Yet although the Auburn disappeared from the automotive scene with the Cord and Duesenberg, it had entered the fray long before — before Cord and Duesenberg were anything other than family surnames. No history of Auburn should exclude those early years.

The first Auburn automobile — a single-cylinder, solid-tired, tiller-steered runabout — was built in 1900 by Frank and Morris Eckhart, brothers and partners in the Eckhart Carriage Company of Auburn, Indiana. That same year they established the Auburn Automobile Company, capitalized at $2500. Two years later they were in the swing of manufacture, modestly at first — production in 1904 totalled fifty units — but they expanded slowly thereafter, adding another cylinder to their car in 1905, a four-cylinder model in 1909, a six in 1912. The Eckharts were proud of their cars, justifiably so; they were certainly well built. But they were also rather pedestrian in appearance, and this may have been one of the factors which plunged the company into financial trouble by 1918. The

Eckharts' story was fairly typical for that day — good intentions and a good car weren't enough to make it in the automobile business. Whatever it took, the Eckharts no longer had it, and in 1919 they sold out to a group of Chicago financiers who would soon discover they didn't have it either. The new owners, headed by Ralph Austin Bard and including William Wrigley, Jr., of Juicy Fruit renown, made numerous changes, the most noteworthy being the introduction of the Auburn Beauty-six, the model name of which may or may not have been an intended slur on previous Auburns but was in any case reasonably apt. Yet despite expanded facilities, an enlarged advertising and sales program and an improved product, the situation at Auburn remained much the same. From 1919 to 1922 a disappointing 15,717 cars were sold. By 1924 the Auburn factory was producing a dismal six units a day and more than meeting the demand.

There's an old saying pessimists enjoy puttin to the frankly miserable, that things always loc gray before they become totally black. So th situation seemed at Auburn. But the perpetrat of that bit of congenial prose — and indee Auburn itself — never reckoned with the lik of Errett Lobban Cord. E. L. Cord, defined various times by *Time* magazine as a "profan bespectacled capitalist whose life has been garage mechanic's dream" and "an astut scheming, self-effacing businessman who know how and where grand parsnips can be found an buttered." E. L. Cord, less waggishly called th "boy wonder" or "golden boy" of the Twentie and when that decade turned darkly to th Thirties, as a "leading entrepreneur of th Depression." He was all that — and much more

Born in Warrensburg, Missouri, in 189 Cord's early career had ranged from buildin "racing" bodies out of junked Fords operating a trucking concern hauling alkali o of Death Valley. By his own admission he mad and lost $50,000 three times — all before he wa twenty-one. Now he was thirty, with a hundre thousand dollars saved from yet another en terprise in Chicago. As he later said, "I starte looking around. I wanted to do something wit that $100,000."

In 1924 he and Auburn got together. Cord wa brought into the company as general manage without pay, presumably, but with the optio that if he put the company on its feet, he woul be given an opportunity to buy control. His im mediate problem was apparent — moving som 700 unsold and presumably unwanted Aubur touring cars that were idly standing in the fa

*A 1921 Model 6-39R Beauty-*SIX *roadster.*

ry parking lot awaiting obsolescence. A little ylish nickel plating, some flashy repainting, a w minor modifications and the problem was lved. A half-million dollars was netted; uburn's debts were paid off. E. L. Cord had

proven himself. He became a vice-president.

Two years later he was president of the Auburn Automobile Company. It was scarcely unexpected. Company sales had doubled in 1925, and before 1926 ended they would double once

again — 8500 cars for a net profit of close to a million dollars. Moreover the Auburns being sold were entirely new.

The 8-88 made its debut late in 1925 and was improved yearly for three years thereafter. Its

A 1929 Model 8-120 speedster.

A 1927 Model 8-88 four-door sedan.

stiff, pressed-steel "twist-proof" frame, semi-elliptic springing front and rear, and three-speed "racing crash box" were joined by 1928 with such other commendable features as hydraulic four-wheel brakes and Bijur lubrication, which ordinarily was used on only the most expensive automobiles. But the 8-88 wasn't expensive — it just looked it. Its coachwork had a dash and distinction all its own. Particularly appealing was the roadster, with its flowing two-tone color scheme highlighted by a beltline gracefully sweeping over the hood. A snugly fitting top, wire wheels, a sloping windshield and a rumble seat with a special entry door on the right side completed the picture — and a pleasant picture it was. The car was uncommonly low — the result of nineteen-inch diameter wheels as well as body design — and, moreover, it looked

A 1933 Model 8-100 four-door sedan.

A 1931 Model 8-98 Phaeton Sedan.

greeably European. Its price: $1695.

Were all this not sufficient, the Auburn was now a sporting performer as well, and Cord wanted to make certain that this fact was not lost on the car-buying public. In 1927 he sent a sedan and two roadsters to the Atlantic City Speedway, where they proceeded to break all records for fully equipped stock cars, from five to 5000 miles. And on the competition front, Auburn stepped into the tracks left when Mercer quit the scene — as a challenger to the Stutz. Admittedly, Auburn generally followed the champ across the finish line that year, but their competitive baptismal season was sufficiently impressive to make credible the Auburn slogan, "The Car Itself Is the Answer."

Apparently, however, it wasn't for E. L. Cord, because in 1928 he introduced the 8-115, that designation referring to the increased power of the eight-cylinder engine. Auburn celebrated the debut of this new car in a bevy of full-page advertisements with the headline "115 Horsepower" emblazoned in Barnum & Bailey-sized 72 Point Cooper Black type and an illustration of 115 white horses stoutly stampeding off the page. This left no room for a picture of the car — but under the circumstances perhaps it wasn't necessary. Stutz, after all, advertised only 113 horsepower.

Now also was introduced Auburn's version of the raciest coachwork then available to the motorcar: the boattailed speedster. Here was Cord's answer to the Stutz Black Hawk. In March at Daytona one of them established a speed of 108.46 mph over the measured mile, and later in the year another finished twenty-four hours at Atlantic City at a record-breaking average of 84.7 mph. The speedster's single most impressive competitive victory occurred in September when the car set a new record of 21 minutes 45.40 seconds climbing Pikes Peak for the coveted Penrose Trophy. It has since been generally conceded that regardless of horsepower and Pikes Peak, the Stutz was faster than the Auburn. The point is scarcely worth arguing. A Stutz Black Hawk speedster sold in 1928 for close to $5000. An Auburn could be driven out of a showroom for several thousand dollars less, and, with that reality in mind, the loss of a few miles an hour would hardly be missed.

That is the only conclusion that can be drawn by the production figures. The over 22,000 Auburns sold in 1929 represented a 1000 percent increase over sales of a scant five years previous. Cord knew exactly what he was doing. He was offering the public a creditably fast and certainly flashy automobile at prices that could not be equalled. He had a good thing going.

The Auburn could easily have sold itself, but Cord was taking no chances. He reorganized his sales and distributor organization. The basis of Cord's policy was a dealer's dream — the "no-loss" trade-in, and to implement it, he created an artificial shortage of Auburns. Cord was a firm believer in underproduction. For every Auburn delivered to a dealer, there were, in theory, two eagerly awaiting customers willing to accept whatever trade-in allowance the dealer was willing to offer. The car would naturally go to the customer who represented the greatest profit. In 1929 Auburn announced that dealers' stock on hand averaged one and a half cars.

By that time too Cord was also producing the Duesenberg, had introduced another car bearing his own name, and had gathered all the other companies he had accumulated along the way into the Cord Corporation. Then the stock market crashed. E. L. Cord barely winced. True, 1930 wasn't a good year, but by the middle of the year following, from the look of things in the Cord empire, it was hard to believe the Depression had even happened. Auburn sales soared to 28,103, and profit equalled the peak year of 1929. One thousand new dealers entered the fold, most of them abandoning franchises of less popular marques. And Auburn climbed from twenty-third to thirteenth place in retail sales. All in 1931.

The reason for all this was the new Auburn 8-8. It was the hit of the shows. *Fortune* proclaimed it "the biggest package in the world for the price," and *Business Week* concluded "it was more car for the money than the public had ever seen." They were both right. Its 268.6-cubic-inch Lycoming engine was leagues more powerful than anything in its price class. The frame was stronger than ever, featuring "X" cross member bracing for the first time in a

rear-drive automobile. Among the many other noteworthy features, most significant was the introduction of an L.G.S. Free Wheeling unit, then a new item limited primarily to the most costly of cars. The most expensive 8-98 could be had for $1395. Probably no better testament may be made for the car than the fact that insurance companies duly lifted it out of its price class and rated it — by power, weight and speed — with the highest priced cars in America.

Dual Ratio, Bijur lubrication, free wheeling and a price in the $1000 range were shared by the 1932 Model 8-100 sport coupé at left and the 1934 four-door phaeton sedan pictured above.

Priced at $1800, the 1936 Model 852 convertible shown below is noteworthy for its fold-flat windshield, unusual for a four-door convertible model of American manufacture.

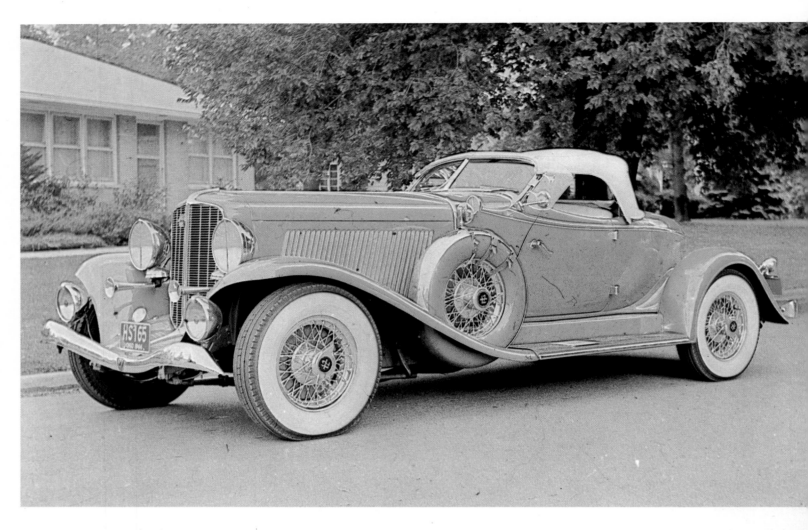

Among the most happily recalled, and today most sought after, models in the Auburn
range was the boattailed speedster. This model had been introduced
in the late Twenties with the advent of the 8-88 and 8-115 series, and was
a popular selling, and competitive, model for the remainder of that spirited decade.
But it was really in the Thirties when the most sensational Auburn
boattail speedsters arrived. Consider the electric blue V-12
speedster above, available for as little as sixteen or eighteen hundred dollars until 1934.
The fabulous 851 below was priced a little higher—about $2245 in 1935.
In either case, there probably wasn't a better sporting buy in America at the time.

But if the 8-98 was a bargain — and assure
it was — it paled in comparison with the V
offered the following year. It was inevitable t
Auburn would enter the multi-cylinder race
the Thirties and typical, too, that the Auburn
12 — at $975 for a two-passenger coupé
would be the most economical twelve ever
fered to the public. Auburn's unit displaced
cubic inches, developing an advertised 160 h
at 3500 rpm — and one could have it for l
than a thousand dollars. It seemed scarc

lievable — and maybe that was part of the problem. It should have been a good year for Auburn. It wasn't. The V-12 was promoted vigorously, one of the speedster models set up a number of records on Muroc Dry Lake, many of which, incidentally, would stand until after World War II — but at year's end Auburn reported a loss of close to a million dollars.

The following year was even worse; the 11,000 Eights and Twelves produced in 1932 slipped to 6000 in 1933. By 1934 Auburn was struggling to undo what had been done. The V-12 line was phased out, and a six-cylinder series was reinstated. The line of Eights was reduced from ten models to seven. Prices were slashed. Nothing helped. By the end of the year Auburn had dropped to twenty-first place in retail sales.

E. L. Cord, meanwhile, was busy elsewhere in his empire, which by now included shipbuilding and aviation. Then reportedly, kidnap threats against his children motivated him to give up all and retreat to his estate in Surrey, England.

The Auburn company remained in deep trouble. It could no longer afford the luxury of building Twelves, yet it needed an "image" automobile that would generate sales of, hopefully, all Auburns. What would have been Cord's worry was handed to Duesenberg's president Harold T. Ames, who was gratuitously appointed executive vice-president of Auburn. Ames, however, didn't make the move from Indianapolis to Auburn alone; he took with him Gordon Buehrig and August Duesenberg, respectively chief designer and chief engineer of Duesenberg Inc. It was the former's charge to design a sales-generating speedster model, and the latter's to produce an inexpensive but reliable supercharger for it. The result was the Auburn 851 speedster.

What a marvelous car this was! Duesenberg's supercharger boosted the power of the Lycoming Eight from its usual 115 hp at 3500 rpm to 150 at 4000 rpm. Its sound has been described as "audible, but never raucous." Quite true. If a blown Mercedes screamed, a blown Auburn whined. One could get used to that. In looks the Auburn 851 speedster shone too. Set on a wheelbase of 127 inches, it was a big, impressive automobile. Yet for all its massiveness, it was nicely proportioned — a striking radiator grille, a long, low hood, rakish boattail, small cockpit and four finely chromed pipes leading from the side of the engine compartment.

As speedsters go, it was scarcely a practical automobile, strictly and unabashedly a two-passenger car; it had to be that at least, if for no other reason than it took two people to remove and store the pint-sized convertible top. Even luggage space was less than ample, the area being shared by a spare tire, the removal of which required manipulating it over the "X" member in the tail.

But such trivia were soon forgotten once an owner got behind the wheel and got moving — for the 851 speedster could really move. Every one made boasted a plaque on the instrument panel noting the speed at which the car had been tested; it was always a figure modestly in excess of 100 mph — a lively clip for a car priced at $2245.

Like the Auburns before it, the 851 was sent record breaking, this time to the Bonneville salt flats. Both the temperature and the car's performance were well above the 100 mark. The flying mile was taken at 104.17 mph, the standing mile at 51.9 seconds, and 500 miles were covered at an average of 103 mph. No fewer than seventy unlimited and American class speed records were broken, and in the course of doing so, the speedster became the first fully equipped American stock car to exceed 100 mph for a twelve-hour period.

Records indicate that approximately 500 speedsters were built, and the Auburn company lost hundreds of dollars on every one sold. It was virtually a hand-built car, the body section alone comprising twenty-two sections which were hand-filled and fitted. At the price it was sold, profit was impossible. But the speedster did pull people into Auburn showrooms, and many of them drove out in an Auburn — often in a less expensive model of the 851 line or in one of Auburn's six-cylinder cars which sold for as little as $795.

It was all for naught, of course. The Auburn ostensibly was already dead. E. L. Cord had returned to the United States. It wasn't a happy homecoming. The Securities and Exchange Commission was taking a stern look at his empire, and in August of 1937 he sold his holdings to two Wall Street firms and a group of his former associates headed by L. B. Manning. In September Manning hinted that Auburn might retire from the automobile business to concentrate on parts, accessories and air conditioning — no Auburns had been built in that year at all — and in October "informed Wall Street sources" announced that manufacture of Auburn, Cord and Duesenberg automobiles would be discontinued. The sources were obviously well informed.

Should one wish to affix blame for the demise of the Auburn, it's easy enough. A good many people believe that had Cord's interest been focused more on the automobile than the empire the company might have survived. In truth, had it not been for Cord, the Auburn story conceivably would have ended some ten years before it did. And maybe the car was doomed anyway. Why? Simply because it offered too much for too little. It was, as advertised, "Above the Mass Class." Should its price have been commensurate with its looks and performance? Perhaps. Perhaps the fact that the Auburn line was so diversified — that a six-cylinder utilitarian car and a high performance speedster carried the same name — was distressing to those who would rather buy an image than a car. Perhaps people were — and are — so cynical as to doubt anything that seems too good to be true, even when it's proven. Perhaps, on reflection, we deserved to lose the Auburn.

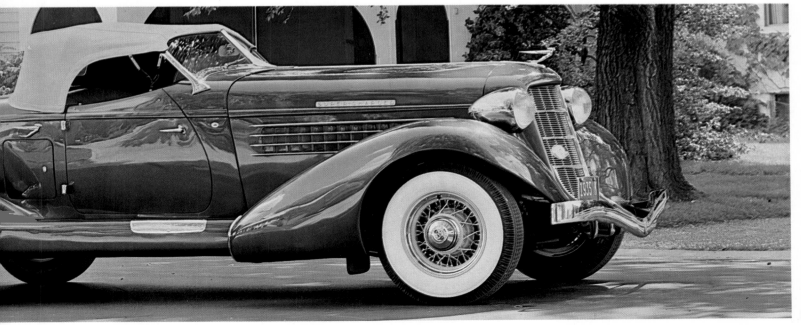

PUNGS-FINCH INDEED!

Whoever heard of a Pungs-Finch?

The Pungs-Finch had a problem. It was credibility. To hear the story as they told it shortly after this century turned, but for them the automobile would probably never have made it at all. Builders of automobiles since 1888, nearly ten thousand engines bearing the Pungs-Finch nameplate chuffing away in all corners of the globe, now nobly putting together cars without peer, every part from "pump to piston" being built in their Albert Kahn-esque factory in Detroit: They were real pioneers, those Pungs-Finch people.

Yes, indeed — were all the foregoing true. Unfortunately, for those who wrote Pungs-Finch promotion, truth was something to be used only with the greatest discretion. This, of course, poses a problem for the historian. One begins to feel safe only in concluding that yes, there was a Pungs-Finch — and it was a car. The unlikely name derived from W. A. Pungs and E. B. Finch. They were a father/son-in-law duo, although it appears that Pungs provided Finch with little more than money, a factory site, a daughter and something to put before the hyphen. Finch was the engineer, and a very good one, having studied the art at the University of Michigan and having built his first car around 1902. Come 1904, he and his father-in-law organized the Pungs-Finch Auto and Gas Engine Company in Detroit, locating at Pungs' boat-building works on Jefferson and Baldwin Avenues, and taking into the fold the Sintz Gas Engine Company.

Just what they acquired, tangibly, in the Sintz deal is a mystery. Certainly not Claude Sintz, who would play no part in the Pungs-Finch story. Probably not, for practical purposes anyway, the Sintz factory in Grand Rapids: No Pungs-Finch would exit from there. But what they did acquire was a past, one which would prompt the touted Pungs-Finch tradition of motorcar building.

Claude Sintz, of course, had been in the engine business for a good many years and had almost made it to the *Chicago Times-Herald* contest in 1895 with a car of his own design. The Pungs-Finch New York agents pounced on this bit of retroactive news, mantling the Sintz tradi-

tion — without credit to Sintz — around Pungs-Finch. And they didn't stop there. In subsequent brochures they dared to even picture the Pungs-Finch "past achievements" — some of these vehicles looked curiously European and one, an "1894" omnibus, was unquestionably the behemoth built by Milton O. Reeves in 1897, powered, admittedly, by an engine Reeves had bought from Claude Sintz. All this was rather removed, one might say, from *nuda veritas*.

And it was surely unnecessary, too, for while the Pungs-Finch selling agents were toying with tenuity and truth in New York, out in Detroit E. B. Finch was coming up with some cars interesting enough to stand on their own merits. The first production Pungs-Finches had rolled out on Jefferson Avenue as 1904 passed into 1905. They were the models D and F — experimental cars no doubt having been awarded the preceding alphabetical designations — the former being a bit bigger than the latter, and the latter actually becoming the former the following year.

Granted, the Pungs-Finch did look rather much like any other $1850 four-cylinder, side-valve, twenty-odd horsepower tourer, but add to its specification shaft drive and sliding gear transmission, and it's evident that Detroit's forward thinking was considerably more commendable than New York's backward reveries. Mr. Finch had built a nice car; even so, he wasn't satisfied.

"Substantial construction," as *The Horseless Age* would put it, was a "conspicuous feature" of the Pungs-Finch. And a creditable performance was too. Early in 1905, with "five passengers up, two tollgate stops and a six-mile rate through the village of Birmingham," the Pungs-Finch finished a test trip of twenty miles from Pontiac to Detroit in thirty-four minutes flat. That was very strong driving, as Hugh Dolnar, inveterate journalist of the *Cycle and Automobile Trade Journal*, concluded, but not strong enough for Mr. Finch, "who wants to feel some life under him when he drives a car." And thus was conceived the ultimate Pungs-Finch: the P. F. *pièce de résistance*, a motorcar the truth of which is even more incredible than the

*Few, certainly, and this
is the only example known to exist.*

colorful fiction of Pungs-Finch history.

Completed in late summer of 1905 for the 1906 season and dubbed the Finch "Limited," the car would have been noteworthy if only for its ample measurements — 5¾ bore by 6½ stroke for a piston area of 132 inches per cylinder. Heady enough stuff right there. But, the four cylinders sat in a row and — now heed this — carried inclined overhead valves in hemispherical combustion chambers operated by a single gear-driven overhead camshaft! Mr. Finch, Dolnar averred, "had always liked the valves on top and had also disliked the long lifters and top levers needed if the valves are placed on top with the camshaft in th[e] crankbox." At the time few engineers anywhere thought that way too. Mr. Finch was somethin[g] of an innovator.

But, alas, although "limited" was affixed [to] the car's name because of its identification wi[th] the speed and power of a locomotive, as [it] turned out, it more correctly forecast the car['s] future. It was limited — only the one prototy[pe] was built. Just why is not known. With a pri[ce] tag in the $3500 range, attractive styling, [a] guaranteed better than 50 hp and 55 mph, [it] could have been one of the better buys of th[e] year. Henry Ford told Mr. Pungs it was th[e]

car he had ever seen.

it was what Mr. Pungs was telling Mr. — and vice versa — that posed the real m, were not their overzealous selling sufficient cause for alarm. They simply get along, and Mr. Finch finally left in a irst to work in the technical department at d, then Chalmers, finally in 1910 to give that mechanical nonsense and become the ers dealer in Cleveland.

he interim Mr. Pungs went on producing rlier Pungs-Finch tourer, as well as the 40 hp model his son-in-law had developed his departure. But not for long. By 1910

the company was out of business. Mr. Pungs without Mr. Finch was rather like Mr. Rolls would have been without Mr. Royce. Nowhere.

Total Pungs-Finch production during its six years in the automotive vale is not known. Several hundred has been estimated, but that, at best, is just a guess. Only one of the cars is known to exist today, and this fortunately is the Limited. It belongs to Henry Austin Clark, Jr., and is on display at his Long Island Automotive Museum in Southampton, New York. When people ask him what it is, he tells them. They think he's kidding. There was a lot of that going on when the car was being built, too.

The magnificent engine of Mr. E. B. Finch, measuring five and three-quarter inches (bore) by six and a half (stroke) for a total of five hundred twenty-eight cubic inches.

ROLLS-ROYCE:
THE IMMORTAL LINEAGE

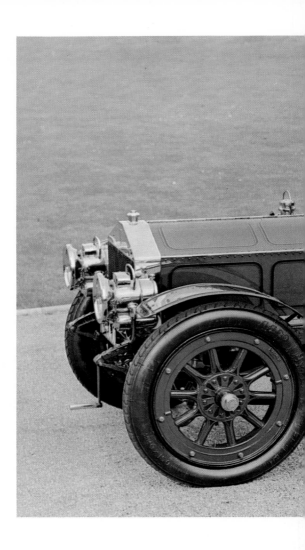

Rolls-Royce. Stand any other name in automotive history next to that one and it pales into near-transparency. There may have been more expensive cars, bigger cars, perhaps even better cars, but the Rolls-Royce reputation remains inviolate and undiminished, the standard against which every other luxury car is inevitably measured.

Among motoring connoisseurs, Rolls-Royce is the tall and solitary standard-bearer of perfection, whose loneliness in the world of motorcar manufacture is viewed with awe and wonder, as tribute to a reputation for exclusivity which has withstood the onslaught of wars, social revolution, tottering empires and other man-made disasters for more than sixty-five years. In short, it is in a class quite by itself.

The "Spirit of Ecstasy" statuette which evolved into the Flying Lady, the splendidly simple R-R monogram, the cacophonous Rolls-Royce clock, the coin on the radiator, the fables and myths, lore and legends — all are part of the Rolls-Royce saga. And it all began so simply that day in May of 1904 when a wealthy motoring and ballooning enthusiast by the name of Charles Stewart Rolls met a brilliant mechanical engineer named Frederick Henry Royce at the Midland Hotel in Manchester, England.

The results of that meeting are history, and in the portfolio that follows are presented some of the cars that have transformed that history into legend.

The Silver Ghost and Before

The noted British magazine *The Autocar* reported the event thusly in its December 6th issue of 1906: "Anything appertaining to automobile mechanism which issues from the works at Manchester under the direction of the finished and talented engineer, Mr. Ed. Royce, is certain to attract the immediate attention of the motoring world." One must forgive the lamentable gaffe of either editor or typesetter, but although the magazine failed to get the name of the engineer right, they were certainly right about the engine. It was the new 40-50 hp six-cylinder powerplant from Rolls-Royce, Ltd. — and it was the heart of a new car that would be named the Silver Ghost.

Above: The 1905 30 H.P., with rakishly-striped two-seater coachwork by Jarvis of London.
Below left: A 1907 Silver Ghost, with replica coachwork of an original Barker tourer.
Right: The 1912 Silver Ghost limousine by Hooper, originally owned by Lord Wavertree.

The company itself was barely a year old, though the partnership between the son of Lord Llangattock and the engineer from Alwalton had already weathered two years, and several Rolls-Royce models. C. S. Rolls and Co., as the London automobile dealership was called, had agreed in 1904 to purchase all the cars built by F. H. Royce and Co. of Manchester and to market them as Rolls-Royces. The inevitable consolidation to Rolls-Royce, Ltd. had followed on March 16th, 1906.

Produced during this period had been the 10 hp two-cylinder car, of which sixteen examples were built; the 15 hp three-cylinder car built in six copies; the 20 hp four-cylinder car with production numbering forty units and the 30 hp six-cylinder car with a total production of thirty-seven. Then, too, there were the V-8 Legalimit and Invisible Engine models. But soon all this was to change.

By 1908, when the company had outgrown its tiny Manchester plant and had moved to Derby, the decision was made that henceforward Rolls-Royce would be a one-car company — and that car would be the Silver Ghost. All previous models were discontinued.

The man behind that decision was probably neither Rolls nor Royce, but Claude Goodman Johnson, originally partner to Rolls in the London dealership. Indeed much of the credit for early Rolls-Royce success must go to the enterprising Mr. Johnson. One long look at the new car and a glance at the results of rigorous tests it had already undergone were enough to convince Johnson that the 40/50 hp model was the stuff of which motoring dreams are made — and he set out at once to prove it to everyone else.

The thirteenth chassis was handed over to him, fitted with a touring body painted silver and a simple silver-plated brass plate on the dash carrying the name "Silver Ghost." The car was then driven for 2000 miles, under Royal Automobile Club observation, plotting the course for the forthcoming 1907 Scottish Trial. Then it was entered in the trial itself, after which it continued with trips between Glasgow and London until 15,000 miles had been covered. Because a minor fuel tap closure caused a one-minute delay at the 629th mile, Rolls-Royce could advertise only "14,371 miles non-stop." But that was sufficient.

The Silver Ghost Rolls-Royce was produced for nineteen years thereafter, with but minor modifications. Claude Johnson obviously knew a winner when he saw it. What the Silver Ghost proved was that a quiet car need not be slow (as electrics were), that a gasoline car could be as smooth-running as a steamer — and that speed was not necessarily a deterrent to reliability. Even economy was stressed. "Is your car costing you too much?" asked one advertisement — suggesting that, in the light of Rolls-Royce's amply-demonstrated dependability standards, it probably was.

The Silver Ghost — its side-valve engine with non-detachable cylinder heads and unenclosed stems, tappets and springs — has since been viewed by some as old-fashioned even for its day. Let the critics be gone. The Silver Ghost's day lasted nearly two decades, and it established standards for refinement and workmanship that others would be hard put to emulate. There's nothing old-fashioned about that.

Originally Silver Ghost-mounted, this landaulet was installed on its 20 H.P. chassis in 1923. Below: A 1914 Silver Ghost, sporting the London-to-Edinburgh-type touring coachwork.

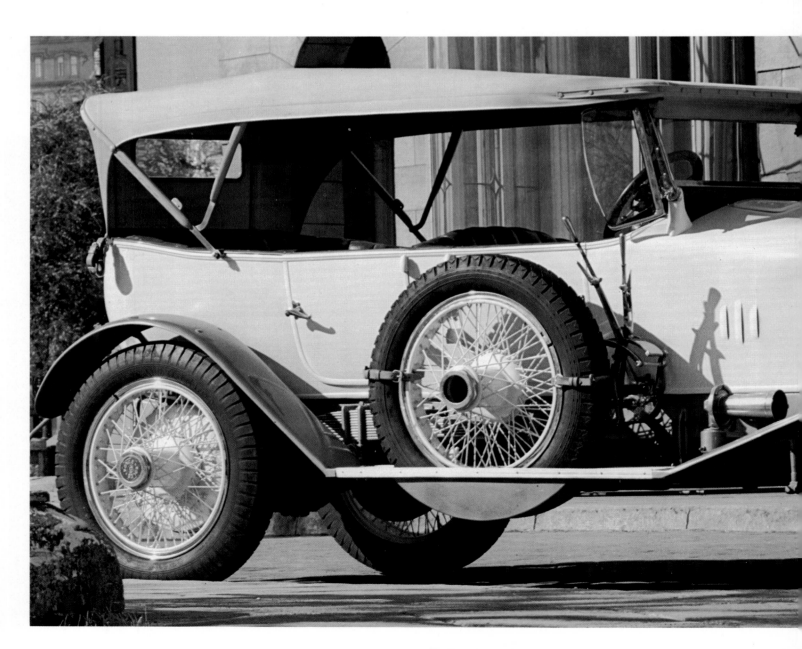

The Phantom I

They had, they said, developed a V-12, an in-line eight, an overhead cam six. They'd even tried a supercharger, rejected rather quickly as noisy, complicated and extravagant. And so, after seven years of testing and experimentation, Rolls-Royce said, with almost desperate restraint, ". . . the 40/50 h.p. six-cylinder Phantom chassis emerged, and is offered to the public as the most suitable type possible for a mechanically propelled carriage under present-day conditions."

It was 1925. Only now would its predecessor become officially known as the Silver Ghost. It had previously been referred to merely as the 40/50 H.P. The successor, known initially as the New Phantom, would with time and descendants become known as the Phantom I. This explanation as to nomenclature is, by the bye, given only incidentally, and simply because when speaking of Rolls-Royce one feels obligated to be quite as proper as the car.

The Ghost and the Phantom were offered side by side at first, though the former faded from the scene within a year of the latter's introduction. Indeed the New Phantom was essentially a Ghost with an overhead valve engine displacing 7668 cc (468.14 cubic inches) as opposed to the time-honored side-valve's 7428 cc (or 7036 for the earliest Ghost models). The new engine made for perhaps twenty-five percent more power, though Rolls-Royce themselves never bothered with providing such information, nor would it appear did any of the motoring journalists of the day go to the trouble of calculating it. As with all Rolls-Royce engines — both previous and to come — the new six was gradually increased in output during its life, and most historians since have concluded its developed horsepower to be between ninety and one hundred.

Rolls-Royce claimed seventy-five miles an hour for the car. *The Autocar* headlined its performance as "Not 'Very Fast' but Quite Fast Enough!" — commenting, "it will run quite comfortably at 70 m.p.h. without giving the slightest suggestion that any part of the chassis is working hard." In most versions a maximum of eighty was certainly possible, and in the short-chassis "Continental" model, admittedly fitted with a specially designed lightweight body, ninety miles an hour could be topped. Anything faster than that would probably have seemed undignified to a Rolls-Royce owner anyway.

"The man who goes to Poole's for his clothes, Purdy for his guns and Hardy for his rods, goes to Rolls-Royce for his car." This inspired, and certainly appropriate bit of prose, had been penned by Rolls-Royce advertising men during the Ghostly years, and it would remain ever as apt during the reign of the Phantom I.

The Phantom — like the Ghost — was built in America as well, Claude Johnson having founded Rolls-Royce of America in Springfield, Massachusetts, in 1919. (The Depression, among other factors, would force its closure in 1931.) The American Phantoms were incredibly expensive, $11,750 for the chassis alone. "A Rolls-Royce, like a fine residence, is a permanent investment," quoth the advertising department in New York, thus mitigating the fact that the

British version just about doubled-priced mo_ American variations on the luxury theme. A_ parently it sufficed. A respectable number _ Phantoms were built in this country — 1241 _ fact. A goodly portion of them survive to th_ day, not unsurprisingly; it was scarcely a ca_ one would simply discard.

Below: A Brewster-designed playboy roadster on the Phantom I chassis. This car was built in 1931 by Rolls-Royce of America, Springfield, Massachusetts. At right is the uncompromisingly sporty Phantom I boattail speedster built by Barker in 1925 as a hunting car for the Maharaja of Bikaner.

But no car improperly maintained could be immortal, and Rolls-Royce were rather emphatic on that subject. "Before a Rolls-Royce chassis is sold," the Phantom handbook reminds us, "it is very carefully tested and adjusted by experts. It will run best if no attempt is made to interfere unnecessarily with adjustments." With that quasi-polite admonition the company proceeded to tell the owner just what he *should* have his chauffeur do to ensure the proper maintenance of his Phantom. A Rolls-Royce chauffeur certainly earned his wages.

Of all Rolls-Royce models through history, the Phantom I was the shortest-lived — 1925 to 1929 in England, 1926 to 1931 in Springfield, Massachusetts — and only recently has it come to be looked upon with favor by Rolls-Royce connoisseurs. In its day, however, the Phantom I was certainly very well received, and some notable — and incredibly opulent — examples survive.

Consider the brougham on these pages, built

The Phantom I,
of singular opulence,
built in 1927
by Clark of Wolverhampton.

by the coachbuilding house of Clark of Wolverhampton as a present from C. W. Gasque of Hamstead, London, to his wife. Mr. Gasque, a devotee of French furniture of the Louis XIV period, asked that the car reflect this style, and indeed it does. The back seat is a sofa, the bow front cabinet concealing the auxiliary seats as well as decanters for sherry and brandy, glasses, silver tray, and containers for cigarettes and potables. The upholstery was specially made at Aubusson in petit point needlework. It alone cost £600. (The cost of the entire car is not known.) Drawn thread work was featured in the curtains, and fittings of genuine Battersea enamel were included in the companions on either side of the seat. France also provided the artist to paint the ceiling, door panels et al. All appropriate external parts were silver plated, the interior metal fittings gilded.

Such splendiferous coachwork might have seemed faintly absurd on another chassis, but on the Phantom I it seemed merely apropos.

Before standardization each "Flying Lady," as at left, was individually cast.

The Twenty and the 20/25

With the turn from the Teens to the Twenties, Rolls-Royce, who were never really out of the news, found themselves in a particularly vigorous eddy of it. Rumors forecast that they were about to introduce a new model, a "baby" Rolls of about 16 hp. Like most rumors, they were just half right. *The Motor* was somewhat more specific. In September of 1921 they noted that "in the Sussex district a 20 hp car has been seen which bears certain characteristics of radiator shape and control which might lead to the supposition that it was a 20 hp Rolls-Royce." The supposition as to horsepower was taken from the prominently displayed RAC taxation disc, and they noted further that the car had four cylinders (!) and semi-elliptic springs front and rear (as opposed to the 40/50's and later New Phantom's cantilever rear springs). Even a picture of the car was included. But thus whetting the appetite of Rolls enthusiasts, the magazine admonished readers not to write the works about the car, because the Rolls-Royce company would advise *The Motor* and the world of their plans when they were quite ready themselves, thank you.

They did, a year later. Actually *The Motor* had been quite right about the car, save for the number of cylinders. The 20 H.P. (or Twenty) Rolls-Royce was an overhead valve six, which was, *The Motor* was delighted to report, "a high efficiency unit capable of giving off well over 50 bhp." Rolls-Royce, apparently, had a sometimes-we-will-sometimes-we-won't attitude toward divulging power output.

The 20 H.P. Rolls was produced for seve[ral] years, until 1929 when it evolved into and wa[s] superseded by the 20/25 H.P. The new car ha[d] a larger engine, with a RAC rating of 25.2 h[p] (as opposed to its predecessor's 21.6); in th[is] case, however, the factory didn't bother wi[th] developed horsepower figures. Perhaps no on[e] asked. As one road tester noted, the car was on[e] "from which the most critical would derive re[al] pleasure in handling, and a passenger would [be] even more satisfied." Who would discuss vulga[r] horsepower after such a remark?

Right: The 1932 20/25 H.P. with sports saloon coachwork by Thrupp and Maberley.

The Phantom II

The Best Car in the World — Rolls-Royce, incidentally, didn't say it first, a motor journalist did — drove blithely through the Depression, the same Depression which saw a good many firms on both sides of the Atlantic forced out of business. And they did so without the distasteful compromise of an "economy" model or a lowering of standards — either of which would have been anathema to the company and the image. Indeed, no doubt the tradition already well established assisted Rolls-Royce through the difficult period — that and their aero engine production.

The Rolls-Royce was probably not "The Best Car in the World" — an audacious phrase certainly, whatever it means — but overt challenges to the claim were few, and put forward with a respect bearing on the reverential. Only retrospectively, and comparatively recently, have critics come forward, with a joyous propensity for idol-smashing, and declared, for example, the Rolls-Royce Phantom II a "rough old lorry." Stuff and nonsense.

The Phantom II was introduced in 1929, amid considerable speculation in the press that Rolls-Royce were about to put forward — ah, heresy — a sports model. Nothing of the sort. As Rolls-Royce themselves said in announcing the car, it "is not intended to compete with racing or ultrasporting types of cars, nevertheless it will more than maintain the position the 'Phantom' has achieved amongst its owners of being the fastest genuine touring car in the world."

Although it was the successor to the Phantom, the Phantom II was in essence a scaled-up Twenty. It carried the Phantom engine, although Royce had redesigned its cylinder head on the crossflow principle, which allowed for extra power at higher revolutions and thus a more sporting performance, yet also improved slow running. The mating of engine and gearbox was borrowed from the Twenty (the Phantom and its predecessors having an independently-mounted gearbox), as was the semi-elliptic springing all round (as opposed to the rear cantilevers previously used.) The propeller shaft, heretofore enclosed in a torque tube, was now, like the Twenty, open and of lighter construction.

The Phantom II was decidedly a faster car than its predecessors, and in short-chassis "Continental" guise that was quite fast indeed. "Speed, Silence, Tractability, a Wonderful Top Gear Performance, and Unsurpassed Controls" headlined *The Autocar* in its road report on one of these cars in 1933, commenting that "during the times test the speedometer held a steady reading of 95." It might be, as historian Anthony Bird so charmingly put it, that "at high speeds some mechanical effort from the engine could be both heard and felt." It probably even kept the clock quiet.

Left: A 1930 Phantom II, featuring boattail 5/6-seater coachwork by Douglas Wood.

The Phantom III

By the time the Phantom III made its first appearance at the Olympia Motor Show in November of 1935, Sir Henry Royce was dead. (He had been knighted in 1930.) The last of the triumvirate who began the Rolls-Royce enterprise was gone. (C.S. Rolls had died in a 1910 flying accident and Claude Johnson had worked himself into an early grave in 1926.) But just as Johnson and, for his short tenure, the oft-maligned Rolls were responsible for the commercial success which perpetuated the marque, so too did the engineering genius of Royce live beyond him. The general design of the Phantom III might be said to be Royce-inspired; the influence of his legendary aircraft engines was most certainly indicated in the formidable unit which powered it.

The rumors circulating before its arrival centered around the probability of Rolls-Royce adopting a vee engine formation, and the rumors proved correct. The Phantom III was indeed vee-engined, and the cylinders numbered twelve. It was an altogether impressive unit — though complicated — with a capacity of 7340 cc. Output had been considerably upped — and here Rolls-Royce provided some figures. In 1937 they declared 165 bhp at 3000 rpm, though this was subsequently developed to about 180. The pro-digious torque of this massive unit, however, was never publicized.

With this model Rolls-Royce introduced independent front suspension, having experimented for some years previous with various systems (rather in the same way that four wheel braking, introduced by them in late 1923, had been preceded by extensive investigation).

The company called the car "at once the most luxurious road vehicle ever produced," and though one might demur somewhat, there can be no doubting that the Phantom III was everything a discerning motorist of the Thirties could possibly have desired. Its top speed was, like the Continental Phantom II, in the nineties; the 100 mark, however, could be reached by the less ponderously-bodied versions, and exceeded by the "overdrive model." In acceleration and cornering, the Phantom III was eminently superior to its forebears. (Zero to 50 was recorded in 12.6 seconds.) According to a reporter from *The Times*, "The acceleration is like the swoop of a bird down the wind." The only thing that could threaten the Phantom III was the war. Production was discontinued in 1939.

Two Phantom III's from 1938. Right, with town car body by Barker. Below, with close-coupled saloon coachwork by Thrupp and Maberley.

The Wraith

The "baby" Rolls — somehow the term "personal" seems more appropriate — had evolved from the Twenty of 1922-29 to the 20/25 of 1929-35 to the 25/30 of 1936-38. And in October of 1938 it became the Wraith.

The years from the introduction of the smaller Rolls-Royce had seen a steady increase in power and performance (the original was barely more than a mile a minute, the 20/25 could do seventy-five, the 25/30 better than eighty) — and total production for the decade and a half had neared 8000 units.

Interestingly, if the Phantom II might be called a scaled-up Twenty, the Wraith might be appropriately termed a scaled-down Phantom III. Its engine remained an overhead valve 4¼-liter six, although considerably refined from the 25/30 which had preceded it. But the chassis design for the car was largely P-III, including the new independent front suspension.

All the superlatives for which Rolls-Royce had already become so well-known were showered upon the Wraith at its introduction. It would surely have been a resounding commercial success. Four hundred ninety-one Wraiths were built. Then the world was plunged into war.

Below: A 1939 Wraith, with two-door sports saloon body by James Young & Co., Ltd.

The Phantom IV

Of all Rolls-Royces, the Phantom IV was the most exclusive. Only sixteen were built and to be allowed the privilege of purchase, one had to be royal of birth or head of state. The car was never sold to the public.

It was born in 1950 on a foot-stretched (to 145 inches) Silver Wraith chassis, powered by a war-developed straight eight which had seen service in various army vehicles and Dennis fire engines and would subsequently be found around English airports towing huge aircraft to their appointed sites. Though performance figures for those various applications of the engine are of no consequence here, installed in the Phantom IV it provided a top speed around the 100-mile-an-hour mark.

The first Phantom IV went to their Royal Highnesses the Princess Elizabeth and the Duke of Edinburgh. General Franco had two, and others (as the 1955 Mulliner-bodied limousine at right) went to a variety of oil potentates in the Middle East. Production was discontinued in 1959; its market had, after all, been rather severely limited.

The Silver Wraith

In 1946 Rolls-Royce returned to automobile manufacture, announcing in April of that year their new Silver Wraith. It would be built for the next dozen years.

The Silver Wraith was powered by an all-new six-cylinder engine with overhead inlet and exhaust valves. Developed horsepower was recorded as 122 in 1946, but in the years that followed this was raised substantially, as had been Rolls-Royce practice throughout their history.

Considerable comment began to rise during the late Sixties that the Silver Wraith may well have been the best car that Rolls-Royce had ever built. In refinement and road handling, it was virtually perfect, and more than the equal of any previous Rolls. It was also a markedly simpler design than some of its predecessors.

Some consider the Silver Wraith the last of the great Rolls-Royces. It was described in its day as having "an indefinable something about it." And so it has remained. A car like the 1957 Hooper-bodied sedan below will ever remain the sort of vehicle about which one could compose fugues in its honor.

CHADWICK: REMEMBER THE NAME

To the cynical any car called "Great" one year and "Perfected Great" the next must be suspect. A scandalous misuse of the language surely — even for advertising copywriters. More prudent perhaps, to call the product — as it also was — "The Car of Exclusiveness," "A Car of Class," "The Quality Car of America." There's a pleasant innocuousness — born of belabored familiarity — to all that. However, to imply further that it is *nulli secundus* in the areas of safety, power, luxury, dependability, strength, simplicity — and to top that off with the blatant

sertion that it's the fastest car in the world. ow that is audacity. But cynics be warned. One speaking here of the Chadwick — and it was erything its builders said it was.

The Chadwick was with us for only about a cade — and that was more than half a century o. Fewer than 300 were built —and only two e known to survive. But neither of these mentable facts should obscure what the adwick was: one of the finest cars built in nerica during those exciting early years of the tomobile industry.

Lee Sherman Chadwick was quite a fellow. One could say, rather literally, that his career began in the laundry and ended in the kitchen. As a twenty-four-year-old engineering student at Purdue University he invented a driving mechanism for a commercial laundry machine manufacturer, and thirteen years later he began an association which was to endure for nearly three decades with the Perfection Stove Company, first as a designer, later company president and chairman of the board. His years in the automobile business were sandwiched in be-

tween. Quantitatively, they were few — but what years those were.

The Chadwick was not, incidentally, his first car. That laundry machine venture in 1899 had attracted the attention of a gentleman named Whitney, president of the then money-losing Boston Ball Bearing Company. Joining that firm as general superintendent, Chadwick had them making money within a year, and managed, too, to build a couple of experimental cars, ostensibly to demonstrate the use of ball and roller bearings. But when Whitney sold out,

Chadwick was out of a job. He went to Philadelphia and Searchmont, then builders of low-powered auto buggies. Again he perked up the business, expanded it, bought a plant near Chester, Pennsylvania, and set about redesigning the Searchmont two-cylinder cars. The Searchmont company appeared in good shape, financed as it was by a conglomerate of mightily successful businessmen, among them the redoubtable Spencer Trask. They all stood four-square behind Chadwick, and were more than a little enthused with his idea for a four-cylinder car. They wanted a hundred of them right away. Parts were ordered, some work began. But it was 1903 — Wall Street became a little shaky — and, as Chadwick later recalled, "Spencer Trask got pinched in the stock market . . . and the rest of the gang just quit." So much for Searchmont.

Undaunted, Lee Chadwick bought up a wagonload of engine parts and other components for the proposed four-cylinder Searchmont, and took them to a small foundry shop on Third Street in Chester where he promptly came up with a 4½ x 5 four-cylinder 24 hp sixty-mile-an-hour car that was the first Chadwick. It was a quick seller — Frank Kennedy, president of the Logan Iron and Steel Company bought it for $4000 — which money Chadwick promptly invested in machinery, tools and an old stable on Callowhill Street in Philadelphia which he named the Fairmount Engineering Works. Here, as he later said, "I repaired foreign cars and built Chadwick four-cylinder cars and engines." By the time about fifteen Chadwicks were built, the old stable had proven itself inadequate, and in 1905 Chadwick relocated in a larger building on Spring Garden Street, where about twenty-five more fours were built. In addition to the 24 hp model, the line now included a bigger 5x6-inch 40 hp tourer.

This latter car was described in the August, 1906, issue of *Cycle and Automobile Trade Journal*, by the intrepid Hugh Dolnar: "This car and its motor were designed by Mr. L. S. Chadwick, who has had an extended practical experience with cars and motors, is an ingenious machine designer, a thoroughly competent constructor, and has in this car achieved a safe and happy combination of thoroughly tested elements, in forms meeting the fashions and requirements of the period, with some novel details of obvious value designed by himself, which are amply sufficient to give a distinctive individuality to this large and speedy touring car, which is powerful enough to go at any pace, and well enough put together to stand up under pushing on the roughest roads."

Mr. Dolnar then took a breath — and went at it again; unwavering, he proceeded for another seven pages of unabashed panegyrics about the car. Not that Mr. Dolnar was alone in his enthusiasm. Hardly. More open-mouthed perhaps but fulsome praise was the norm in press commentary about the Chadwick. Pick up any automotive periodical of the day — *Motor Age*, *The Automobile, Motor, The Horseless Age* — and search out the articles on Chadwick cars. You will find yourself confronted with a medley of hosannas that are almost embarrassing. You should have heard them when Lee Chadwick came out with his six.

The Great Chadwick Six is, of course, the car just about everyone thinks of when mention of Chadwick is made. Lee Chadwick built it, typically, because he thought it would be a better car than the four. He was an inveterate improver. Chadwick built his first six, appropriately enough, in 1906 — and in later years the company advertised that in that year too they began building sixes exclusively. This would seem somewhat misleading. Most contemporary publications for 1906 indicate that fours were to be among the Chadwick models offered for the 1907 season, and Chadwick themselves advertised only that "a large portion of our 1907 models will be six-cylinder cars."

But there would appear to be a logical answer. For a couple of years previous Lee Chadwick had been toying with the idea of a six, recognizing its advantages of more constant torque and

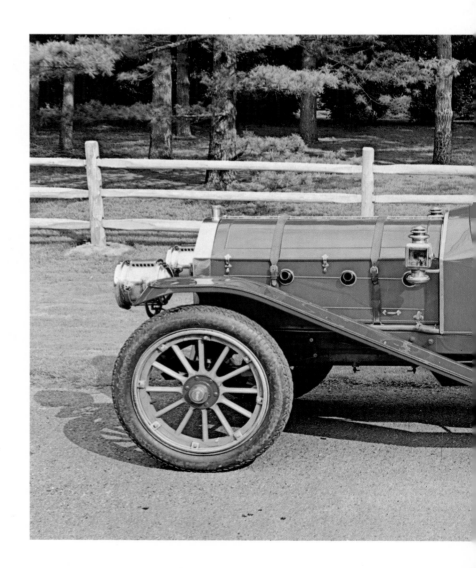

moother running. And when he came up with ne to his liking, he boldly decided to discontinue fours altogether. Lee Chadwick was looking to the future. Conceivably the fours already built, or in the process thereof, might have been offered in 1907. But that would have been the extent of it. Lee Chadwick's mind was already made up.

This would put Chadwick in the forefront of what *Motor Age* called "the six-cylinder invasion," which had not, so they commented in July, 1907, "stormed the American market so strenuously during the present season as it has the European field." It was Chadwick, together with such other luminaries as Franklin, Stevens-Duryea, Pierce-Arrow and Peerless, that would see to it that thereafter it would.

There is one firm date that can be set down regarding the Chadwick Six, that of the first road test of the first production car. Several experimental models had preceded it, this particular car had been run out on previous occasions in various guises, and the company was already launched into regular production at the scheduled rate of four a week — but this was the first running of a Chadwick Six "out of doors with its seven-passenger body on the chassis." Hugh Dolnar was there, and bless his copious heart, he recorded all. It was Saturday, April 27th, 1907, 11:34 a.m., "the day was fine, and

the warm, springtide air prest very hard against our bodies as we flew over that down and up mile." Sales manager Harold B. Larzelere took Mr. Dolnar along for the excursion, which lasted exactly four hours and sixteen minutes, and carried the pair from Philadelphia to Jenkintown, through a tangle of curves and crossroads where Larzelere got lost and "where a nickel toll has to be paid about every two minutes with a quick car." A leisurely stop for lunch "at a delightful oldtime wayside inn" and the two drove back to the factory, the only untoward incident on the entire trip having been the moment when the hood flew off the car. This hadn't unnerved Dolnar unduly, that sort of thing being not unusual for a "first" production car. Indeed the Chadwick bodymaker later accused Larzelere of taking the car before "it was finisht." Besides nothing could dim Dolnar's enthusiasm for those moments in the Chadwick "at a really fast clip, probably sixty-five miles good, for a mile and a half or so, a piece of the swiftest and smoothest and stillest running in the writer's experience, and this with the throttle not more than half open."

Initially the car was called simply the Chadwick Six. Then the company realized what they had, and forthwith the change to Great Chadwick Six. They were right. Lee Chadwick had outdone himself, with an exemplary six, in-

corporating many of the "novel details of obvious value" which had been the hallmark of his fours. Most prominent among these were the cylindrical copper water jackets enclosing the upper part of each pair of cylinder castings — thus surrounding valves, stems and guides with water. This resulted in greater efficiency, the impossibility of warping and the minimization of carbon deposits and, most important, three to five times the cooling capacity per cylinder above the norm at that time. Overheating was a virtual impossibility. It was an expensive proposition, to be sure, and some competitors scoffed at the value of the design. Lee Chadwick simply removed the fan from one of his cars and sent it to a race — which it won. Nothing more needed to be said.

Before proceeding with the other outstanding features of the car, perhaps we might first look inside those water jackets — and throw the Chadwick specifications at you in one impressive sweep. Cylinders were five inches bore by six inches stroke for an overall displacement of 706.86 cubic inches, which one reviewer commented "can probably show 70 to 75 hp at about 1100 rpm." The heaviest of Chadwicks was guaranteed to do 65 mph, the runabouts were good for at least 80, and if any owner cared to make the few necessary revisions, he could try to equal the stripped runabout's demonstrated

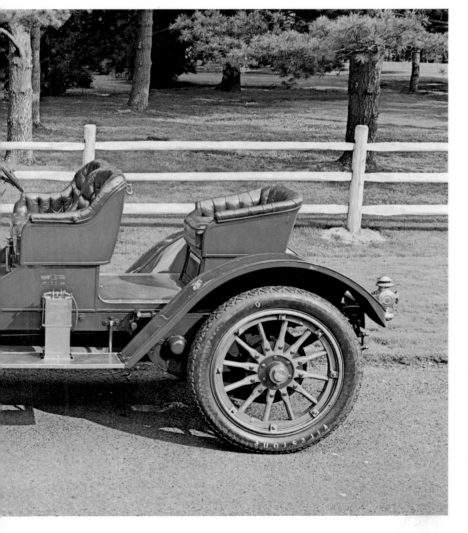

GREAT CHADWICK SIX
THE MODEL 19
RUNABOUT

The Chadwick appearing here and on the two pages previous was built in 1910. It was the runabout model which Chadwick so successfully raced through 1910, and to which the historic supercharger had been added. However, should a customer have desired it, he could have had the supercharger fitted to his runabout for about an extra $375. Whether any ordered one is not known. It probably wasn't necessary. With a few comforts removed the car was capable of 100-plus mph without it.

speed of one-hundred-plus miles an hour.

Any car capable of such speeds in those days had to be strong and yet flexible — and the Chadwick was, every part, every inch of it. The carburetor, "a pet design of the maker," so *Motor Age* said, is a case in point. It provided the correct mixture of fuel at a greater variation of speeds than hitherto demonstrated on any other car, every variation of the throttle acting directly on the jets, insuring correct gas mixture. A mixture regulating lever, located on the dash, permitted the driver to coordinate fuel jet opening with accelerator setting, a feature allowing Chadwicks to idle smoothly at low rpm and yet accelerate quickly.

The Chadwick carburetor was patented, as was the water jacketing system. Another patent (dating back to 1903) covered the direct drive double bevel gear transmission which Chadwick originated. It was one of the semi-selective-type; the rear end of the countershaft carried a bevel gear, as did the rear end of the mainshaft, these bevels being constantly in mesh with a double bevel on the differential crown wheel. It had four speeds forward, the gearshift lever being provided with a positive latching device which prevented even the most amateurish of drivers from passing through a gear or improperly meshing it. Also patented was the clutch; it was of the internal expanding variety — a cone in-

side the flywheel, the face of the aluminum male portion being covered with a sheet of phosphor bronze, rivetted and then machined smooth.

And that's not the end of Chadwick's patented features. There were the aluminum dust-proof cases which enclosed the double chain drive. Considering the progressiveness of Chadwick design generally, it is interesting that Lee Chadwick preferred chain to the then-becoming-popular shaft drive. But as far as Chadwick was concerned, shaft drive would not provide the elasticity and flexibility he deemed of paramount importance in any car. And besides, one of the principal advantages of shaft drive — quiet running — he believed he provided anyway with the Chadwick's "absolutely silent double chain drive."

By 1907 it was apparent that Chadwick had outgrown the Philadelphia plant. And on March 7th of that year the Chadwick Engineering Works was incorporated in Pottstown, Pennsylvania, that city having been chosen because of its industrial advantages — and the persuasiveness of one Edward S. Fretz, who headed the Light Foundry Company which was to make and machine all the aluminum and bronze castings for the Chadwick. By spring of the following year *The Horseless Age* reported that the new Chadwick factory was ready for occupancy by its staff of some ninety men.

"Built up to a Standard — Not down to a Price" was one of many Chadwick slogans. The standard was absolute integrity, and the price $5500. Lee Chadwick was of the let's-build-the-car-first-and-then-see-what-it's-worth school: The Great Chadwick Six was not overpriced. Properly cared for, the Chadwick company guaranteed that its car would transport its owner reliably, comfortably and safely wherever he was going — and that he could get there faster in a Chadwick than in any other car on the road. The Chadwick had, one automotive writer of the day noted, "Speed enough to satisfy the most reckless of drivers," and although the company didn't condone excesses, they were pretty much aware that most owners wouldn't hold back — much. In their manual they advised prospective Chadwick drivers only to "learn how before you try to perform stunts."

Chadwick performed a few of those themselves. Actually the Chadwick competition record wasn't particularly long, nor was it terribly comprehensive — but what they did do they did awfully well. This is, of course, when the Chadwick supercharger — ah, controversy — enters the picture. There shall probably always be historians who doubt its existence, who believe that the bulge on the right side of the hood of certain racing Chadwicks was for a picnic basket or such. But sufficient documen-

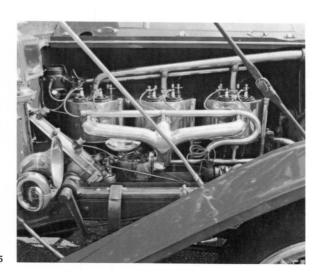

ation has been unearthed to indicate that Chadwick did work up in 1907-08 first, a single-stage, then a three-stage centrifugal blower, that he did apply it to a racing car, which did win races. It was the world's first supercharged racing car. Moreover, around 1909 or 1910, the supercharger was available for an extra $375 on the production runabout, for those customers desiring the extra oomph. That was certainly another first. How many Chadwick buyers ordered one is not known. Probably not many. Practical the supercharger might have been, but attractive it was not.

Chadwick built the supercharger because he wanted to win races — and win races he did. Willie Haupt was his principal driver initially, a young man, barely twenty, fast and "rather reckless," so Lee Chadwick thought, adding "he was a pest to handle, as he would not follow instructions." Haupt remained with Chadwick for two years, if for no other reason than that he won races — a lot of them — and in the process the Haupt-Chadwick combination came to be known, so *The Automobile* reported, as "the fastest thing in the hill climbing line in the country, if not the world."

The hill climb was the Chadwick's especial forte, although it acquitted itself admirably in road races as well, one of which is deserving of particular attention: the third Founder's Day Race at Fairmount Park on October 8th, 1910.

Willie Haupt had left Chadwick at the end of the '08 season, his place being taken by Len Zengle. Lee Chadwick was delighted; Zengle had an endearing way of following orders, and was a proven winner as well. And he provided Chadwick with their greatest triumph.

Chadwick came to Philadelphia's Fairmount Park in 1910 probably better prepared than for any other race they had ever entered. They had two cars — one for Len Zengle, the other for his teammate Al Mitchell — and Lee Chadwick had a strategy. He knew speed alone wouldn't be the key to winning this particular race; instead, steady, consistent pressure would be a deciding factor. He so instructed his drivers. Chadwick stationed himself in the pits; beside him was Harvey Samuel Firestone, Sr. The tire company had recently decided to go racing, and they had decided to try it first with Chadwick. Firestone's brother and chief engineer were with him at Fairmount Park, but as Lee Chadwick later recalled it was Harvey who was "on edge all the time — as nervous as a rabbit's nose."

Once the event was under way, so was Lee Chadwick — for Al Mitchell, with Hauptian enthusiasm, decided to run his own race. He bounded into the lead, stayed there for five laps, dicing with Erwin Bergdoll's huge Benz and Ralph Mulford's Lozier, enjoying himself immensely — until on the sixth lap when he hit a tree, plunged into a ditch and overturned. He came out of it fine; the car was a wreck. "Crazy driver," Lee Chadwick muttered. Later he would refine that comment somewhat — it was an error of judgment, he concluded, to try to take the treacherous curve on Neill Drive at 70 mph. Meanwhile Zengle was running a smooth race, exchanging third place every now and then with De Hymel's Stoddard-Dayton, allowing the Bergdoll Benz and the Mulford Lozier to fight for the lead ahead of him. By the 16th lap, the Benz, which had led since Lap 6, was out, the Stoddard-Dayton was faltering — and the race was now between Zengle's Chadwick and Mulford's Lozier. With nine laps to go the lead was now changing back and forth. Mulford was driving beautifully as always, the same steady consistent race Zengle was running, but his Lozier was considerably less powerful than the Chadwick. Indeed Lee Chadwick later admitted that "I almost caused [Zengle] to lose the race by holding his speed down to far below what the car could have made."

But as the car came down to start the last lap — nine seconds behind the Lozier — Lee Chadwick gave Zengle a signal to "beat it," which no doubt pleased Zengle immensely, for as *The Automobile* reported, "the big car reared like a living thing" and charged off after the

GREAT CHADWICK SIX
THE MODEL 16
SEVEN-PASSENGER TOURING CAR

The Chadwick appearing here and on the pages following was built in 1907, during the first model year for the company's new six-cylinder car. Its body is aluminum, fitted onto a massive steel frame riveted to a wooden underframe. This practice was followed throughout the Chadwick history. The car is as solidly built as it looks, magnificent testimony to the incredibly high standards which Lee Chadwick set for himself and his cars. The car was certainly worth the $5500 price it commanded.

Lozier. Then the unforeseen — one of the Chadwick's tires blew, it was quickly changed, and the car was away again for the last six or so miles of the race. When the dust lifted, and the checkered flag was lowered, the race belonged to Len Zengle, by 5.4 seconds, the narrowest margin then in road racing history. Harvey Firestone's nose stopped twitching — it was a victory for him too, over Michelin, as the press duly reported. Len Zengle said only, "I am tickled to death." Lee Chadwick was absolutely beside himself.

For sheer drama, few races of the day matched that Fairmount Park event, and it was a fitting conclusion to Chadwick's racing history. It was the marque's last important triumph — indeed their last important competitive try. Back at the factory Lee Chadwick found other matters weighing heavy.

The Light Foundry Company had decided to discontinue the machining of Chadwick castings, and the Chadwick company was unexpectedly put to considerable expense developing facilities to do it themselves. Then there was the conflict

between Lee Chadwick and his financia[l] backers. His Great Chadwick Six had evolve[d] into the Perfected Great Chadwick Six — i[t] wasn't changed, simply refined. And Chadwic[k] firmly believed even the Perfected Great Chad[-] wick Six could be made better, and he had lo[ts] of ideas how. His financial backers didn't agre[e,] nor did they agree with his plans for an exte[n-] sive dealer network. Inventories were high, sale[s] low — and no one seemed able to agree on jus[t] what to do about it. In 1911 Lee Chadwic[k] walked out.

Lee Chadwick's cars continued to be built without him for a while at Pottstown — changes were minimal. The price remained the same: $5500 ($6500 for the limousine, a price tag it also shared for a season or two with the fast runabout). Just how long Chadwicks were made is not known. The *Cycle and Automobile Trade Journal* issue of December, 1915, includes Chadwick among the "models to be manufactured for the coming season" — but that might have been wishful thinking on either the magazine's or the company's part. Other information indicates the Chadwick company was bankrupt by this time — their plant taken over by an armaments manufacturer.

The two cars pictured in these pages — the only Chadwicks known to exist today — are in the collection of William Pollock, noted historian and past president of the Antique Automobile Club. While restoring his

Chadwicks, Mr. Pollock became a close friend of the man who had built them and his enthusiasm for the cars — it remains boundless — obviously elated Lee Chadwick. In one of his letters to Mr. Pollock in 1954, written four years before he died, Mr. Chadwick wrote wistfully: "If I had had a few men like you with me in the past the old company would still be doing business." One can only wish that it might have been so. To use a phrase which is altogether trite, yet particularly appropriate here, they just don't build them like that anymore.

DUESENBERG

A Legend That Will Live As Long As Men Worship Beauty And Power On Wheels

Devotees of every grand marque are distinguished by at least some degree of fanaticism, but the victims of "Dementia Duesenberg" are almost rabid. Some will admit that the Duesenberg was not the best automobile in the world in every respect. But to a man they will insist that it was simply the best of its era on the American scene. And that it was. It was the most glamorous car one could own, and it far excelled its contemporaries in stamina and brute strength. To cite examples, the then-current 1929 Cadillac boasted one-fourth of the power potential of the 265 hp Model J, and nearly two generations were to pass before even a racing equivalent of Duesenberg's mighty double overhead cam engine would be built by another American maker (Ford, in 1965).

Some comparisons would be unfair, of course, for the cheapest J sold for twenty times the price of the least expensive Model A Ford. The Duesenberg buyer was paying for prestige as well as for superlative craftsmanship. And though he received — as he had a right to expect — a high-quality product, the question whether Duesenberg was "The World's Finest Motor Car," as it was often touted, deserves analysis, as does the story of the men who were its creators.

Fred S. and August S., the legendary Duesenberg brothers, were not educated formally, but as self-trained engineers they stretched their skills and plumbed their talents to such an extent that they became renowned as pioneering geniuses. Their achievements spanned four decades and encompassed success in modes of transportation that ranged from bicycles to airplanes. So varied were their activities that any of their competitors could have paraphrased Ettore Bugatti's classic evaluation of Bentley automobiles by remarking, "Those Duesenberg brothers build the fastest *tractor* in the world." Although it is little known, even today, the Duesenbergs produced tractor engines among the array of powerplants that bore their name. What other small producer made two-, four-, six-, eight-, twelve- and sixteen-cylinder varieties, not to mention double-eights and parallel-twelves? The giants of motordom have since emulated most Duesenberg innovations, but a great many of them have yet to appear on modern passenger cars.

What other automaker at the time was so consistently and successfully associated with speed? It was hardly a secret that Duesenberg was a three-time winner of the Indianapolis 500 — in 1924, 1925 and 1927 — a consistent multiple-place winner there and at all major tracks, the holder of many land speed records, and of course the only American marque ever to win the French Grand Prix. The latter achievement was the work of driver Jimmy Murphy in 1921. Some European automotive writers still soft-pedal Duesenberg's victory, it being the only lapse in European trophy-taking at the event. Yet, such a performance as took place at Le Mans in 1921 should have been sufficient to incite a universal mania for the marque, but for a while, at least, Europeans remained cool. One look at an old photograph of Murphy taking the checkered flag without a single Frenchman's hat being doffed or a Gallic hand waving in salute is enough to cause the rabid to growl.

Duesenberg has had its doubters and detractors — what marque hasn't? — but even they have been impressed by the fact that where engineering was concerned, the Duesenberg brothers believed in making everything double, triple or even quadruple, insofar as was practicable. Fred and Augie did more for high performance American machinery than any other pair of individuals in the business. They were among the first proponents of dual-throat carburetion, dual points, dual condensers and coils, not to mention the inclusion of one mechanical plus three electric fuel pumps, and the noteworthy four valves per cylinder.

When the captious point out that Duesenberg cars are high on fuel consumption, a stock answer might be, "Better mileage per ton mile than a new Buick." The reply might cause an eyebrow to raise now and then, but the fact the Big D scales out at around three tons compared with the modern car's two-ton average. The factory asserted that the car's average fuel consumption would be eleven to thirteen miles per gallon for high speed driving, which was certainly possible in the factory era when low octane fuel was used.

Obviously those who bought luxury cars that time were little concerned with the cost fuel, or with whether the custom bodies they ordered could accommodate two or three persons abreast. They bought a car because they liked and if they were rich enough — and most them were, in those pre-Depression years — they owned automobiles of assorted passenger capacities and coachwork for use on different occasions.

Myths are common to all great names, and Duesenberg is no exception. The most widespread canard is the virtually impossible-to-squelch belief that the car is of German origin. In reality, all that is Teutonic about it is the fact that the Duesenberg brothers were born Germany (they grew up in Iowa, however) and that its engineering (including safety features) was meticulous and thorough down to the last detail. Neither fact of which, of course, surprises the Duesenberg devotee.

The origins of the Duesenberg mania should rightly be traced to the early days of Fred and Augie's career, for their initial efforts are noteworthy, relatively speaking, as creation the enterprise that produced the J's and SJ's. From 1897 to 1899 the duo won fame in Iowa builders and winning riders of racing bicycles. (In 1898 Fred set the world's two-mile-bicycle speed record and the three-mile motorcycle mark.) As the Twentieth Century began, the brothers were gaining experience in actual auto construction and road testing — at the Wisconsin factory of the original Rambler company. It was in 1904 that they first indulged their desire to build a car of their own. They had opened a garage in Des Moines in 1903, and the following year launched their automotive venture. The spirited two-cylinder car they built which was named after their financial backer, attorney named Mason, was highly successful a hill climber, and after 1907 as a racing car.

In 1910 the fledgling company was purchased by Maytag, the firm that built washing machines, and the name of the car was changed — first to Mason-Maytag, ultimately to Maytag. The brothers remained independent, however and continued to build cars on their own. It was under the Mason name, which they reclaimed that they began producing 230-cubic-inch, four-cylinder-engined racing cars, one of which came close to qualifying for the 1912 race at Indianapolis, and went on to perform well in other

ove: A Model A roadster by Millspaugh & Irish.

Below: A Model J convertible berline by Murphy.

big races that year.

In 1913 the infant Duesenberg Motor Company, operating now in a modest establishment in St. Paul, Minnesota, began to earn recognition for its line of small, high-speed engines. Soon the brothers were building marine powerplants in addition to racing cars. A notable early achievement was their design and construction of two twelve-cylinder marine engines of 200 hp each in a tandem setup that enabled a Chicago speedboat to be first in the world to exceed the nautical mile-a-minute.

Until military preparations intervened, and America became a participant in World War I, Duesenberg racing cars continued to account for a remarkable series of victories. These provided a springboard for many of the men who were to become racing hero-drivers — Eddie Rickenbacker, among them. The struggling Duesenbergs couldn't afford to advertise then. Thus it was an undeniable boost to their enterprise that the motoring journals of the day were so often to report that a Duesenberg racer had come in first. The brothers' reputation, and the magic of their name, began to emit an estimable glow.

By 1917 — after sojourns in Chicago, and Edgewater, New Jersey — the Duesenbergs were

in their own new plant in Elizabeth, New Jersey. There their initial work on the famous Liberty aviation engine brought them contracts to produce not only the 500 hp sixteen-cylinder Bugatti aviation engine, but also the purely Duesenberg-designed Model H. This 900 hp V-16 job was the biggest aircraft engine ever attempted until then and one that represented a considerable change from the Duesenberg's basic marine design. Four of these giant engines were completed before the Armistice; two were geared and two were direct-drive types. For variety, Fred and Augie simultaneously produced a number of 500 hp V-12 aircraft engines (similar in design to their marine types) as well as a sturdy 160 hp four-cylinder tractor engine!

The brothers delivered more than two hundred 400 hp marine engines to the navies of American allies, and as long working hours were never of concern to them, they somehow found spare moments to dream of someday building a passenger car of their own. This one, they agreed, would bear their own name. Some of their wartime advertising carried the slogan, "The Power of the Hour," which they adapted thusly in 1919 to tantalize a car-hungry public: "Out of the wrack of war comes the ultimate car,

the car you have dreamed of, and its motor THE POWER OF THE HOUR."

Their vision began to take shape when the succeeded in raising a modest amount of capit from the sale of their war plant to Will Motors, plus the sale of the rights to their rac powered Model G four-cylinder engine to th Rochester Motor Company. After this paring their enterprise, the Duesenbergs transferred a tivities from Elizabeth to Indianapolis, whe temporary quarters housed the birth of the fir 183-cubic-inch straight-eight overhead can valve-in-head Duesenberg engine. Only fo were built in 1920; three of them were mounte in cars that placed third, fourth and sixth their premier appearance in the Memorial D event at the Speedway that year. As the racin season progressed, and the cars continued perform well, the Duesenberg mania began gather impetus. It received additional e couragement with the breaking of the La

Although restricted by a chassis that never change from year to year, by Duesenberg's characteristic radiator configuration and by the need to accommodate that big straight eight, each coachmaker added his particular stamp. Below, a Model J convertible coupé and club sedan by Murphy; right, an SJ convertible coupé by Rollst

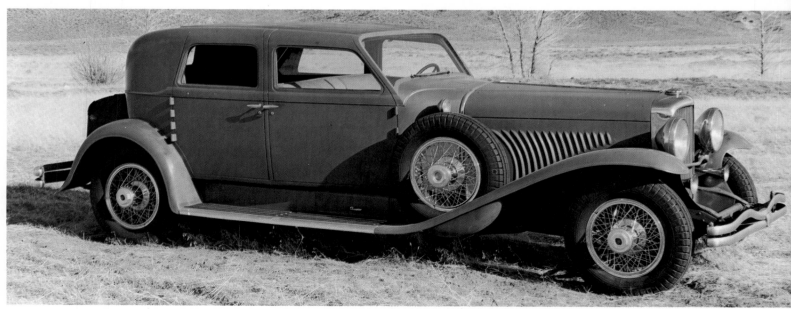

peed Record for racing cars. Tommy Milton averaged 156.04 mph at Daytona in a car in which the Duesenbergs had mounted two 300-cubic-inch eights side by side — no mean feat of engineering in those days, by the way. Soon the Duesenberg company could bask in the glory of that is still a unique distinction, that of holding speed marks for both passenger and racing cars. Eventually Duesenberg held sixty-six world records for all distances, ranging from one kilometer to a twenty-four-hour endurance run. There is a lapse, now, in the story of Duesenberg, where history becomes haze. The first Duesenberg passenger car made its debut at the Automobile Salon in New York City's Commodore Hotel in October, 1920, but there is considerable doubt that the initial display cars — those produced the next year contained the actual Model A engine — or even its racing predecessor. According to Duesenberg authority Marshall Merkes, the actual Model A design came into being sometime in 1921, with delivery of the first car in 1922. He adds, "This does not mean there were no prototypes built or running in the earlier years, but the cars were simply not Model A types."

The construction of eight prototype passenger cars got under way in New Jersey, but actual manufacture did not begin until the company had moved to Indianapolis and was functioning as the Duesenberg Automobile & Motor Company. The new car bore the unmistakable earmarks of its racing heritage, stealing a lead on the auto industry with such features as hydraulic brakes (the first to be used on an American production car) and a race-proved straight-eight engine with single overhead cam and gear drive to the camshaft.

In ads published in 1922, the Duesenbergs showered their Model A with superlatives: "Built to outclass, outrun and outlast any car on the road" and "The most consistent performance of any automobile manufactured." They also boasted that seven of the eight Duesenberg cars entered in the Speedway events that year had finished in the money. The impact of this achievement, which followed Jimmy Murphy's earlier epochal win in the French Grand Prix, did a great deal to stimulate public interest in the Duesenberg passenger car.

Interest, and the mania too no doubt, was whetted still further by the then-startling performance of a stock Model A touring car that made a nonstop "coast to coast" run of 3155 miles at an average speed of better than 62 mph — all on the Speedway oval in April, 1923. Its only stops were for tire changes, and even under those circumstances the engine was kept running at a tachometer speed equivalent to 30 mph. Fuel was added, and drivers were changed, from a service car traveling sometimes as fast as 90 mph. A description of the perils of changing a spark plug at speed would be an epic in itself. Heavy rains, an accident and a fire on the track — plus servicing problems — all held down the average, but at times the car did reach 105 mph. This grueling endurance run, whose record was unbroken for a decade thereafter, must have had a direct bearing on sales in 1923. That year 140 cars were marketed, a notable increase over the ninety-two cars that had been sold in 1922 and an all-time record for the marque.

The Duesenberg brothers repeatedly conceived "crazy" innovations, and these invariably turned out to be significant automotive engineering advances to be admired, and ultimately copied. Among the "firsts" were heat-treated molybdenum steel chassis, ground instead of cast transmission gears and lightweight tubular axles. The massive crankshafts of later models were damped by attaching mercury weights in

copper-lined containers. Most significant, perhaps, was the fact that the A was America's first straight eight and the first overhead-camshaft production car. In actuality it was a slightly detuned version of a Duesenberg racing car, and it boasted remarkable low-speed torque that enabled a driver to pull away from a dead stop in high gear — smoothly.

No one knows exactly how many A's were built. A fair estimate would be under 500. The car's advanced engineering and high quality notwithstanding, the typically drab styling of the early Twenties and Duesenberg's lack of press-agentry didn't help the A reach anywhere near the pinnacle of glamour enjoyed by later, luxurious giants. Certainly the J surpassed it.

"The mighty dream," as author-historian J. L. Elbert has described the fabulous J's design and development, was brought to fruition by the Horatio Alger-like rise in the automotive world of E. L. Cord. With a genuine flair for salesmanship, publicity and corporate empire-building, Cord acquired the Duesenberg enterprise in 1926 and joined it with Auburn and his other business interests. The genius of the Duesenberg brothers lay in their inventive engineering ability, not in administration or profit making. They never acquired wealth, in fact disdained it. The varied abilities of young E. L.

Bohman & Schwartz convertible coupé on an SJ chassis.

Cord complemented those of Fred Duesenberg and made a reality of the Duesenbergs' dream of producing the biggest, fastest and most powerful stock automobile the world had ever seen — and on a "no-expense-is-to-be-spared" basis.

Building the Model J involved a lavish ex-

penditure of funds — so much that the company, by that time called Duesenberg, Inc. never did make money. It was a prestige operation and a "loss leader" for the Cord automotive empire. The firm's financial statements often seemed a red-ink manufacturer's dream. On

Dual cowl phaeton, originally a Model J, by Murphy.

marque. Monetary considerations aside, the new combination certainly succeeded in this aim.

The debut of the J evoked a torrent of superlatives. The car quickly became the darling of the moneyed and the mighty, and to everyone the vision of owning a Duesenberg became the *ne plus ultra* of status symbols. Small wonder the wealthy and sports-minded were attracted to the car, or that the newly-coined exclamation "It's a Duzy!" would connote a spontaneous tribute to anything superb. During the J's production years, 1929 to 1936, the heroic proportions plus the individuality of this Xanadu-on-wheels offered the discriminating buyer the prestige that went with sheer luxury and the performance that went with high horsepower.

And the car's promised performance was assuredly delivered. According to J. L. Elbert, "Hot-shot operators of the various existing makes were quick to discover that attempting to pass the new Duesie was as ludicrous as a dog barking at an express train. The owner of a Duesenberg, whether his was a 5250-pound sport phaeton or a stately limousine tipping the scales at 6750, was passed only when he was willing to be passed." The 112-to-116 mph J, with its 265 horses, gave 374 pounds-feet of torque at 2000 rpm and peaked at 4200 rpm — a thousand more than any contemporary seven-liter engine, and with a compression ratio of 5:25 to 1.

The elite clientele of the new glamour buggy clamored for a wide variety of custom bodies by their favorite coachbuilders. Some customers bought chassis only and had bodies built to suit their own individual tastes. But normally the factory arranged for the coachcraft with any of a number of renowned American firms. At least nineteen coachbuilders had a hand in determining the exterior adornment of the J and later SJ chassis. Only a few of the cars were purchased by affluent Asians or Latin Americans, but some fifty of them were sold in Europe, whose carrossiers were ecstatic over the potential for rakish, sporting and sometimes sensuous body designs.

The Model J was Fred Duesenberg's "baby," but the SJ, introduced in 1932, was his masterwork. Supercharged, the engine had a 320 hp output (at 4750 rpm) and could propel the car from a standstill to 100 mph in seventeen seconds. As a matter of fact, the SJ could pass the 100 mark in second gear! Duesenberg was the first classic American car to use a supercharger. The device had been developed for the SJ after being tried out at Indianapolis in 1923. It was a noiseless, centrifugal vane type blower, mounted vertically on the exhaust (right-hand) side of the engine.

ch annual report shows a cost-of-production gure exceeding that of total sales, exclusive of verhead, administration, etc. The aim of the ompany was to produce a custom-built luxury r of marked distinction to compete with Euro-ean cars in a class above any other American

Speedster-bodied Model SJ by Weymann.

Above: SJ speedster by Gurney Nutting of England.

Below: The Duesenberg Special record car of the mid-Thirties.

The powerful SJ's — and the few J's equipped with high speed differential — will hit an honest 130 mph. All Big D's, though truck-like when it comes to parking (because of their 142.5-inch or 153.5-inch wheelbase), are a delight to handle on the highway. And their finned brake drums with power-assisted braking (yes, quite standard on all!) are entirely adequate. When the brakes are adjusted properly, the sensation of braking is not that of stepping on a rock-hard pedal, but akin to pressing one's foot down on a pillow. Incidentally, the man-size chromed hand brake operates on the drive shaft. It alone has been known to serve drivers adequately when the hydraulics have become inoperative. The hydraulic system has shut-off valves in its brake lines. These valves serve to cut off braking on one or more wheels if a failure should occur in a single brake cylinder. A brake-pressure gauge on the instrument panel shows the efficiency of the brakes at a glance.

It is no secret that the magnificent J's and SJ's were Fred Duesenberg's creations, reflections of his taste, engineering skill and perfection. But while Fred dwelt in the limelight, his brother Augie remained contentedly in his shadow. It should not be forgotten, moreover, that Augie was responsible for a number of engineering achievements, among them the superchargers for both the Auburn and Cord. Also, all Duesenberg racing cars produced after 1926 were Augie-built in an enterprise that functioned separately, and years later he made four-, six- and eight-cylinder marine engines under the banner of A. Duesenberg Marine Motor Company.

Stories about the original prices of Duesenbergs are usually exaggerated. Generally prices ranged from between $13,000 and $19,000, with a very few in the "Twenty Grand" category. Only two of the American-bodied J's reached the $25,000 mark. These were the very modernistic Walker-Legrand coupé of J. K. Lilly, Jr., and the Bohman & Schwartz "Throne Car" made for the use of evangelist Father Divine. Both cars are still in existence, the latter registered in the name of one of Father Divine's disciples and in possession of the church. Technically, the late religious leader did not have ownership of any material thing.

Figures are not available as to the prices charged by deluxe coachbuilders in Europe, but it is reasonable to assume that the final selling price of the products mounted on the costly imported chassis was considerably higher than their all-American-built counterparts. Incidentally, before being shipped to coachbuilders, every chassis was speed-tested at Indy, with little more than an old cowl and a seat bolted on.

As is so often the case with men of genius who attain the lofty heights of achievement, Fred Duesenberg bore an unhappy burden throughout his lifetime. He was physically handicapped, crippled by arthritis from the time of his early manhood. And it is believed that he was suffering from cancer at the time of his death at fifty-five in 1932 — a death caused by pneumonia following an accident he had in a Murphy SJ convertible. One could easily speculate on the additional contributions he might have made to automotive progress if he had enjoyed a full life span, and if the automotive empire of E. L. Cord had not been dissolved by its new owners in 1937, wiping out Duesenberg, Inc. with it.

The much-debated question of exactly how many J's and SJ's were made can probably never be answered accurately or satisfactorily. Duesenberg, Inc. was known to sell cars in several categories, aside from completely brand-new units. Wrecked cars were dismantled for salvage, and there were chassis referred to as "reworked units," which were guaranteed as though new. A used car might be resold with a new engine or an exchanged body, sometimes new and sometimes used. The origin of a car might be unknown to anyone but those persons involved in its reconstruction. Thus there can be no doubt that Duesenberg's total sales in units must have been somewhat in excess of the maximum number of new cars that were built.

Marshall Merkes has placed the figure of cars built at 470, concluding after extensive research that "the total sales in units, if larger than 470, should be explained as renumbered or rebuilt cars." The attrition of time has not been great, fortunately. A total of some 360 J's and SJ's exist today, of which two-thirds are fairly complete and original cars and about half either in use or readily drivable condition. Many of the balance are in the process of being restored. Durability was a natural and inbuilt characteristic of the distinguished Duesenberg, a fact which the passing of decades only tends to confirm. Most of the Big D's being driven today bear six-figure mileage totals.

Ken W. Purdy once wrote a treatise on Duesenberg that was subtitled: "A legend that will live as long as men worship beauty and power on wheels." Additional praise would be superfluous. He has aptly summed up a grand marque.

LAGO-TALBOT

*Major Antony Lago's
Stable of
Magnificent Thoroughbreds*

Their ancestry goes back to the Nineteenth Century and proceeds from there in a maze of begetting on both sides of the channel: Darracq, Clément-Bayard, Clément, Clément Talbot, Talbot — and finally in 1920 the Sunbeam-Talbot-Darracq empire with factories in Wolverhampton, England, and Suresnes, France. Within fifteen years the S-T-D combine was to break up, with the Rootes Group acquiring Wolverhampton and British rights in the names of Sunbeam and Talbot, and Major Antony Lago taking over the Suresnes branch with rights in the name of Talbot and Darracq.

From 1936 to 1958 the automobiles built in Suresnes came to be variously identified as

lbot-Lagos in France, as Talbot-Darracqs in lgium and Luxembourg and as Darracqs in gland, the latter designation used to dis-guish them from the English Talbots. That ne of this confusion was felt in the parent ganization is evidenced by a postwar Suresnes ochure: Following the opening page with notation "manufactured by Automobiles rracq-Talbot S.A." is the foreword which vises, "To avoid confusion, cars exported in rtain Countries by Automobiles Talbot S.A. c] are now known as 'Lago'." All this makes e wearily acknowledge the truth of Coleridge's hat are names but air" and decide the easiest y out is simply to designate Suresnes auto-

mobiles from 1936 to 1958 as the cars that Tony Lago built.

Major Antony Lago was born in Venice, Italy, in 1893. Educated at the Turin school of engineering, he served as an officer in the Italian army during the First World War and at war's end travelled to England, where he stepped immediately into the automobile world. He began initially by selling Isotta-Fraschinis in London. In 1923 he joined Lap Engineering of London as technical director, and two years later secured a similar position with the Wilson company, for whom he assisted in perfecting the ex-traordinary Wilson self-changing gearbox. Two years later he became associated with

Armstrong-Siddeley, acquired the foreign selling rights for the Wilson gearbox from Sir John Sid-deley, and drove with the works team in the 1932 Alpine Trials. That same year he was en-gaged by the English branch (Sunbeam-Talbot) of the S-T-D combine as assistant director. The condition of S-T-D on either side of the channel was far from healthy. In 1933, after the board of directors in London assessed the French situa-tion as more critical, they dispatched Lago to the Suresnes branch with the hope of transfus-ing new blood into that ailing outpost. It has been variously reported that during the S-T-D era, the British hand, with the exception of year-ly financial statements, never knew what its

*The 1939
Type 150C-SS
two-place teardrop
coupé by Pourtout.*

ench hand was doing. In any event, when the eakup came, Antony Lago was the natural heir the doddering organization in Suresnes. He signed his Wolverhampton position and took er control of Société Anonyme Darracq cum tomobiles Talbot.

A quick glance around him was all Lago eded to assure himself that what he owned as almost a corpse. The products of Suresnes re viewed with apathy by both the French car-ying public, and even by the company person-l. Nonetheless Major Lago plunged into his rk with characteristic élan. Speed and luxury re his guidelines, and racing — regardless of e contemporary rigorous competition — was s goal. Within eighteen months the old apathy as to be replaced by pride and enthusiasm.

Lago had an excellent base from which to rk: the Talbot-Darracq three-liter Type K78 th its seven main-bearing, six-cylinder engine d in-line pushrod-operated overhead valves. A ecial high performance cylinder head was veloped by Lago and built to the designs of s chief engineer, Walter Becchia. Its orthodox and ingenious feature was the valve-ar that used cross-pushrods of unequal length, us providing a relatively inexpensive and un-

complicated hemispherical head layout. As such it was patented by Lago. In competition two-Solex-carburetor form, output of the Lago Special powerplant was 165 bhp at 4200 rpm. The car's chassis was of rugged, heavy con-struction with solid rear axle and independent front suspension by a transverse leaf and A-arms. And, of course, it used the combination friction clutch and oft-maligned Wilson prese-lector gearbox, both operable with the one pedal.

With his four-liter cars completed, Major Lago was ready to go racing. To him racing was not only his finest laboratory, but his most ef-fective sales campaign as well. Were neither of these factors to be considered, Antony Lago would have raced nonetheless — for the sport of it. Racing was his all-consuming passion. With gusto and perhaps a bit of presumption, he journeyed to Italy and persuaded champion driver René Dreyfus, then with Ferrari, to join and manage his team in its debut racing year.

During that first year the Lago team was largely held together by speculation. The Lago engine: Would it last? Almost everyone, in-cluding Major Lago, feared it wouldn't. Still with the dawning of June's last Sunday in 1936, the Lago cars — these came to be known far

and wide as Talbots, or Talbot-Lagos, or Lago-Talbots — were readied for the French Grand Prix at Montlhéry. After a frank appraisal that the car probably wouldn't be able to last the race, Major Lago advised Dreyfus, "Your job will be to stay ahead of the Bugattis for as long as you can. That's all I want." And he got it. After hanging onto the Bugattis for a respect-able distance, Dreyfus' car ended the race with a noticeable limp. The final result didn't daunt Major Lago — his three cars finished eighth, ninth and tenth — he could remember a few glorious laps. And the picture was to brighten the following year as his cars finished the French GP spectacularly, placing first, second, third and fifth; in the Tourist Trophy first and second, with wins as well in the Marseilles and Tunis Grands Prix.

According to magazine reports of the Paris Salon that year, the Talbot-Lago exhibit virtually shone with the sweet glow of success. And well it might, for the same engine that made a place for Lago in the world of racing was also being used in Gran Turismo cars with rakishly unorthodox, beautiful, and oftimes flamboyant, bodies — and a touring speed of about 115-plus mph. The Lago automobile was soon dubbed by the French, "The car that beguiles . . ."

In 1938 Lago bored out the engine of his com-petition car to 4½ liters (240 bhp) and mounted it in a quasi-Grand Prix car. By adding or taking away fenders and other road equipment to meet various racing requirements, the car could be run in both sports and Grand Prix events. There has been, in fact, some dispute as to whether this unsupercharged 4½-liter machine was a thinly disguised GP machine or merely a "converted" sports car. As a GP car, despite its reliability and light fuel consumption, it was of course no match for the German brutes. This was evident in 1938, and the same engine modified the following year to bring power out-put up to 250 bhp did not bring the car any closer to the Grand Prix Masters. The two Lago cars entered in the 1939 French Grand Prix finished a punishing third and fourth, albeit many miles behind the winning Auto-Unions.

On September 3rd, 1939, France and England declared war on Germany, and everything changed. Previously Major Lago had created a company for the manufacture of aircraft engines, and with the outbreak of hostilities he equipped his Suresnes factory for production of Pratt and Whitney power units. After the fall of France, of course, war production ceased, and the factory shut down. Antony Lago's Italian na-tionality prevented the Germans from seizing the plant, however.

With the war over, Lago determined to pick up just where he had left off in 1939 and brought out from retirement his experimental 4½-liter engine. Among other improvements, its single camshaft was replaced by two camshafts set high in the block, à la Riley. The inclined valves were worked through short pushrods and

vo Lago-Talbot jewels from the Thirties with coachwork by Figoni et Falaschi. he coupé, above left, was built in 1939. The 1937 two-place cabriolet, below, s equipped for competition, with a dual braking system and higher compression.

ckers, thus greatly reducing the weight of the lve gear and providing more efficient action. his engine — the largest passenger car ·werplant then built in France — provided the ·wer for both standard and racing cars. Their ·annel-section chassis frames featured in- pendent front suspension by a lower ·ansverse leaf spring and a hollow upper shbone, and a one-piece rear axle mounted on ·mi-elliptic leaf springs. In the Grand Prix ·rs, the transmission was stepped to the right that it ran alongside the driver's seat to an ·fset differential assembly. In Grand Sport ·rm the engines were mounted within a longer,

heavier chassis; with regular coachwork a speed of 125 mph was claimed. In each of these versions the handy Wilson gearbox was standard equipment.

Lago competition cars were soon headline material in the racing press. The competition, of course, was considerably less formidable than in the prewar years, and this accounts for much of the Lago success. But success viewed from any angle is impressive. First-place finishes in five Grands Prix and the Coupe du Salon in 1947 were a healthy beginning. Then there were six racing firsts in 1948, five in 1949 and ten in 1950. Among these, the 1950 win at Le Mans saw

the Lago car driven by Louis Rosier and his son break every course record.

It was not that the Lago cars were fast; their 240 bhp was not really a match for the super- charged Alfa Romeos, Ferraris and Maseratis. But a nine-mile-per-gallon running consumption made them two or three times less thirsty than the Italians, and the ability to run through a Grand Prix nonstop was a decided advantage.

The cars Lago placed on the circuits were largely the same automobiles he placed on the road. His Grand Sport was just that — a sports car in the grand manner — and in 1946 the Lago Record made its debut, a striking car utilizing a modified Grand Sport engine. But the postwar French taxation system was not favorable to builders of luxurious grand touring cars — and compromise was necessary for survival. This was done via the more popularly- priced Lago Baby, and later Lago America.

Despite these efforts, Antony Lago was being spun in an eddy of financial difficulties. Pro- duction dropped from around 1000 cars a year to under 100. In 1951 Lago was forced to give up his works racing team. But not racing.

In the annals of motor sport, there are a few races that will live as long as men remain at- tracted to speed. One of these was Le Mans, 1952. Tony Lago never forgot it. Neither did driver Pierre Levegh, who had commissioned Lago to build him the car. Levegh was deter- mined to drive the race himself—for the full twenty-four hours — and win. The full works teams of Jaguar, Aston Martin, Mercedes-Benz ιand Ferrari opposed him. Nevertheless at the end of twenty-three hours it appeared that Levegh and the Lago car would be the first combination ever to win Le Mans without a driver change. They were ahead and by a wide margin, but the driver behind the wheel had become a robot. Disregarding the pleas of his wife and Lago to turn the car over to his co-driver, failing to recognize even the men in his own crew, Levegh took off — with twenty-five miles between him and the nearest Mercedes and only forty-four minutes to go. Shortly afterward an official car brought an almost lifeless form back to the pits, and a loudspeaker announced the breakdown of Levegh's car. The mechanical failure — a broken connecting rod. The reason — an almost unconscious driver engaging a lower gear than he had intended, when accelerating away from the corner at Arnage. For years Lago carried the broken bearing bolt in his pocket — a reminder of a glorious moment that might have been.

The odds were, of course, against that mo- ment, and as the years wore on, they mounted against Tony Lago as well. He had remained longer than most of the small exclusive French motorcar manufacturers, but in the end he, too, was enveloped in the complex machinations of the French industrial scene. In 1959 Automobiles Talbot Darracq S.A. was quietly absorbed into the Simca organization. One year later Major Antony Lago was dead.

ft: The 1950 Grand Sport, a two-place touring coupé by Pennock of the Hague.
low: A competition-type tourismo from 1948, with coachwork by Figoni et Falaschi.

HENRY'S "T" AND EDSEL'S "A"

Ford

As a factory worker later recalled of that da[y] "Every time he'd meet somebody, he'd give hi[m] a kick in the pants or a punch between t[he] shoulders." Henry Ford had just returned fro[m] his first ride in the new Model T. With u[n]abashed enthusiasm, he glanced around h[is] coterie of similarly exuberant associates a[nd] beamed, "Well, I guess we've got started!" [He] had a legend.

A year or so previous to that epochal rid[e] Henry Ford had analyzed the automobi[le] market: "The automobile of the past attaine[d] success in spite of its price because there we[re] more than enough purchasers . . . T[he] automobile of the present is making go[od] because the price has been reduced just enou[gh] to add sufficient new purchasers to take care [of]

The 1910 Model T town car.

e increased output . . . The automobile of the ture must be enough better than the present r to beget confidence in the man of limited eans and enough lower in price to insure sales r the enormously increased output."

Ford had, of course, been producing cars of e present since 1903. The Ford Motor Company had been formed that year — following ven years of experimental work by Henry, a cing interlude and a rather unfortuitous sociation with several Detroit financiers in hat was successively called the Detroit utomobile Company and the Henry Ford Company. Since 1903 Ford production had ranged rough Models A, B, C, F, K, N, R, S — and ter the S, the T. It was Henry Ford's car of e future.

In 1908, the natal year of the Model T, there were 200,000 cars in the United States. A scant five years later there would be that many Model T's on American roads; by 1915 the figure would be a million, and before Henry Ford was through, there would be some fourteen million more than that.

Some historians have since called the Model T Ford a bad car. Imagine! A more blatantly absurd notion would be hard to come by. The Model T was — and perhaps still is — the most famous car in the world. Defining the automobile in a practical sense as an efficient and economical means of transport of wide application and availability, it must be viewed as, historically, the most important. And it remains among the most endearing. It's a unique

automobile that cannot be compared with any other. The Model T Ford stands quite alone.

The car was one of revolutionary simplicity. The four cylinders — with their water jackets — of its engine were cast en bloc, with the upper half of the crankcase also integrated with the cylinders. It was a side-valve layout with a single gear-driven camshaft, having bore-stroke dimensions of 3 3/4 x 4 inches for a displacement of 176.7 cubic inches (2.9 liters). It developed 20 bhp (and 65 lb/ft of torque) at 1600 rpm. Lubrication was via an ingenuous combination gravity and splash system. The first T's featured centrifugal water pumps, soon to change to the thermosyphon system, however. Noteworthy was the low tension magneto built into the flywheel — familiar to Europe but

The 1914 Model T speedster.

rather innovative for an American car — which with the engine, transmission, and universal joint were all enclosed in one solid casting.

The chassis was light and of blessed simplicity. Transverse semi-elliptic leaf springs front and rear served for the suspension. The arrangement for stopping the first Model T's featured two pedals and two levers, the wheel brake and reverse band actuated by individual hand controls, but this system was abandoned by late February of 1909 in favor of the soon-to-become-famous three-pedal system. Equally famous was the Ford two-speed epicyclic transmission system, about which novelist John Steinbeck was to later write that two generations of Americans knew more about "the planetary system of gears than the solar system of stars." Wheelbase was 100 inches, track fifty-six inches, chassis length 128 inches. And that was the way it stood — for the next nineteen years.

The loathness to change that has come down to us as a hallmark of the Model T — and its creator — is part myth. True, Henry Ford was most definitely of the opinion that to change "what we can't make enough [of] as it is" was

The Model T touring car, above from 1909, below right from 1926. Below left is the Tudor sedan from 1926. Almost from its inception the T was supplied with a wide variety of bodies by independent builders, the most popular being the depot hack, as the 1921 car above right.

folly, and as late as 1924-25 some Model T's were still exiting Dearborn with the little oil taillamp and no self-starter. But there had been modifications through the years. For example, the earliest T's had linoleum-covered wooden running boards. And embossed on the front of the radiator was the Ford script, borne on wings. But steel running boards were soon substituted, and the wings were removed from the Ford logo. Prior to 1911 the Tin Lizzie had a body made of wood, afterward it was a sheet-steel-covered wooden frame, and the steering wheel — at fifteen inches — was two inches bigger. By 1912 much of what had previously been brass became black, as would the entire body after the following year. The any-color-as-long-as-it's-black policy endured through 1925.

Electric lights replaced the acetylenes, the flat rear fenders became curved, and the cherry-wood dashboard had given way to a curved steel cowl by 1915. Two years later a black steel shell finally replaced the brass radiators, all fenders became curved and crowned, and an electric horn replaced the hand klaxon which itself had replaced the original bulb horn in 1915. By 1920

self-starters and demountable rims were available as extras, and the steering wheel was now sixteen inches across. A half decade later balloon tires were available, and the company had coined the words "Fordor" and "Tudor" for the sedan body styles introduced two years earlier. For 1926 — when customers again had a color choice — the radiator shell was nickel-plated, the gas tank on most models was moved forward into the cowl, and the coil box — wooden until 1913, steel thereafter — was removed from the dash and put under the hood. The steering wheel was given still another inch.

None of the foregoing can be construed as sweeping change. Indeed probably the most massive alteration of the Model T during its lifetime was its price. It began in October of 1908 as an $850 car, and was thereafter price-revised almost yearly, to a low in 1924 of $290! This was perhaps the most revolutionary of all Model T changes. For it brought within the budget of mass America an automobile that was durable and reliable — and simple: to maintain, to operate, and to understand.

Early in his political life Woodrow Wilson had castigated the motorcar as flaunting idleness and conspicuous consumption in the faces of hard-working, hard-pinched men. That was before the Model T. It has to be the most democratic automobile ever built. Millions of Americans could afford to own one, and anyone who could manage that also had the wherewithal to maintain it. A new fender might cost two and a half dollars, a new muffler half that.

"Every man is his own mechanic with a Ford," advertised the company. And they were quite right, provided the owner had access to waxed twine, bailing wire, chewing gum, a monkey wrench, a screwdriver, a stove pipe, a paper clip — few tools more complicated than this were needed to keep a Model T going strong. A solution of kerosene and old candle ends would keep the engine chuffing, should there be a temporary shortage of gasoline. It was "The Universal Car." Perhaps it shimmied, heaved, rattled and wheezed, but the Model T racked up more driving miles — over probably more varieties of surface — than any other car in history. In June of 1927 the last one was built.

Of all the interesting facets surrounding the Model T's successor, probably the most telling that it was conceived not because of but rather in spite of Henry Ford. Indeed it was force upon him, by his son Edsel, backed up by mo of the board of the Ford Motor Company.

Henry Ford had been a munificent father, b despite his generosity it was evident that he ha withheld from his son nearly as much as he ha given. Edsel had received a million dollars gold on his twenty-first birthday, and at twent six — in 1919 — he had become president of t Ford Motor Company. He was like a fairyta hero, except that in reality, though he bore t title and wore the crown, he was as much paw as king. His father still ran the company.

Henry and Edsel were opposites in eve possible way. Edsel Ford was an egalitarian, man of considerable taste and charm, businessman with an engineer's regard f design. His father was an autocrat, a rugged individualistic product of the Nineteenth Ce tury. The difference between the two can likened to that between an instrument honed precision by machine and a tool fashioned fro stone by human energy. Both may do the sam

The 1928 Model A phaeton.

ob well — but differently.

By the mid-Twenties what Edsel most wanted to do differently was the Model T. But Henry wasn't having any of that. He was completely satisfied with his car, and he believed everyone else in the country should be too. "The Model T is the most perfect automobile in the world," he once said — and for years his faithful nodded in agreement.

Now they were nodding no more. Model T production remained high, to be sure, but unsold cars were accumulating in dealers' lots and showrooms. It is easy to see why Henry Ford thought his judgment indisputable. Since he had been right before in introducing the T, and since nearly half the cars on the road were Fords, there was no reason for him to suppose he was any less right now than he had once been. Though a shrewd man with a discriminating and canny business sense, he ignored the signs suggesting that his Tin Lizzie's days were numbered, but numbered they were.

The American public no longer agreed with Mr. Ford. They wanted more power, more performance, a more pleasant package. They didn't want a car already more than a decade and a half old. Ultimately it was Edsel who — together with reality itself — managed to convince his father that what the public wanted was a Ford all right, but not the Model T. And so on May 25th, 1927, newspapers across the country carried the announcement that production of the immortal Model T would be discontinued.

Almost immediately numberless farmers, businessmen, housewives and salesmen wrote passionate letters of protest, imploring Ford to continue manufacturing the car. And, so legend has it, an elderly New Jersey lady purchased and stored seven new Model T's so she would not have to change cars for the rest of her life. The rest of the country sat back and waited to see what in the world the Ford company would come up with to replace the T.

The assembly line stopped. Henry Ford had insisted that a new car project should not get under way until the last Model T had come out of the shops. Several ideas had been under development during the Model T's last year, but little progress was actually made until the spring of 1927. Then the pressure was on. The Ford Motor Company was going to lose more than $100 million during the shutdown period, but this bothered Henry not nearly so much as did Edsel's interference.

Edsel had his own ideas of what the new Ford should be, many of them in opposition to what his father wanted to do. There were times when antagonism between the two men was so strong that intermediaries had to dart between offices, conveying messages back and forth, striving to keep father and son in communication, but apart. Not all the messages were actually delivered. One of those that was not directed Edsel to go to California and remain there until summoned back. Characteristic of cold wars, the conflict between father and son took its toll in time. As Edsel and Henry Ford wrangled over such points as brakes and transmission, the production date of the new car was driven farther and farther ahead.

Although the months passed and funds continued to drain away, there was no waning of interest on the public's part. Rumors appearing almost daily in the press kept public enthusiasm alive. Despite the lack of official information,

The 1929 Model A station wagon.

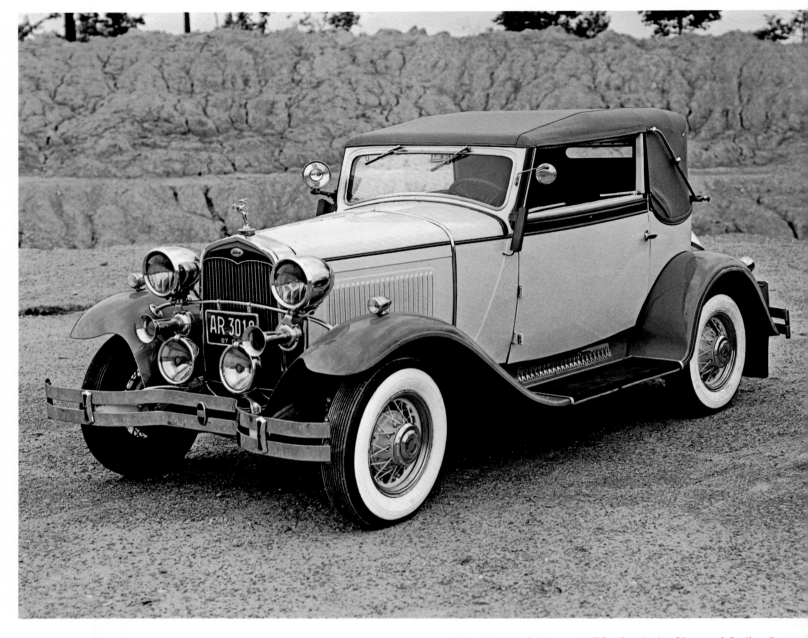

The 1931 Model A convertible victoria by Glaeser of Berlin, German

anticipation ran so high that half a million people ultimately paid deposits on the car before they had seen it or found out its price. And everybody waited.

Ford neither confirmed nor denied any of the rumors. It was reported that the car was to be a mixture of Ford and Lincoln and thus would be called a Linford. It was also reported that the car would be named after one of Henry Ford's oldest and dearest friends, Thomas Edison. The first story earned more acceptance than the second after a newspaper published the "fact" that a nameplate manufacturer in Columbus, Ohio, was engaged to turn out Linford emblems. Other rumors had it that the new Ford would be radically different and cheaper than the T, still others that the car would be "purely defensive" and would cost much more than the T.

The new car was neither a Linford nor an Edison, nor was it revolutionary, nor was it an imitator. It was named after the first Ford production car of 1903, a designation also designed

to indicate that a new generation of Fords could be expected from Dearborn. At its public showing in New York in January of 1928, the police were called out to hold back the mobs surging into Madison Square Garden. Fifty thousand New Yorkers placed orders and paid cash deposits on the new car. In St. Paul, Minnesota, twenty-five thousand people turned out, despite sub-zero temperatures. In Cleveland, mounted police had to be summoned to protect show windows. Elsewhere in Denver, Berlin, Madrid, London — the enthusiasm was the same. In the United States alone, according to estimates, ten million people inspected the new car in its first thirty-six hours on display.

What they saw was a certainly admirable car. Not ahead of its time, the Model A was clearly of it — it was precisely the right car at the right time, though it was not to be that for long.

Henry Ford had dictated the Model T: He "approved" the Model A, or at least most of it. The only vestiges of the T remaining in the A

180

The 1931 Model A convertible sedan by Briggs.

The 1931 Model A deluxe roadster.

were the Ford emblem and transverse springs. The new four-cylinder engine (3⅞ x 4¼ inches displacing 200.5 cubic inches) developed 40 hp at 2200 rpm, nearly twice the power of the Model T. Rear-wheel brakes had been replaced by four-wheel mechanicals; flywheel magneto by coil-and-battery ignition. Significantly, the Model T's planetary transmission was discarded in favor of a standard three-speed gearshift. Henry Ford had been against that; he called the sliding-gear transmission a "crunch gear," considered it imitative of what other manufacturers were using — this was anathema to him — and would have preferred to have retained his nearly two-decades-old three on the floor. He had even toyed with the idea of an automatic planetary transmission, but the development time necessary would have been prohibitive, and Edsel had talked him out of it.

Even Edsel Ford admitted, "There is nothing radical about the new car." More important, of course, was the fact that it was an all-new car.

The car-buying public, and Ford dealers as well, were more excited by the car's arrival — at long last — than by any single facet of its design. Generally the A contained most of the refinements the public had been clamoring for, and it was priced right. But the Model A was not in a class by itself. It presented a challenge its competitors quickly met. Within a year the Chrysler Corporation brought out its new Plymouth, which featured better brakes (hydraulic) and, later, the much-publicized "floating power." In 1929 Chevrolet introduced their six-cylinder engine and geared a potent sales campaign to the notion that six cylinders could now be had for the price of four.

In 1932 the Model A passed quietly from the scene. Its demise would bring a wave of respect and affection for the car it had been, which has endured to this day. As for Henry Ford, he was about to make news again — and astound all his competitors, and the motoring public alike — with the unveiling of the first low-priced V-8.

LAGONDA LG6

Some people think it's the best car Lagonda ever built.

Not many people these days are aware of the fact that one English company which during the Thirties produced automobiles expressing the very essence of the British vintage idiom was founded by an American from the Midwest who really wanted to be an opera singer. Wilbur Gunn, son of a successful manufacturer of sheep shearing equipment, eventually pursued his singing career to England during the late Nineties. He abandoned his pursuit there and the turn of the century found him building motorcycles and small two-cylinder three-wheel vehicles at Staines, in Middlesex. The company which he founded there took its name from the small Ohio town, now part of Springfield, where Gunn was born: Lagonda Creek.

Around 1910 Gunn began building four-wheelers, and curiously enough virtually every example built for the next two years was sold to Czarist Russia, where their reliability was widely appreciated. All of these early Lagondas were built entirely in Gunn's own shops, carburetors only being purchased outside.

After Gunn's death in 1920 Lagonda's ownership, fortunes and prospects altered more or less with the seasons, one high point being the introduction in 1926 of the twin-cam two-liter "Speed" model which was fairly successful in competition up through the late Twenties. Six-cylinder Meadows-engined models were also introduced during this period, but these and other developments were but stepping stones leading to the adoption in 1934 of a massive 4½-liter Meadows six which ultimately resulted in what a good many people think are the greatest Lagondas of them all: the M45R Rapide, the LG45 and the LG6.

These were big, strong, powerful machines now, more like Bentleys than anything else, and it seemed only natural that W. O. himself should be tempted away from his Rolls-Bentley affiliations to work his special magic on this new range of Lagondas. Most recently the Staines firm had been acquisitively eyed by Rolls-Royce, who had of course acquired Bentley Motors back in 1931. But this was 1935, and a totally unexpected thing happened in June of that year; a Lagonda Rapide won at Le Mans.

With this altogether surprising victory Lagonda had suddenly become a highly desirable pro-perty, but for once Rolls-Royce were outmaneuvered — the ownership of the Lagonda company now passed to a London lawyer by the name of Alan Good.

Good was very aware of how little use Rolls-Royce had been making of Bentley's enormous talents, and what a considerable asset he could be to Lagonda's future. Discussions between the two had actually begun before the company had changed hands, and W.O. was installed as technical director only a few days after the sale was completed. Lagonda's golden age had just begun.

Bentley's first project was to banish some of the roughness from Henry Meadows' big six,

vamp the suspension, add synchronizers to the
p two gears, and make countless improvements
 the structure of the car. *The Autocar* was
oved to observe that this new model, the LG
, was "a great deal better." But the best was
t to be.

 Once W.O. had got the old M45 into a state
here he could live with it he immediately set
out designing an entirely new car from the
ound up — this time to be powered by what
 himself still feels *could* have been his finest
gine design of all: his overhead-cam short-
roke V-12.

 Alas, this engine was not a success, or, more
curately, it was introduced sooner than it

should have been. Though extremely smooth and quiet, the V-12 had a somewhat disappointing power curve, requiring rather more use of the transmission than should have been necessary with a multi-cylinder touring engine of its size (4480 cc). This would have been a simple matter to overcome with a bit of development time, but Good and his backers were hungry for sales now and had little patience for those who spoke of developmental periods and product testing (techniques which by now Rolls-Royce had raised to a veritable art form). The car was put into production anyway.

But if the V-12 engine was less than it could have been, W.O.'s new chassis was everything and more. "Remarkable," "exceptional," "superb . . ." enthused contemporary journalists over the new car's handling, ride and all-round refinement. Though the new chassis had been designed with the V-12 in mind, the now vastly improved six was still available with it, and in that form was designated model LG6. The big Meadows engine was now as smooth as silk up to its limit of 4000 rpm, at which point the cars would be sailing along at a shade over 100 mph. Enormous Lockheed two-leading-shoe hydraulic brakes and a beautifully tuned suspension system with an independent torsion-bar front and long half-elliptics at the rear, coupled with adjustable hydraulic shock absorbers and very precise steering, rendered the LG6 supremely comfortable and highly controllable — a good deal more so than the Bentleys that R-R were building then. A better Bentley had been built, and Lagonda had built it! To W.O. the taste of vindication must have been sweet.

1939
LAGONDA LG6
SPECIFICATIONS

ENGINE
Type: six-cylinder in-line overhead valve
Bore x stroke, mm: 88.5 x 120.64
Displacement: 4480 cc
Horsepower developed: 130 (approximately) at 4000 rpm

TRANSMISSION
Type: G10 four-speed
Ratios: 1st 11.63:1
2nd 5.98:1
3rd 4.48:1
4th 3.58:1

DIMENSIONS
Wheelbase: 10 feet 7 inches
(available also in 11 feet 3½ inches)
Track, front and rear: 5 feet
Tire size: 6.50 x 18
Overall length: 16 feet 5 inches
Overall width: 6 feet
Weight, dry: 4144 pounds
Ground clearance: 7½ feet
Turning circle: 37 feet, 9 inches

The Lagonda LG6 chassis was priced at £875. The 1939 Vanden Plas roadster pictured is in the collection of Mr. and Mrs. Gerald P. Roeser of Lahaska, Pennsylvania.

MODULO
by
Pininfarina

It may seem a bit odd to regard the Modulo as a classic. Still, in twenty years or so, when most production cars may well have descended from it, perhaps it won't be so difficult.

During its long and illustrious history, the Italian coachbuilding house of Pininfarina has consistently produced automobiles distinguished by tremendous vitality, flawless good taste and perfect logic — admirable qualities all. The Modulo provides still another one. It is nothing less than a milestone, a genuine automotive breakthrough on the order of Pininfarina's famous 1948 Cisitalia. Interestingly, however, the Modulo is so pure of line, its elements so thoroughly integrated, that it is quite easy to overlook its many extraordinary qualities.

Consider first the name: Modulo. This means simply that the car is built up from modules or identical units. Why? First, economy. The exterior shell can be made up from one pair of dies, cutting tooling costs by as much as twenty to thirty percent. Second, efficiency. A customer need only advise the manufacturer how he wishes the car to be set up — a huge, powerful engine with two seats, or perhaps a compact V-6 with four. Why should they differ externally? This common-sense approach to design has been accepted in the boating world for decades.

A few words now about space utilization, of which the typical full-size American car is a living, rolling monument to its misapplication. In the Modulo maximum volume is reached precisely at the seating position, exactly where it should be. And in touring version there would be room enough for a raft of suitcases tucked neatly into the tail of the car. In short, the Modulo is extremely roomy. But it is less than thirty-seven inches tall.

Among the Modulo's best features are its doors, or rather the lack of them. The entire upper frontal section slides forward, allowing passengers to walk in standing straight up, and then seat themselves. Wonderful. Noteworthy, too, is the spherical module mounted to the driver's right and orientable so he can put the controls at whatever attitude is most convenient.

But most memorable is the way the Modulo looks. On the road it appears to float like some Bradburyesque visitor from an alien world come to show us how much we still have to learn. It is futuristic, yes, but soundly engineered, wonderfully practical — a brilliant exercise in modern sculpture. This car cannot be praised enough. It is a masterpiece.

THE REMARKABLE RUXTON

Only about five hundred of these unique cars were ever built—and enthusiasts are the poorer for it.

The Ruxton production roadster, 1930.

It was early in 1929 when it appeared, casually parked one blustery day in midtown Manhattan. Even blasé New Yorkers were startled. The car was so low and sleek that it would have attracted attention anyway, but one glance at its radiator badge and even the mildly curious were set to wondering. Emblazoned there was not a name but a question mark! It would prove remarkably appropriate. For the car that began its life as the Question Mark would end it pretty much the same way.

William J. Muller and Archie M. Andrews — those were the two men behind the project. Born in Brooklyn and educated at Brooklyn Polytechnic, Muller garnered a wealth of practical engineering experience over a decade of work as racing mechanic to some of the top drivers of the pre-World War I era. After a brief association with Willys-Overland he joined the Edward G. Budd Manufacturing Company of Philadelphia, makers of automobile bodies, as an experimental engineer late in 1920. In the course of his work he proposed building a prototype front wheel drive car in hopes of persuading some manufacturer to produce such a machine — with bodies by Budd, of course. After several delays the car was finally completed in the fall of 1928, and a striking job it was. Lower than its contemporaries by many inches, the sedan was mounted on a 130-inch wheelbase with thirty-one-inch diameter wheels. Economics required the use of existing mechanical components wherever possible, so a six-cylinder Studebaker engine was employed, powering the front wheels through a modified Warner gearbox. Befitting its speculative status the radiator bore an intriguing question mark instead of a name.

Now there entered on the scene the intrepid Mr. Andrews. Quite a wealthy financier and promoter, he had amassed a fortune in the machinations of Wall Street and real estate. During his business career he had become a member of the boards of directors of several corporations including Dictagraph, Trans-Lux, Hupp and Budd. Highly enthusiastic over Muller's design, Andrews was convinced that America was ready for a front-drive car and persuaded the Budd company to allow him to market it. He logically planned to have the Hupp Motor Car Corporation build the car, but was thwarted by the Hupp management who had ambitious schemes of their own at the time.

Therefore Andrews decided to form his own corporation to market the car and in April, 1929, a new automobile company was announced — New Era Motors, Inc. A Delaware closed corporation, New Era had neither plan nor dealers — but plenty of ambition. Corporate offices were established in New York City, with Andrews and Muller as president and vice-president respectively, and a distinguished board of directors including automobile manufacturer Fred W. Gardner, metallurgist C. Harold Wills of Ford and Wills Sainte Claire renown, and a stockbroker by the name of William V. C. Ruxton. It was Ruxton whose name was chosen for the car, possibly with the hope that, thus flattered, he and his associates might invest in the new company. As it turned out, they wouldn't.

While New Era was being formed, Andrews was busy demonstrating the new experimental car to the press and prospective distributors in New York and California. At the same time in Philadelphia, Muller was hurriedly designing and finishing the production prototype, and on August 1st, 1929, it was ready.

The supercharged Ruxton (above) built in 1929 as Bill Muller's personal car.

Replacing the Studebaker six was a Continental Model 18S L-head straight eight which would develop 100 horsepower at 3400 rpm. Nelson-Bohnalite pistons were fitted, as was a five-bearing crankshaft and a Zenith dual-throat updraft carburetor. Generator and fuel pump were located on the left side of the engine, while the right side was clean except for the starter and battery. Locating the battery under the hood was somewhat of a novelty inasmuch as conventional cars still carried this unit under the floorboards. The engine was supported on the frame at four points: two rigid mountings forward, two rubber mountings at the rear. The power unit was reversed in the chassis with the flywheel bell housing forward, driving the front wheels through a unique Muller-designed three-speed transmission.

Perhaps the heart of the Ruxton design, this transmission was a brilliant solution to a tough problem. While testing the experimental Budd model, it became apparent that the engine had to be moved forward in the chassis in order to bring sufficient weight over the front wheels. Remember that front-drive cars were prone to slip and break traction on steep hills because of light front ends and transfer of weight rearward. Bringing the engine forward avoided this problem, but the long, eight-in-line motor in vogue at the time left little space for a conventional transmission. Anxious to avoid an excessively long car forward of the cowl, Muller decided to split the gearbox. Low and reverse gears were put in front of the differential, second and third behind. In addition, a unique worm gear and wheel, whose design was aided by Wills, replaced the conventional ring gear and pinion. The telescoping of these formerly bulky units into a compact transaxle brought about a reduction of nearly one foot in the driving gear, a remarkable achievement.

But it was the striking body design that made the Ruxton a truly impressive car. Mounted on a 130-inch wheelbase, the Ruxton was a mere 63¼ inches high, while providing ten inches of ground clearance. Rear-drive designs of the period by contrast were fully ten inches taller and had less clearance. This drastic reduction in height enabled the body to be so lowered on its chassis that the hood was nearly as low as the graceful front fenders. An unusual design, this hood was arranged so the top raised while the sides remained stationary, through removable. The Ruxton was so low that running boards were eliminated. Scorning the flat front ends of most contemporary cars, the Ruxton's chrome and paint radiator shell housed a Long-built core of five-gallon capacity with a false vee-shaped front. Gone was the question mark, and replacing it on the radiator, tire covers and large, oversize hubcaps was a stylized griffin. This was Andrews' idea.

The design staff had done an excellent job producing a distinctive, different-looking car with seemingly excellent sales possibilities. This opinion was echoed by the engineering community, who greeted the Ruxton with much interest. Fielding questions at a meeting of the Society of Automotive Engineers in November of 1929, Muller reported that on a trip from Philadelphia to Indianapolis, the Ruxton exhibited especially good hill climbing ability with traction loss held to three percent on a fifteen percent grade. A tendency to pick up speed in turns, partly because of driver confidence, was reported, but in 12,000 miles of testing, the Ruxton displayed no shimmy or wheel fight. This was confirmed by W. F. England, chief engineer of the F. B. Stearns Company, who added that the Ruxton could be driven around corners faster than any rear-drive car he had ever seen.

The 4000-pound sedan had 2125 pounds over the driving wheels and 1875 over the rear, with unsprung weight held to 390 pounds front, 280 pounds rear, an overall ratio of nearly 6:1. This compared most favorably with the recently-introduced 4710-pound front-drive Cord L-29, whose ratio of sprung to unsprung weight was 5.2:1. Of course, the higher the ratio, the better the ride and roadholding. And, too, the Ruxton carried proportionally more weight than the Cord over its driving wheels, with attendant superior traction on steep inclines.

Early press releases from New Era in the spring of 1929 stated that 12,000 Ruxtons would be produced during the remainder of the year in unnamed plants in Detroit, Cleveland and St. Louis. Deliveries were to begin on July 1st. Rumor was running rampant by this time. Just who was going to build the Ruxton? From Cleveland, Peerless admitted that they might. From Detroit, Hupmobile said emphatically they would not. Finally the matter seemed settled when from St. Louis, Gardner said that they definitely would. In June Fred Gardner made the announcement.

With one problem solved — a plant site — Andrews and New Era set about tackling others: creating a distributor organization and latching onto favorable publicity through lavish display of prototypes.

But suddenly everything changed and New Era was back where it had started — sans factory. For some unknown reason Andrews and the Gardner brothers were unable to work out a mutually satisfactory agreement for Ruxton production. But Gardner remained very much interested in the front-drive concept and decided to build a FWD car of their own. Only a sing[le] prototype was ever built, but that is anoth[er] story. The question was, without Gardner whe[re] would the Ruxton now be built?

Marmon looked promising. Andrews arrange[d] to have the car shown to officials of the Marm[on] Motor Company in Indianapolis, and they e[x]pressed some interest in taking over the proje[ct]. In fact Marmon's chief engineer sent Muller [a] telegram enthusiastically stating that the Ruxt[on] was practical, even ingenious, and had gre[at] commercial possibilities. But the Ruxton was n[ot] destined to be a Marmon product eithe[r]. Ominous clouds were beginning to appear on t[he] automotive horizon. While the Ruxton was [on] view in New York, ironically the financi[al] catastrophe that was ultimately to end the who[le] project occurred with the collapse of the sto[ck] market — and with it the Marmon negotiations.

It was now November, 1929. No Ruxtons ha[d] been manufactured or sold, only a handful [of] sample cars existed. Once again there was t[he] question — where would the car be built? A[nd] again there was an answer. Another one. Moon.

The Moon Motor Car Company was an e[n]terprise similar to that of the Gardner brother[s]

aring St. Louis as its manufacturing site. Like ardner, Moon was an outgrowth of a buggy mpany — and like Gardner, it was both old ne and small time. Production never was high; peaked in 1925 with the building of approximately 13,000 Moon and Diana cars. hereafter the company began a slow downhill ide, vainly trying all the while to find a winning combination in a bewildering succession of odels, but quite unsuccessfully. Apparently oon officials viewed the front-drive Ruxton as panacea for their many ills.

In late November it was official. Moon had ken over Ruxton production and would stribute the car through its dealer organiza-n. Plans were being finalized. The stage was t for Ruxton manufacture in the Moon plant, at the same time backstage the scene was ie of considerable corporate commotion.

And again rumors spread. By March of 1930 ord had it that New Era was planning a merger th Moon, Kissel, Gardner, Jordan and Stutz. iat was news to Stutz, or so the company said; ey denied everything. Jordan executives ad- itted to the fact of some discussion, but thing more. At a meeting in Boston the

Gardner distributor for that city was informed of merger plans, although at the same time such plans were being denied at the factory. The clouds of rumor and counter rumor finally gave way — to a cloudburst. It was early April. The scene was St. Louis.

First there was the announcement of a Moon-Gardner merger. It was a grand plan — the consolidation of their respective sales and engineering staffs to design and market the Windsor and Gardner rear-drive and Ruxton and Gardner front-drive automobiles. It looked good on paper, and that's precisely where it remained, for the reason behind the merger apparently was to prevent the taking over of the Moon company by Archie Andrews and New Era — and Andrews had really already seen to that. The Moon company didn't have a chance. In exchange for the Ruxton rights and patents they had traded new issues of their stock to New Era. Now, of 350,000 shares of outstanding common stock, Andrews and his associates held 240,000. But the Moon people stubbornly chose to ignore that fact, and reportedly when Andrews requested a seat on the company's board of directors they simply said no. Andrews, understandably annoyed, called

a special board meeting in the East on April 7th, where an increase in the number of directors from seven to fifteen was approved. The eight new directors were Andrews' men, of course. Less than a week later all of the old Moon officers found themselves out of their jobs, their positions taken over by New Era men.

Completely stunned, and refusing to recognize the legality of the new regime, the former Moon executives were determined that, although Andrews had captured the company with comparative ease, he would not get the factory — at least not without a fight, be it in the courts or otherwise. Accompanied by armed guards they barricaded themselves in the Moon plant, a futile gesture. Andrews armed himself with a court order — and his men simply broke in. When the smoke cleared New Era emerged firmly in control.

Meanwhile Andrews had approached the management of the Kissel Motor Car Company in Hartford, Wisconsin. The Kissel brothers had been building small numbers of quality cars since 1906, but the company was finding the going rough in the mass-production world of 1930. But they had an excellent plant — much

The Ruxton sedan, the most prolific of the Ruxton body styles.

Only two examples of the
Ruxton phaeton, the
loveliest car to carry
the name, were built.

perior to that of Moon — and other such useful equipment. The idea of using Kissel production facilities to supplement those of the Moon plant was attractive to Andrews and particularly to Muller, who was rather appalled by what he had found at the Moon factory. Consequently Andrews and George Kissel worked out an agreement whereby Kissel would receive new financing from New Era in return for which they committed themselves to the production of 500 Ruxtons a year, as well as all transmission and drive assemblies for the car. Further, were the Kissels not to live up to their part of the bargain they were to pass over control of the company to Andrews in exchange for New Era preferred stock.

It was June of 1930 before the first Ruxtons rolled off the assembly line at the Moon plant. J. Roberts, general manager of the Moon company, reported that demand for Ruxtons exceeded expectations and that orders on file would keep the factory running at capacity for some time. While cars were being shipped across the country, suits and countersuits over the control of Moon raged through the St. Louis courts. New Era was fighting an uphill battle in promoting the Ruxton, faced with the beginnings of the Depression and following on the taillight of the Cord, which had stolen much of Ruxton's thunder. Although the new car was finally in production, Andrews' empire was in shaky condition. In mid-September, the beginning of the end was signalled in Hartford. Kissel collapsed.

Failing to meet its mortgage payments, the company was placed in the hands of receivers at the request of its president, George A. Kissel, due in part to his reluctance to have control in the hands of Andrews. An attempt was made to continue production in receivership, but this was not possible. Tooling for Ruxton final-drive assemblies and related parts was tied up at the Kissel plant, and the resulting parts shortages caused the Moon factory to close its doors November 10th. Moon was losing money on the Ruxton and production was suspended on the advice of creditors. In domino fashion, companies involved with New Era followed Kissel's downfall. On November 15th Moon was placed in receivership. In early December New Era itself filed a bankruptcy petition. Although no longer involved with the Ruxton, the Depression had hit Gardner too, and that company suspended operations early in 1931. A sad sight indeed, watching three tradition-laden companies — Kissel, Moon and Gardner — all buckle within a short six months.

Just how many Ruxtons were built? The generally accepted estimate today is about 500 units, of which Kissel produced about twenty-five, with Moon building the rest during the summer and early fall of 1930. Given the rudimentary state of front-drive engineering in the late Twenties, the Ruxton was truly a brilliant car. Had it been sponsored by a financially stable manufacturer and produced in larger quantities it would undoubtedly have had a greater impact on the industry. Unfortunately a suspicion of fraud has surrounded the project these many years and Andrews' motives in promoting the Ruxton have been questioned. But there can be little doubt he was genuinely interested in marketing the car and was not simply using it to build an automobile empire. Granted, some of his methods in obtaining plants in which to build it were pretty ruthless, but all the companies involved would have failed eventually, Ruxton or no.

And so the Ruxton remains a curiosity today, a victim of the times and one of the stranger stories in the history of the automotive industry. It deserved a better fate.

MARMON: A QUEST FOR PERFECTION

Its virtues were restraint, solidity, performance—and matchless quality.

The 1912 Model 32 speedster.

Quiet, mild, retiring Howard C. Marmon seems to have been too shy. And somewhat logically, this trait has rubbed off onto his cars. They are hardly ever seen today. At classic car meets where Lincolns, Cadillacs, Packards, Duesenbergs might abound, a Marmon appearance is an occasion. Yet though few

Marmons remain extant, few enthusiasts have forgotten their existence. No mystique has attached itself to the Marmon, as it has to many other cars. There is no Marmon aura. Instead there is simply appreciation. No historian worth his nuts and bolts can afford to neglect the marque.

To begin with, the name has been part of America's industrial heritage for well over hundred years. Covered wagons were still heading for California and gold in 1851 when Daniel W. Marmon, in partnership with a man called Nordyke, established himself in a factory in Richmond, Indiana. It was a shed of a store

The 1914 Model 41 speedster.

d a half; its equipment, a single forge; the business, making millstones. The firm prospered nd in 1876 relocated in larger quarters in Indianapolis. In that year, too, Daniel Marmon's wife Elizabeth gave birth to her second son, oward.

By the turn of the century Nordyke and Marmon had a strong claim to being the world's ading producer of milling machinery. The Marmon brothers grew up surrounded by this technological background. Howard Marmon ould quite easily have remained content merely inherit the business and continue its long-established activities, as was his elder brother alter's inclination. But Howard was burning ith enthusiasm for that newfangled gadget alled the automobile. During 1898 he had rafted out some ideas for a car, and the follow-g year he managed to convince his father to low him a corner of the plant to build it.

Frequent design revisions delayed completion the car until 1902, but it was worth waiting r. The car was powered by an air cooled, erhead valve V-twin engine. Though symbolic advanced thought, a V-type engine had been sed before by others. But no precedent existed the automobile industry so far as the Marmon's lubrication system was concerned. It sed a gear pump with pressure feed to the ngine bearings via a drilled crankshaft. The ormal practice in those early days was dipper-d-splash, but Marmon realized the shortcom-gs of this for the high-speed engines that were und to evolve, and he adopted the pressure ed used in marine steam engines — thus mak-g possible higher rpm and higher efficiency. Marmon's frame/suspension design showed con-

siderable ingenuity too. A sub-frame, suspended on hangers from the body frame in front, carried the engine, its longitudinal members tapering to a pivot point at the rear axle. The "single-three-point suspension" system was used to obtain straight line shaft drive without the complications of universal joints.

Highly pleased with the technical success of this first car, Howard Marmon continued with a second. This one carried a V-4 engine, the revolutionary lubrication system was extended to include the piston pins as well, force-feed becoming full-force-feed, and the frame and suspension now had a "double-three-point" layout — a pivot in front replacing the sub-frame hangers. This was the production Model A, and it was followed by Models B, C and D.

By now Marmon was well on his way to becoming the most comprehensive promoter of light alloy aluminum construction in the industry. From the cast aluminum front seat structure in the earliest V-4, Marmon had proceeded to the point where not only the entire body was in aluminum but much use was made of the light alloy in the running gear as well. All in all, the Marmon was a most impressive package.

A starting price of $2500 might help explain why only six Marmons were sold in 1904 — mostly to Howard's friends — and only twenty-five in 1905. But the company might have been expected to do better as the car's merits became known. They didn't, however. There may be an explanation. Although mechanical details were quite different, the Marmon goals — scientific lightweight construction, ultra-flexible suspension and utmost simplicity in engine cooling — were the same as the Franklin's. And

Franklin had got there first: Indeed, thirteen Franklins were built and sold in the same year Marmon completed his first car. In the stiff price field Marmon had selected, someone else had run off with the air cooled sector. With air cooling now meeting a lot of public resistance, only Franklin seemed to have the know-how and managerial touch in that line. The bulk of the over-$2000 market was being grabbed by Packard and Pierce-Arrow with water-cooled four-cylinder machines. Marmon decided to join that majority. From 1909 forward, all Marmons were water-cooled. Howard came up with a new but orthodox car, simpler in design. Yet in this new Model 32 he still held to two of his original principles: perfect lubrication and light alloy construction. For the rest, the car resembled many a contemporary in its frame, suspension and engine.

How to publicize the new car was the problem. And it was solved handily. Howard sent one in 1909 to the new Indianapolis Speedway, where it acquitted itself admirably. And for the highly-touted inaugural Indianapolis 500 in 1911, he built a special, the Marmon Wasp. When it was declared the winner of that event, Howard left the speedway with $16,000 prize money, incalculable prestige and more orders than he could handle. Now, it seemed, the company was really going someplace.

By 1913 the Marmon staff included two talented engineers, Fred Moskovics and Alanson P. Brush, and with Marmon they proceeded to develop an entirely new car. The instructions from the executive committee included this fortuitous note: "Cost is of secondary importance." That is an engineer's dream. Howard

The 1920 Model 34 cloverleaf roadster.

had never been happier, and his team went to work with a will. Already well grounded in aluminum, Marmon decided to go the whole way to save weight. The only cast iron components of the main engine structure were the cylinder sleeves and the one-piece "firing head." Clutch cone wheel, transmission case, differential housing, the entire body, fenders and hood, even the radiator shell — all were in Howard's favorite metal. But "scientific lightweight" did not stop there. A unique "Z" frame eliminated heavy body sills and combined body splashers and running boards with a light but very strong chassis. This made the body and frame virtually a unit and considerably lowered the center of gravity. The whole package weighed only three-quarters that of contemporaries its size and price — 3295 pounds. Even styling had been thought of; the crowned fenders and rounded body lines were certainly well ahead of their time.

The car was designated the Model 34, and it took the 1916 National Automobile Show by storm. Priced at $2700 and up, it was, like the new Packard Twin-Six, aimed at the market created by the pioneering Cadillac V-8. These cars were a different animal to the crude machines of the first decade, a new and altogether superior breed. There were others, too, the Peerless and Cunningham V-8's and the intriguing Premier all-aluminum six. Unfortunately, for many of them, technical promise was not automatically followed by great commercial success. Although Packard's V-12 carved out a substantial market for itself, none of the others, including Marmon, were able even to approach the Cadillac success story. In Marmon's case, there are several possible explanations and one certain reason. Firstly, Howard Marmon never shone in production, nor did he bother to find someone who did. Secondly, the Marmon's design was perhaps a little far out for many luxury car buyers — different in almost every detail. Advanced though Cadillac and Packard were, their designs could still be classed as straightforward, and therefore acceptable. And, to a considerable extent, the cautious *were* right. There *were* hidden bugs in the Marmon 34's engine.

Howard Marmon, however, wouldn't be able to do much about it for several years. His company was soon working for Uncle Sam, filling military contracts, and Howard himself became a lieutenant colonel in the Air Corps. With the close of the war, Howard was back with his engine problems, and by 1920 had come up with a redesign. Throwing away the all-alloy block, he replaced it with two cast iron three-cylinder units. Aluminum was retained for the crankcase, but composite pistons of aluminum and cast iron were now used — Howard being determined to overcome the troubles of the "trouble metal." He was successful, for the engine was to stay for eight years with only minor changes.

Unfortunately, the company was now in financial backwater, drifting, it seemed, toward

Nineteen twenty-four and the year following was the short era of the Model 74, a fine car developed from the Model 34. A speedster 74 from 1925 is shown above. The Model 75 was its successor, the last six-cylinder car offered by the Marmon company. Below left is a 1926 roadster, below right a 1927 victoria coupé.

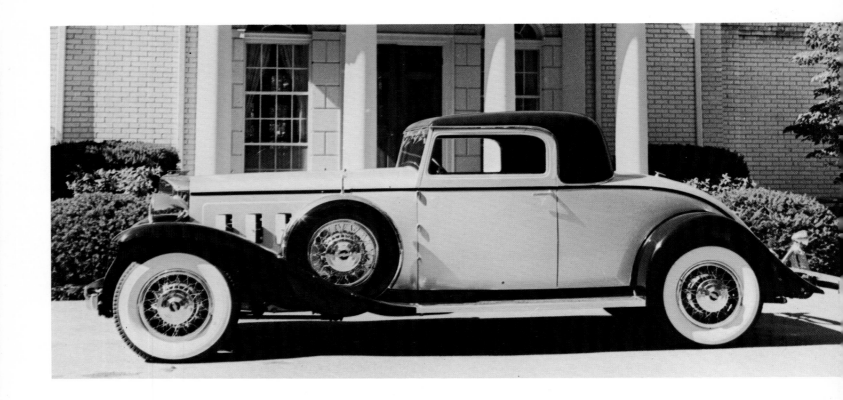

stormy seas. Resignations and an executive shake-up ensued. Earlier Brush had resigned, in 1923 Moskovics left as well. Howard remained as vice-president and chief engineer, but his brother Walter left the presidency for the board chairmanship, and in his place came George M. Williams. It was Williams' assignment to make Marmon's management broader and more flexible. And he did it with a vengeance. He concluded firstly that the big six was "out" and the straight eight was "in" — which was logical enough. But then he concluded, too, that Marmon could not survive with its exclusive fine car policy. Consequently he hired former Locomobile engineer Barney Roos and put him to work on a smaller straight eight for the under-$2000 market. The Roos project publicly appeared in 1927 as the Little Marmon, although Barney himself, disliking the Indianapolis setup, had already gone to head engineering at Studebaker. To replace Roos, Williams took on former Lincoln engineer Thomas J. Litle and placed him in charge of Marmon's new straight-eight-across-the-board program. Marmon was now to produce not one or two, but three separate lines, straight eight coverage in all price fields.

Howard Marmon was devastated. His world turned upside down and inside out, his engineering judgment questioned, he could garner no enthusiasm for an economy car policy. Gradually he withdrew from company affairs. In semi-retirement, he began pondering his own "car of the future." Several of the new Marmon eights were good enough cars — better probably than most on the market — but they were so banal in engineering design that it hurt to see them carry his name. They were certainly not even an attempt for leadership in the fine car market. He had to do something about it.

The penultimate Marmon—and assuredly the greatest
of a truly great line—was the Sixteen,
introduced during the month of November, 1930.
In two-passenger coupé guise, as on the 1931
Model 141 shown at left, it could be had for $5200.

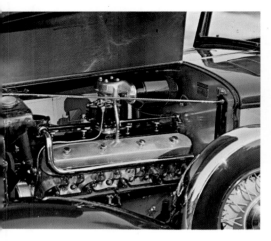

During its three years from 1930 to the spring of 1933, just 390 Marmon Sixteens were produced.
Among the most stately—and costly—of body styles available was the limousine. This Model 147
seven-passenger example from 1932 was capable of a genuine but very dignified 100 miles an hour.

Meanwhile back at the Marmon plant Williams' idea for a "straight eight General Motors" was resulting in a new addition every year. Eights began to be issued almost like bank checks, ranging from under $1000 to more than three times that figure. For a while profits began to flow again, then they ebbed.

Marmon's expansion had been too recent, and its public image too confused to weather the Depression. At least when the Marmon brothers were running the company, everyone knew what a Marmon was. But in the late Twenties the name could mean anything. Consequently, Marmon had no lasting success against those long established in the lower price echelon, while the cheaper Marmons delivered a critical blow to the marque's previous fine car image. The Marmon story would have ended as a dreary fizzle here had it not been for the Colonel himself. It was doomed regardless, but at least Howard Marmon would make the Marmon name go out with a bang and not a whimper.

Sixteen cylinders. Two hundred horsepower. Almost five hundred cubic inches. More than one hundred miles an hour. And priced below

$5000 too. That was Marmon's dream — and he realized it all, save the price tag. The Marmon Sixteen was an altogether fabulous automobile, largely justifying the slogan that went with it — "The World's Most Advanced Motor Car." But it had taken five years to do it. And Cadillac had got there first. It was a familiar story.

The Marmon Sixteen's base price was $5200, $150 less than the Cadillac's. The Marmon was ten miles an hour faster than the Cadillac. But the Cadillac got away from the production line more quickly. The Marmon was styled for the early Thirties rather than the late Twenties. But the Cadillac collared the market. Before a single Marmon Sixteen had ever been shown, General Motors' premier division had already sold 2887 of their V-16 Cadillacs. And Marmon's problems hadn't eased after the late introduction. The next problem was delivery. Prototype handbuilt cars had been displayed at automobile shows during December of 1930 and January, 1931. But the first buyer did not get his car until April, 1931, a delay of almost six months from the original announcement in November of 1930. Many buyers refused to wait, and went

elsewhere — frequently to Cadillac. That is, th[e] luxury car prospects who had refused to go int[o] hiding: By mid-1931 the country was ap[p]roaching the absolute pit of the Depression.

Difficulties faced Marmon everywhere. Im[p]ortant men left the firm, and internal politic[s] were strife-ridden. The proliferation of cheape[r] models had generated a widespread belief tha[t] Marmon had abandoned the fine car field. Ac[t]ually the company was preparing to do just th[e] opposite — abandon the low-priced range an[d] return to fine cars exclusively. This took plac[e] in 1933, when the Sixteen was the only car th[e] company listed — and at reduced prices. Eve[n] this drastic move failed. By May of 1933 th[e] Marmon company was in receivership.

Ironically, it seems that Howard Marmon wa[s] always either too early or too late — too ad[-]vanced, sometimes, for the times, other times no[t] quite quick enough to take advantage o[f] marketable advances. Yet, for all this, he di[d] succeed in producing some uncommonly fin[e] cars. And though few in number, those that re[-]main aptly serve as reminders of his talent an[d] dedication.

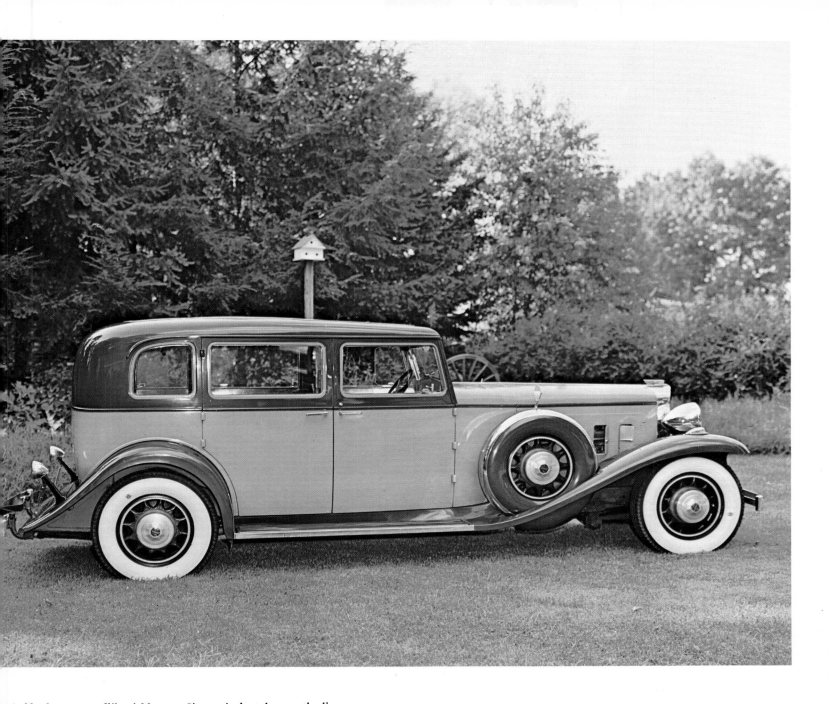

robably the most prolific of Marmon Sixteen body styles was the five-
assenger sedan, designated Model 149. Two examples from 1933
ppear above and below left. On the facing page is a custom-built
pen phaeton produced by Waterhouse in 1932. The Marmon story did not,
owever, end with the Sixteen. Its sequel appears below right, the V-12
rototype. Howard Marmon financed the project largely by himself,
e company cupboard being virtually bare by this time.
he car had independent suspension front and rear, tubular backbone frame
nd a way-out body style by Walter Dorwin Teague, Jr.
he V-12—only one was ever built—was completed in April of 1933,
ne month before the Marmon company found itself in receivership.
t was tested, and most successfully, on the Indianapolis Motor Speedway,
ut Howard Marmon could find no potential investors to put the car
to production, and it remained with him until his death in April of 1943.

SYDNEY ALLARD'S FABULOUS J2X

In his youth Sydney Herbert Allard raced an became enamored of Morgan three-wheelers, s when he later applied bellows and anvil to th construction of real rectangular cars it wasn surprising that they shared two of the Mog' time-honored traits: crudity, mitigated b enormous effectiveness. As their road and trac record shows, too, Allards were outstandin allrounders. Among many other speed and er durance exploits, they broke a twenty-one-yea spell of British non-success in the Monte Carl Rally, winning it outright in 1952; placed thir at Le Mans in '50; scooped the hard-fough British hill climb championship in '49; won th Watkins Glen GP the first time it made the in ternational calendar.

Sydney himself, founder and chairman of th Allard Motor Company, had an insatiable in

uiring mind. As well as being the marque's most skillful and ubiquitous competition driver, e was also its chief designer. In this capacity, kely to his commercial disadvantage, he often uldn't resist putting new irons in the fire efore removing old ones. Some of his ideas bore ttle or no relation to production car realities, ut Sydney, as undisputed boss of Allard, and e other family firms affiliated thereto, could end as much time as he liked on projects with ttle prospect of a direct and tangible return. In stice, though, there wasn't a dilettante bone in is large, loose limbed body. Without giving any npression of haste or harassment, he kept imself as busy as a contact breaker the livelong ay, fitting his racing, rallying, hill climbing, ar designing and development work into any me left over from the directing of one of Lon-

don's biggest Ford dealerships.

Sydney formed the Allard Motor Co. Ltd. in 1946, with premises at Clapham, London, just a short walk from his Ford dealership. Toward the end of the year he launched a range of three models. These were the J1 competition two-seater, the K-1 touring two-seater and the L four-seater touring car. Common denominators were the 3662 cc Ford V-8 side-valve engine, developing 85 horsepower at 3800 rpm, and a three-speed gearbox and other staple mechanicals of the same origin. Although the performance of these old flatheads was pretty soporific by the bhp criterion, their torque was impressive and the Allards they powered were light; the J1, for instance, weighed only 2350 pounds dry. Although not pretty, the early Allards had an appealing pugnacity. Stylistically, they were dis-

tinguished by a vertically barred and forward cascading frontispiece, suggestive, apart from its chromium finish, of a baronial coal scuttle.

In the sellers' market conditions of the late Forties and early Fifties, Allard felt no great compulsion to make design changes for change's sake. True, the XK-120 Jaguar, introduced in 1948, was a far better looking car than any past, present or foreseeable Allard, as well as possessing such allurements as a dohc engine of classic type, superior i.f.s. and four-speed transmission. On the other hand, the XK's 160 bhp engine was outpowered and out-torqued by the various and much bigger rocker-box V-8's that the J2 Allard and its descendants were drafted to accept. Such comparisons, however, were more or less mean-ingless because both makes, whatever their merits, could sell more cars than they could

build. During this export-or-die chapter of Britain's economic history, H.M. Government reduced Sydney Allard's problem to very simple terms: As long as he could sell x percent of his output for dollars, his ration of steel would keep right on coming, and if not, not.

Sydney's reaction, coinciding with the launch of the de Dion-axled and otherwise updated J2 model late in 1949, was to give this car the elasticity necessary for the accommodation of various American engines with transmissions to match. Cars were built at Clapham to U.S. dealers' individual order, shipped across the Atlantic and postnatally fitted with powerplants of the customers' choice — Cadillacs, Chryslers, Mercurys, Dodges or whatever.

And that's how it all began. To adequately describe the cars that resulted, one would have to say that the J2 Allards were the Carroll Shelby Cobras of their era. Both cars were of the

"Anglo-American sports bastard" variety, and each in its time was the fastest genuine sports car in the world. In their beginnings neither of them could handle very well, but they were so stupendously fast that they rendered that issue virtually irrelevant. Remember all those pictures of Phil Hill, Dan Gurney and Ken Miles squirreling Cobras around corners with all four wheels meeting the road at every imaginable angle except straight up and down? Well, the Allards produced some angles too that were uniquely their own, never seen before and seen on nothing else since.

Sydney Allard devised his unique-split front axle back in the Thirties in an effort to keep both front wheels of his specials on the ground while storming up muddy hillsides during the "trials" events which were so popular in Britain then. It worked pretty well too, but on ordinary roads it was a poor substitute for real i.f.s., or

even a well located front axle. All the same Sydney Allard liked it, and with his announcement of his first production cars in 1946, to no one's surprise they had split front axles also

On the original K-1 and K-2 series this hadn't presented much of a problem, but with the entrance of the fabulous J2 on the racing scene the split front axle's shortcomings were suddenly mightily apparent. Even so, this didn't prevent the Cadillac-powered J2 from finishing third in the Twenty-Four Hours of Le Mans that year — Sydney and Tom Cole driving — behind two bare-faced Grand Prix Talbots converted into sports cars for the occasion by the addition of lights and fenders.

For the next couple of years brave Allard conductors were stomping Jaguars, Ferraris, et al, all around the United States. It wasn't surprising. It might be truthfully said of the J2's that their chassis lagged behind the more powerful

ngines fitted to them. But one reason they were ard to beat in all forms of competition for which they were eligible was that they attracted two-fisted, scareproof breed of driver, like for nstance the late, flamboyant and not exactly introvert Erwin Goldschmidt. Laurence Pomeroy, igh priest of Britain's technical automotive writers, extolled the J2's "outstanding controllability," but his praise might have been more measured if he'd attempted to average over 0 mph for fifteen consecutive laps of the Watkins Glen circuit as it was twenty years ago. Firebrand Goldschmidt didn't just attempt this, e accomplished it in winning the 1950 Watkins Glen GP with a J2. Out of twenty-six starters, ighteen either broke, blew up or failed to finish within the time limit. It has been said that merey watching Goldschmidt wielding his J2 around he course should have caused the faint-hearted nlooker to age visibly — what with

Goldschmidt's car in the air for what seemed like half the time and sideways for most of it. Maybe Erwin had a secret there, for surely one of the best possible ways to compensate for poor suspension design is to keep the car at least several inches above the road.

A very simple revision to the J2's front end geometry was effected in 1951 which considerably improved the car's handling characteristics. This revised model was dubbed the J2X, and though it was a lot better now the competition was getting better faster. Bigger and quicker Ferraris were arriving now, along with C-Type Jaguars, XK-120M's and the home-grown Cunninghams, but the tenacious J2X's stood up to them magnificently for still another season, but after that even the pugnacious likes of Goldschmidt, Fred Wacker and Tom Carstens could no longer compensate for the opposition which was growing steadily faster at every race. None-

theless, in its time this Allard was a veritable dreadnaught, and when she finally did go down it was with all guns blazing.

Consider, for the record, what these cars could do — way back in the early Fifties. Goldschmidt's J2X could accelerate from a standing start to 100 mph in twelve seconds. And the Briggs Cunningham-Tom Cole car, the first Cadillac-engined J2, would do eighty miles an hour in bottom gear and a cool one hundred in second. The top speed of the machines varied, of course, depending on which gears were installed in the differential. They ranged from 4.44:1 to 3.20:1 and would offer a maximum from around 112 up to about 140.

The immaculate J2X on these pages — owned by W. E. Bridgeforth, Jr., of Winchester, Virginia — must be one of the few remaining Cadillac Allards in absolutely original condition. Mr. Bridgeforth is a lucky man.

PIERCE-ARROW: THE AMERICAN ARISTOCRAT

Consider, first, all the words of wisdom that have been propounded about names, from the Biblical belief that a good name is better chosen than great riches, to that noted Elizabethan's irreverence in questioning "what's in a name?" Then consider the Pierce-Arrow. Was ever an American marque of luxury better named? To be sure, America has produced an admirable number of luxury vehicles. But do any of them sound as elegant, as refined, as aristocratic as Pierce-Arrow? Were the Pierce-Arrow's only contribution to the American automobile its sophisticated name, it would perhaps be contribution enough. And the story would have ended here. But there was considerably more.

Pierce-Arrow roots ran deep in American history. The founder of the original company, George Norman Pierce, whose ancestors came over on the Mayflower, was born in 1846 in

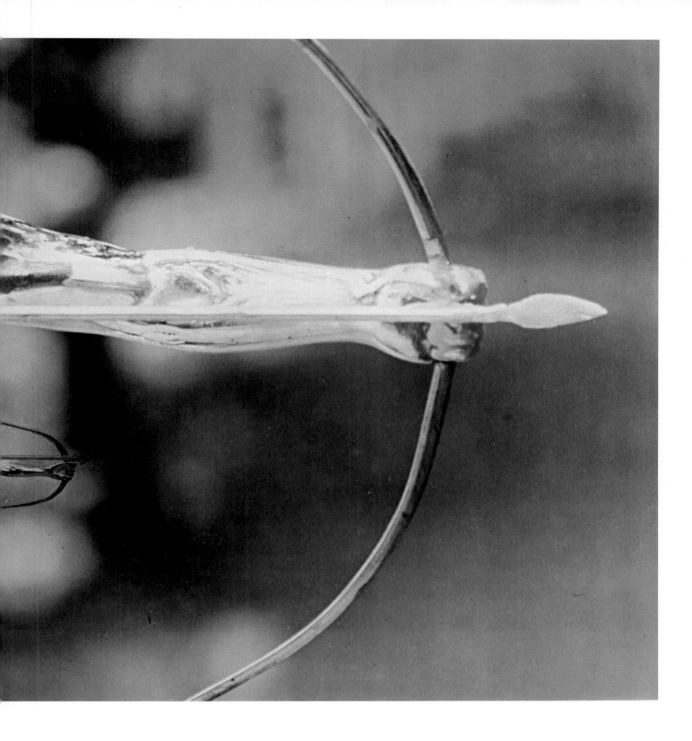

nall town near Waverly, New York, and was
ducated in private schools and business college.
'ith two associates he started a business in Buf-
lo in 1865 to make such varied household
ems as iceboxes and bird cages, obtaining con-
olling interest by 1872, reorganizing as the
eorge N. Pierce Company, later adding
cycles to the line. Brought into the company in
e mid-1890's was one Charles Clifton, who had
en treasurer to the Ball, Lewis and Yates Coal
ining Company, and who was to prove the most
ective business executive in Pierce-Arrow
istory. It was he who, assuming charge of Pub-
c Policy, first began investigating the auto-
obile. There were, of course, few examples
ound at that time for the company to in-
stigate. Finally, early in 1900, the board of
rectors decided that they should experiment
emselves—with both steam and gasoline auto-

mobiles. A steam car, built from drawings supplied by the Overman Steam Car Co., a firm
existing from 1899 to 1902, was readied by
George Pierce's son, Percy, and a couple of
associates. Assembly of the car began in March
of 1900, and after many vicissitudes, the first
drive was made on August 21st that year, the
car being backed out of its assembly barn and
run three times around the block. The ride
lasted a mere five minutes and ended in rear
axle failure. Following a lengthy series of
further road tests, Pierce officials decided that
steam power definitely wasn't for them.

Colonel Clifton, after a trip to Europe to study
the state of the art there, recommended the de
Dion gasoline motor — and by November of
1900 the Pierce people had come up with a
gasoline car which was tested on November 24th,
with further developmental work carried on into

January of 1901. Late in that month a Pierce-Arrow employee noted in his diary: "Mr. D.
Fergusson called to see the carriage today. He
has been working on a car with two speed and
reverse gear."

Thus was the debut of David Fergusson, chief
engineer of the Pierce company for the next
twenty years. He was British born, having served
as chief engineer-designer for an English company organized by Edward J. Pennington and
having come to the United States in 1899 with
that notorious promoter, fortunately severing
connections with him soon thereafter. He was
with Stearns in Syracuse, New York, for a while,
but he found that company too steam oriented to
readily accept the gasoline car idea. After learning about the Pierce difficulties with steam, he
travelled to Buffalo, laid his gasoline-car ideas
before the board of directors and was im-

mediately hired to design and build two cars. He began work on February 4th, carrying out the layout and detail drawings himself. The design was again fashioned on the French "motorette" practice of Pierce's first gasoline car, powered by de Dion motors contracted for by Colonel Clifton in France. The first two cars were completed in May, 1901, and for the rest of the year Fergusson and his staff drove around the United States testing the cars and demonstrating them to the George N. Pierce bicycle agents.

Twenty-five Motorettes were built in 1902 to the original design and a heavier and more powerful version (3½ hp, 725 pounds as against 2¾ hp and 500 pounds) was added later in the year, 125 of those being sold before the end of 1902. There followed by 1903 three more models, a 5 horsepower Motorette and a 6 horsepower and an 8 horsepower Stanhope.

Despite their primitive design, the early Pierce cars were commercially successful, due to the backing of a prosperous and widely

respected manufacturer, an established dealer network, and the favorable publicity accrued from blue ribbons and first class certificates picked up through perfect records in reliability trials which Pierce entered.

Consequently in 1903 still another model was introduced, a 15 hp two-cylinder vehicle built to the Panhard formula, with a vertical engine mounted in front under a Renault-like hood. This was superseded in 1904 by a second model, with the characteristic Pierce radiator, which became known as the "Arrow." Developed from this, also in 1904, was the "Great Arrow," a 24-28 hp four-cylinder car. This vehicle, at 2600 pounds, was 500 pounds heavier than the Arrow, and its price range — $3000-$5000 — indicated that the "luxury" concept of the marque was now well established. Fifty Great Arrows were built in 1904, and in 1905 this car became the mainstay of the company, being offered in three versions up to 40 hp.

This exclusive concentration on the luxury

Above left: The Fergusson-designed, de Dion based, one-cylinder Pierce Motorette of 1903. One of these little cars successfully competed in the Automobile Club of America-sponsored New York-Boston-New York run of that year. Below left: The 40-45 Great Arrow from 1909.

market was a natural outcome of the Pierce company's social and geographical position. The directors were prosperous businessmen and New York State was the center of wealth. Obviously, too, the Pierce directors were as astute as they were prosperous — or so the company's decision to enter the Glidden Tours would indicate.

The first Glidden Tour was held in July of 1905 — a contest to emphasize the reliability and promote the practical advantages of good touring cars. Thirty-four entrants competed, representing twenty-two different marques, of which six were European. Competitors included such notables as Locomobile, Packard, Cadillac, Peerless, Panhard, Napier, Darracq — and a car from the Pierce company. Percy Pierce, driving

bove right: A Great Arrow model from 1905.
t was in 1905 that the Great Arrow became the
mainstay of the company, following its success-
ul introduction the year previous. Below right
: the 1910 Model 36 UU runabout. In the center
: the Model 38 Series 2 touring car of 1914.

28-32 Great Arrow, and accompanied by his fiancée, Miss L. J. Moody, his mother and father, and mechanic George Ulrich, finished the tour with a loss of only four points out of a thousand, making, in the words of the Glidden committee, "an ideal tour of the trip, fulfilling the spirit as well as in the letter the conditions and purpose of the contest." He received the votes of fifteen of his competitors — twice that of any other — and the coveted Glidden Trophy. That was just the beginning. In all, the Glidden Trophy would remain in the custody of the Pierce company five times in five years. And similar triumphs were forthcoming in other touring car trials in the United States, as well as in similar events in Europe.

In 1906 the Great Arrow was offered in two lines, 28-32 and 40-45, refined in light of the Glidden Trophy experience, and continued in 1907 as the "30" and "45." That year they were joined by the first six-cylinder model, the Great Arrow 65 (later 66), of which one hundred were built in 1907. It was to reign for eleven years as the ultimate expression of "damn-the-cost-motoring" — and was perhaps the most successful six-cylinder car in America of this generation. To eliminate crankshaft breakages experienced by the pioneer builders of sixes, Fergusson specified a seven-bearing shaft, forged in chrome nickel steel with a tensile strength exceeding 130,000 pounds per square inch, and all reciprocating and rotating masses in the engine were meticulously balanced. Quietness, smoothness, power, absence of vibration and ease of starting were the result, giving a standard of luxurious travel unequalled by any other marque on the road.

By this time the trade name Arrow had

become a household word, and the directors, recognizing its value, changed their corporate name to the Pierce-Arrow Motor Car Company in 1909. All cars henceforth were to be known as Pierce-Arrows. The only sad note in these years of commercial triumph was the death of the company's founder, George N. Pierce.

There was no doubting the quality of the Pierce product, nor the market to which it was directed. The Pierce-Arrow was a carriage trade car, and its promotion was superbly managed by the capable Colonel Clifton. Advertising copy was lavish and exclusive, and the company offered free, a two-week training course in Buffalo conducted by their technical men at the factory. To enter, one had to merely obtain a letter from a dealer.

By 1909 the company was offering five models, and in 1911 instituted a truck line. Pierce-Arrow were among the first automobile manufacturers to extensively employ aluminum; other unusual characteristics featured in the

Above:
The Model 66
Series 4
seven-passenger
touring car of 1917.

Below:
The Model 48
Series 3
rumble-seat roadster
from 1915.

cars were the engine compartment oil tank with gravity feed (1903-1911), steering wheel gear lever (all cars until 1908) and right-hand drive (retained until 1920). By far the most exclusive feature, however, was the Pierce-Arrow trademark, the famous fender headlamp. It was patented in 1914, by Herbert M. Dawley of the Pierce company, having been featured first on the 1913-14 Model 48 B-2. Although the drum and bracket type headlamps would remain optional through 1932, the majority of Pierce-Arrow owners usually specified the distinctive Pierce-Arrow treatment.

Production of luxury cars in America — ranging in price from $2500-$7000 — totalled 18,500 units in 1913. The two leading manufacturers were Packard (2300) and Pierce (2000), followed by such others as White, Franklin, Locomobile and Peerless. The Cadillac was the leading American marque in the high-priced range ($1500-$2500). In 1914, however, Cadillac moved seriously into the over $2500 group, introducing late that year their epoch-making V-8, a straight-out luxury car with specifications that made all other contemporaries look obsolete. Packard replied with its modern Twin-Six a year later, as did Cunningham with a V-8 and Marmon with its advanced "34."

The Pierce-Arrow engineering department was not blind to this change. Unfortunately the same could not be said for the board of directors. Tradition overrode all other considerations, and the V-8 project upon which David Fergusson had been working was dropped. In July of 1915 the company announced that no radical powerplant change would be made for eighteen months, dismissing eight- and twelve-cylinder engines as "novelties introduced for a more spectacular selling argument." Publicly Pierce-Arrow engineers were stated to be in accordance, although it was a moot point whether Fergusson agreed.

The war years found Pierce-Arrow heavily into military manufacture of trucks, and the war's conclusion marked the demise of the Models 38 and 66. The passing of the mighty 66 was the end of an era, one in which, as a noted automotive historian has commented and others concur, "the Pierce-Arrow was probably the most pleasing American touring or town car" on the road.

Pierce-Arrow began advertising their new engine during the closing months of the war in Europe. It was the Dual Valve Six, introduced in October, 1918. This was the 48 redesigned with two inlet and exhaust valves per cylinder in T-head formation, as on previous six-cylinder Pierces. The dual valve design gave the same effect as a larger, high-lift single valve, but was easy to keep silent because of the softer valve springs. Increased power was thus obtained without a complete redesign. The principle proved so successful that it was retained for the all-new unit-block powerplant introduced in 1921. This new 38 hp had all six cylinders cast en bloc, with a one-piece detachable cylinder head and a separate aluminum crankcase. The clutch and three-speed transmission were in unit with the engine. An advanced feature was the angling of the valve axis to that of the cylinder bores to give more room for valve area. Specifications were 4 x 5½ inches for a 414-cubic-inch displacement, and the rpm range was 200 to 3000 with a power peak of 100 bhp at 2800.

Shortly after its introduction a Dual Valve Six was purchased by the Italian Alfa Romeo firm, to get an insight into American quality car practice and manufacture. Another more notorious utilization of the Pierce-Arrow during the period was by rum runners, who had a marked preference for powering their inshore boats with Pierce-Arrow engines, this because of their reliability and, most important, their extremely quiet exhausts.

Despite the veiled testimony of bootleggers, however, the T-head had become a dead-end design. Sales ranged between 1200 and 2000 annually. This was meager production in comparison with Packard and Cadillac, and poor, too, in relation to Pierce plant investment. The sales totals represented less than one car per year per employee, the Pierce-Arrow company employing eighteen hundred workers in 1921 and thirty-two hundred in 1922.

Pierce-Arrow's new Dual Valve Six engine was introduced in October of 1918. Essentially it was the Model 48 redesigned in T-head formation with two inlet and two exhaust valves per cylinder. Among these Dual Valve Sixes was the 1920 Series ? tourer pictured below left. It is noteworthy as well for the location of its steering wheel. Pierce-Arrow were among the last American holdouts for right-hand drive

Were this not trouble enough, there was considerable dissatisfaction among the top engineers at Pierce as well. The old management had decided to retire at the end of the war, and the new powers-that-be began pursuing plans for a variety of new models that left Fergusson aghast. He resigned, was succeeded by Barney Roos, who also resigned shortly thereafter. His successor was Charles L. Sheppy, and the company also received a new president at almost the same time: Myron Edson Forbes.

Just about everyone in America was making money during the booming Twenties — everyone, it seemed, except Pierce-Arrow. To remedy the situation President Forbes set chief engineer Sheppy to work on a new and smaller six to supplement the Dual Valve, in the same way that Packard had a six complementary to its eight.

The Series 80 Pierce came out in 1924. It was an L-head six, displacing 289 cubic inches and developing 70 bhp at 3000 rpm. It was smaller in size than the Dual Valve Six and lower in price, starting at $2895. In some respects it pointed the way for later Pierce models, particularly in engine design and its Isotta-Fraschini-type brakes, and it was Pierce's most popular model ever, selling over 16,000 units between August, 1924 and the end of 1927.

Not until 1921 did the Pierce-Arrow Motor Car Company put the driver on the left. In that year, too, their all-new monobloc Dual Valve Six engine was introduced, with an output of 100 bhp at 2800 rpm. The new cars, designated Series 33, were set in a chassis measuring one hundred thirty-eight inches. A 1922 touring car is pictured below right. Above is a 1924 rumble-seat roadster, which was priced at a heady $5250.

The year 1928 was a rather unfortunate one for Pierce-Arrow. Sales of the Series 81 — successor to the Series 80 — were just slightly over 5000 cars, considerably less than had been expected. The series had been introduced with enthusiasm by Forbes, and, admittedly, it was mechanically superior to its predecessor. But styling was another story. The noted French designer J. Saoutchik liked it and said so, but although his comments were widely quoted by Pierce-Arrow, the average customer was buying neither the styling nor the car. Conversely, customers were avoiding the lush series 36 Dual Valve Six, not because of its styling, but because of its mechanics. Multi-cylinder engines were the vogue among luxury car buyers of that period, and with just six cylinders the Pierce-Arrow was simply no longer in vogue.

Another era was ending at Pierce-Arrow. The year 1928 also marked the last year of six-cylinder Pierces; Colonel Clifton died and the company ceased to be independent. For some, the merger of Pierce-Arrow and Studebaker was a kind of death too — although in retrospect that hardly seems fair. Studebaker at that time had all the signs of a budding empire — an extensive range of cars and trucks and a president, A. R. Erskine, who was ever searching for ways to expand. He wanted more plant facilities and a high-priced marque to round out his line. Pierce-Arrow wanted stability; they had a luxury car and marvelous facilities, of which full use had not been made since the war. A merger between the two promised to be mutually profitable. For Pierce-Arrow it was perhaps a virtual necessity. Myron Forbes doubted even then that an "isolated automobile unit" could long compete successfully with such giants of the industry as General Motors and Chrysler. And so the deed was done.

Pierce-Arrow continued throughout, however, as an independently operating entity, and it was the Pierce-Arrow engineering staff who came up with the new straight eights introduced in January of 1929. Two lines were offered, both

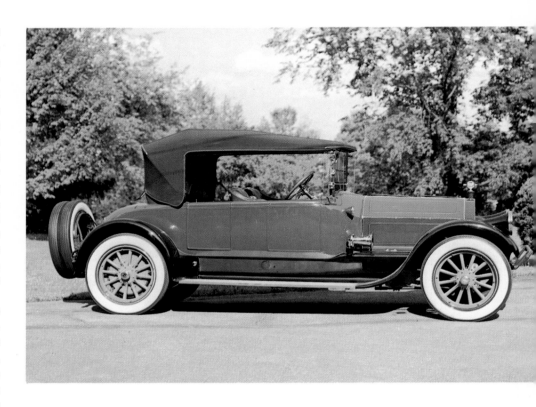

Above: The first generation Dual Valve Six, a 1918 Series 4 four-passenger roadster. Above right: Companion to the Dual Valve Six was the 70 bhp L-head six introduced in 1924 as the Series 80. This was succeeded in 1928 by the Series 81, of which the sport roadster model is pictured. Some five thousand of these cars were built. Nineteen twenty-nine saw the introduction of the new Pierce-Arrow straight-eight engines, which produced 125 bhp. The 1930 Model B rumble-seat roadster is pictured below left. On the right is the 1929 Model 133 dual cowl phaeton.

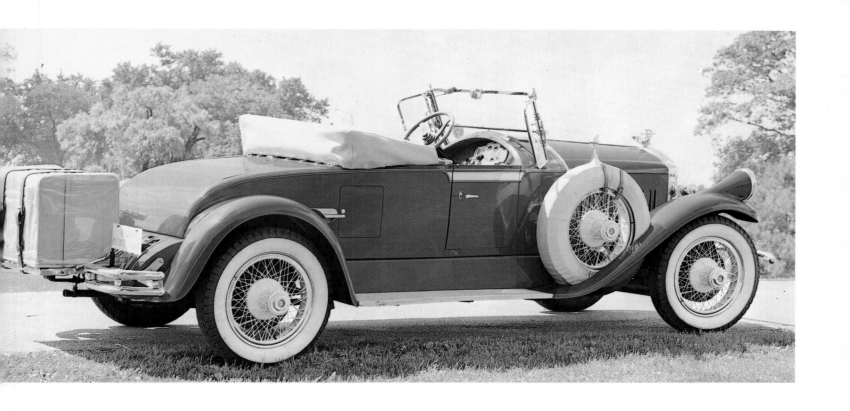

Pierce-Arrows of the early Thirties.
Above: Front and profile views of the Model 54
club brougham built in 1932. Below right
is a Model 43 rumble-seat coupé
built in 1931. Both these cars carried the
eight-cylinder engine. One of the
fabulous Pierce twelves appears below,
the 1933 Model 1247 convertible sedan.
The twelve had been introduced for the
1932 model year, boasting 150 horsepower that
year, subsequently raised to 160 hp for 1933.

powered by the same L-head, nine-bearing 125 bhp engine, and for both the styling was completely fresh and up to date, slimmer and more graceful. They were enthusiastically received, sales doubling in 1929 to 10,000 units.

Meanwhile Pierce-Arrow were headlining their advertisements with "The Tyranny of Tradition" — a latter-day answer perhaps to

Cadillac's "Penalty of Leadership" — and boasting of their determination to put "fineness eternally first." Myron Forbes resigned in 1929 and was succeeded as president by A. R. Erskine. Cadillac introduced their V-16 in 1930, and Pierce chief engineer, now Karl M. Wise, was immediately put to work on a Pierce V-12. It was introduced in November, 1931. Initially in

two sizes, a 398-cubic-inch 140 hp model and a 429-cubic-inch 150 hp model, the former was soon dropped because it could not outperform the current 385-cubic-inch Pierce eights.

The horsepower race, then as always, saw the larger twelve's power boosted the following year — 462 cubic inches, for 175 hp at 3400 rpm. This was the engine — and the car — introduced to the public as the "World's Champion." And the reason was Ab Jenkins — then Pierce-Arrow's test driver — and the Bonneville salt flats. In September of 1932, with a basically standard car which had already seen 33,000 miles in the hands of test drivers, Ab started driving the salt flats, without relief as was his custom. Twenty-four hours later he had piled up 2710 miles at a 112.91 mph average — without any trouble. Fenders, windscreen and road equipment were then returned to the car, and it was immediately driven another 2000 miles across the continent to Buffalo, without a major adjustment of any kind.

This run was followed by two more in 1933 and 1934. For the first, with a convertible stripped of running boards, fenders and other such niceties, and with some modifications to the engine, the meteoric Mormon and his Pierce averaged 123 mph for the first 1000 miles and 117.77 mph for the twenty-four hours at Bonneville. Officially timed, the Pierce broke fourteen records of the F.I.A. (Féderation Internationale de l'Automobile), as well as sixty-six A.A.A. records. For the second — in August, 1934 — Jenkins simply lifted his own previous mark by almost 10 mph to a new record average of 127 mph for 3053.3 miles, again recognized

internationally by the F.I.A. in Paris.

Company literature pointed out, with justifiable pride, that magnificent though the runs were, their great engines would stand much longer tests: "At one hundred hours, wide open, under maximum loads, they function as perfectly as at the start. After two hundred and fifty hours (a continuous two weeks of day and night

running), they developed no major trouble." The engine of the 1932 roadster, in fact, had spent 156 hours on the dynamometer at 4000 rpm before the record run.

Unfortunately, though records were being blithely broken in Utah, no sales records were being posted in Buffalo. And affairs at South Bend were no more encouraging. Suddenly in

1933 Studebaker found itself in receivership. Erskine's dream of expansion had resulted in overextension. He committed suicide in July of that year, and most of his dreams died with him. In August Pierce-Arrow was bought by a group of Buffalo businessmen and bankers — and once again the company was independent. And still in trouble.

The company could break even, it was discovered, with a yearly sales figure of 3000 cars; if 4000 cars were sold, there would be a million dollar profit. Even the latter goal seemed reasonable. But by the end of 1933 sales totalled only 2152, five hundred less than the previous year. Sales of all luxury marques — Packard, Lincoln and Cadillac among them — also fell drastically during the same period, but that was small comfort to Pierce-Arrow.

But the model year 1933 was not without its aesthetic and engineering successes. There was, first of all, the fabulous Silver Arrow, radical, streamlined, a car that would in Pierce-Arrow's words "give you in 1933 the car of 1940." And it was a car whose design was years ahead of its time, but it was not destined to be. On the standard eights and twelves of that year hydraulic tappets were introduced, these being the first of their kind. They were conceived in the early part of 1932 by Carl Voorhies, one of Pierce-Arrow's engine designers, and patented that year by the company. A major technical achievement, but it didn't help.

Neither did the complete restyling of the 1936 lineup, including the first "quad light" treatment and a number of chassis improvements. Again, these were splendid cars, equal to best of the competition, but like almost every other luxury manufacturer, Pierce-Arrow was nearing the end of the road.

What the company needed was eleven million dollars. They didn't have it, couldn't get it, couldn't go on. On Friday the 13th of May, 1938, the *New York Times* reported the sale at auction of the Pierce-Arrow company.

The final car made of the regular 1938 models was built by company test engineer Donald Anson in the summer of 1938 for chief engineer Karl Wise, who had purchased parts along the line from the official receiver. It was a somber and yet appropriate act — a few devoted craftsmen, working in the vast but now silent and deserted plant that had once echoed the voices of thousands of men and the roar of champion engines being test run, carefully assembling and testing the last of a great line. Mr. Anson was the last Pierce-Arrow man to leave the factory.

Pierce-Arrow built magnificent luxury cars. And they did this in full measure, fighting the good fight to the last. A cheap Pierce-Arrow would have been a contradiction in terms. Fortunately, that never happened. We are left today with a memory of a car that was forever fine, and a name that shall forever bespeak the essence of luxury. That is, perhaps, enough.

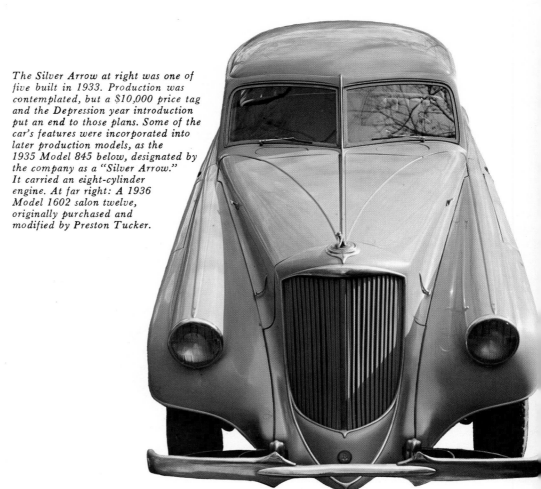

The Silver Arrow at right was one of five built in 1933. Production was contemplated, but a $10,000 price tag and the Depression year introduction put an end to those plans. Some of the car's features were incorporated into later production models, as the 1935 Model 845 below, designated by the company as a "Silver Arrow." It carried an eight-cylinder engine. At far right: A 1936 Model 1602 salon twelve, originally purchased and modified by Preston Tucker.

BIBLIOGRAPHY OF STORIES

The articles in this book were originally published in, or were adapted from or inspired by articles in AUTOMOBILE *Quarterly. Their derivation is shown below. Data given include, wherever pertinent, the authors and titles of the original articles and the volume and number of* AUTOMOBILE *Quarterly in which they appeared.*

ADAMS-FARWELL

Adapted from "Adams-Farwell: You See It and You Still Don't Believe It," by Beverly Rae Kimes, Volume VIII, Number 2.

AUBURN

Adapted from "Auburn—From Runabout to Speedster," by Beverly Rae Kimes, Volume V, Number 4.

CARABO: BY CARROZZERIA BERTONE

Adapted from "About Nuccio Bertone," by Gianni Rogliatti, Volume IV, Number 2; "Notes On My Carabo," by Nuccio Bertone and "Carabo Impressions: Panic in the Streets," by Gianni Rogliatti, Volume VII, Number 4.

CHADWICK: REMEMBER THE NAME

Adapted from "Chadwick: Remember the Name," by Beverly Rae Kimes, Volume IX, Number 2.

CHRYSLER: A HISTORY OF MIXED BLESSINGS

Adapted from "Chrysler: The Early Years," by Cullen Thomas, Volume VI, Number 1; "Chrysler: From the Airflow," by Beverly Rae Kimes, Volume VII, Number 2.

CORD L-29

Adapted from "The Forgotten Cord," by Beverly Rae Kimes, with specifications by Robert Fabris, Volume VI, Number 4.

DE TOMASO MANGUSTA

Adapted from "De Tomaso Mangusta," by Don Vorderman, Volume VII, Number 3.

THE DOBLE STEAM CAR

Adapted from "The Steam Odyssey of Abner Doble," by Maurice D. Hendry, Volume VIII, Number 1.

DUESENBERG

Adapted from "Duesenberg—It's a Grand Old Name," by Raymond A. Wolff, Volume IV, Number 4.

THE ECCENTRIC MASTERPIECES OF ETTORE BUGATTI

Appeared originally as "A Bugatti Introduction," by Ken W. Purdy, Volume VI, Number 1.

1894 BALZER

By Richard M. Langworth, with excerpts from "A Portfolio of Oddities," Volume VIII, Number 1.

HENRY'S "T" AND EDSEL'S "A"

The Model T section by G. P. K. Wheaton; the Model A section adapted from "The 'A' Was For Everything," by Mervyn Kaufman, Volume IV, Number 1.

HISPANO-SUIZA

Adapted from "Hispano-Suiza," by Nicolás Franco, Jr., and José Rodriguez de la Viña, Volume III, Number 1.

LAGONDA LG6

Adapted from "Lagonda LG6," by Don Vorderman, Volume VII, Number 3.

LAGO-TALBOT

Adapted from "The Cars of Tony Lago," by Beverly Rae Kimes, Volume IV, Number 1.

MARMON: A QUEST FOR PERFECTION

Adapted from "Marmon: A Quest for Perfection," by Maurice D. Hendry, Volume VII, Number 2.

M.G. TC

Adapted from "TC—Nostalgic Ramblings," by Don Vorderman, Volume VIII, Number 2.

MISTER TAYLOR'S BUGGY

Adapted from "The Forgotten Steam Buggy of Henry Seth Taylor," by Charles A. Friedric, Volume IV, Number 4.

MODULO

Adapted from "Modulo: The Future Has Arrived," by Don Vorderman, Volume IX, Number 4.

PACKARD

By Richard M. Langworth, with excerpts from "Packard—A Great Name Passes On," by Tom Mahoney, Volume I, Number 3.

PIERCE-ARROW: THE AMERICAN ARISTOCRAT

Adapted from "Pierce-Arrow: An American Aristocrat," by Maurice D. Hendry, Volume VI, Number 3.

PLYMOUTH

Appeared originally as "Plymouth: Walter Chrysler's Trump Car," by Beverly Rae Kimes, Volume V, Number 1.

PUNGS-FINCH INDEED!

Adapted from "Pungs-Finch Indeed!," by Beverly Rae Kimes, Volume VIII, Number 1.

THE REMARKABLE RUXTON

Adapted from "Ruxton: A Superb Automobile That Never Had a Chance," by Jeffrey I. Godshall, Volume VIII, Number 2.

ROLLS-ROYCE: THE IMMORTAL LINEAGE

By Raymond L. Perrin, with excerpts from "Rolls-Royce," by Edgar Allan Jurist, Volume II, Number 1; "The Vanishing Rolls," by Michael Lorrimer, Volume VIII, Number 4.

THE SAGA OF STUTZ

Adapted from the following articles in "Stutz: America's Greatest Sports Car," Volume VIII, Number 3: "The Harry Stutz Era," by Russ Catlin; "The Fred Moskovics Era," by Maurice D. Hendry; "Series BB Black Hawk Impressions," by Don Vorderman; "The DV-32 & The End," by Beverly Rae Kimes.

SYDNEY ALLARD'S FABULOUS J2X

Adapted from "Allard: The Blacksmith's Revenge," by Dennis May, Volume VIII, Number 4; "J2X Impressions," by Don Vorderman, Volume VIII, Number 4.

THE UBIQUITOUS CHEVROLET

Adapted from "Chevrolet: The Winner and Still Champion," by Karl E. Ludvigsen, Volume VII, Number 3.

PHOTOGRAPHY AND OWNER CREDITS

The logistics involved in locating rare cars and arranging for them to be photographed for AUTOMOBILE *Quarterly publications are, of necessity, complicated. The photographs of cars featured in this book are the result of nearly ten years of research and more than fifty individual photographic assignments. Credit is given below to the photographer who took each picture and to the owner of each automobile shown, as of the time when it was photographed.*

THE SAGA OF STUTZ

Pages 8-13: 1912 Series A Bearcat, 1913 Series B Bearcat and 1927 Custom Series AA Black Hawk courtesy of Harrah's Automobile Collection, photographs by Don Vorderman. Pages 14-17: 1928 Series BB Black Hawk courtesy of Tom Lester, photograph by Don Vorderman. Pages 18-19: 1931 Series SV-16 boattail speedster courtesy of A. N. Rodway, photograph by Russel Berry; 1932 Series DV-32 Bearcat courtesy of the Briggs Cunningham Automotive Museum, photograph by L. Scott Bailey. Pages 20-21: 1933 Series DV-32 convertible victoria courtesy of Harrah's Automobile Collection, photograph by Don Vorderman.

MISTER TAYLOR'S BUGGY

Pages 22-25: Courtesy of Richard M. Stewart, photographs by Stanley Rosenthall.

HISPANO-SUIZA

Pages 26-29: Courtesy of Richard E. Riegel, Jr., photographs by Tom Burnside.

CHRYSLER: A HISTORY OF MIXED BLESSINGS

Page 30: 1925 Model Six roadster courtesy of N. A. Billig, photograph by Stanley Rosenthall. Page 31: 1926 Imperial E80 sedan and 1928 Model 72 roadster courtesy of Harrah's Automobile Collection, photographs by Tom Burnside. Pages 32-33: 1929 Model 75 roadster courtesy of Morris Sarnoff, 1930 Model 77 dual cowl phaeton courtesy of Milford H. Gould, photographs by Stanley Rosenthall. Pages 34-35: 1930 Model 66 sport touring courtesy of Seth Pancoast, 1931 Model 6 roadster courtesy of Garvin Weidemoyer, 1930 Model 66 phaeton courtesy of Price L. Reed, photographs by Stanley Rosenthall; 1931 Model 70 roadster courtesy of Philip Wichard, photograph by Tom Burnside. Pages 36-37: 1932 Model 8 convertible sedan courtesy of George Dunning, 1933 Imperial Eight convertible sedan courtesy of Robert M. Perry, photographs by Stanley Rosenthall; 1931 Custom Imperial roadster courtesy of Harrah's Automobile Collection, photograph by Tom Burnside. Page 38: 1936 Airflow Eight sedan courtesy of the Pettit Collection, photograph by William A. C. Pettit, III. Page 39: 1934 Airflow Imperial coupé and 1935 Airflow Imperial sedan courtesy of Harrah's Automobile Collection. Pages 40-41: 1940 Newport phaeton courtesy of William C. Gundaker, photograph by Don Vorderman; 1947 Imperial limousine courtesy of the Pettit Collection, photograph by William A. C. Pettit, III. Pages 42-43: 1942 Town and Country sedan courtesy of Morris Sarnoff, photograph by Stanley Rosenthall; 1948 Town and Country sedan courtesy of the Pettit Collection, photograph by William A. C. Pettit, III; 1957 300C, photograph by Henry Austin Clark, Jr.

DE TOMASO MANGUSTA

Pages 44-47: Photographs by Don Vorderman.

ADAMS-FARWELL

Pages 48-52: Courtesy of Harrah's Automobile Collection, photographs by Don Vorderman.

CORD L-29

Pages 52-53: 1930 three-passenger coupé courtesy of Vincent E. Furnas, Jr., photograph by L. Scott Bailey. Pages 54-55: 1929 phaeton courtesy of the Brooks Stevens Automotive Museum, photograph by Tom Burnside. Page 56: 1931 cabriolet courtesy of Michael Bobek, photograph by Don Vorderman.

M.G. TC

Pages 58-61: Courtesy of the Long Island Automotive Museum, photographs by Don Vorderman.

THE UBIQUITOUS CHEVROLET

Pages 62-63: 1913 Classic 6 Series C touring courtesy of the Sloan Panorama of Transportation, photograph by Don Owens. Pages 64-65: 1916 Baby Grand touring courtesy of William S. Gundaker, photographs by Don Vorderman. Pages 66-67: 1923 Superior utility coupé courtesy of the Long Island Auto-motive Museum, photograph by Henry Austin Clark, Jr.; 1925 Superior Series K touring courtesy of Dennis Boyles, 1921 Model 490 touring courtesy of Charles E. Brown, photographs by L. Scott Bailey. Page 68: 1930 Universal Series AD roadster courtesy of Clarence C. Carson, photograph by L. Scott Bailey; 1928 National Series AB touring courtesy of A. N. Rodway, photograph by Russel Berry. Page 69: 1932 Confederate Series BA special sedan courtesy of George Hornbostel, photograph by Don Vorderman. Pages 70-71: 1929 International Series AC coach courtesy of Robert Nelson, 1931 Independence Series AE convertible cabriolet courtesy of Robert E. Kauffman, photographs by Don Vorderman; 1933 Master Series CA sport roadster courtesy of A. N. Rodway, photograph by Russel Berry. Pages 72-73: 1935 Master Series EA sport coupé courtesy of Perry H. Kremer, photograph by Don Vorderman; 1936 Master Series FA coach courtesy of Joseph Doyle, photograph by L. Scott Bailey. Pages 74-75: 1941 Special DeLuxe Series AH coupé courtesy of Donald J. Edwards, photograph by Don Vorderman; 1946 Special DeLuxe Series KA coupé courtesy of James Edwards, 1947 Fleetmaster Series EK coupé courtesy of Jules Desgain, photographs by L. Scott Bailey. Pages 76-77: 1949 Styleline DeLuxe Series GK coupé courtesy of Roland James, 1952 Bel Air Series KK courtesy of Edward Haegele, photographs by Don Vorderman; 1954 Series One-Fifty sedan courtesy of Pete N. Greco, photograph by L. Scott Bailey.

THE CARABO: BY CARROZZERIA BERTONE

Pages 78-83: Courtesy of Carrozzeria Bertone, photographs by Josip Ciganovic.

1894 BALZER

Pages 84-85: Courtesy of the Smithsonian Institution, photographs by L. Scott Bailey.

PACKARD

Pages 86-87: 1903 Model F touring courtesy of Harrah's Automobile Collection; 1910 Model 30 roadster courtesy of Stan Tarnopol, photograph by L. Scott Bailey; 1904 Model L touring courtesy of, and photographed by, Richard Teague. Pages 88-89: 1909 Model 18 runabout courtesy of W. F. Snyder III, photograph by Henry Austin Clark, Jr.; 1910 Model 18 limousine photograph by Henry Austin Clark, Jr.; 1911 Model 30 touring courtesy of the Frederick C. Crawford Auto-Aviation Museum of the Western Reserve Historical Society. Pages 90-91: 1912 Model 6-48 special victoria courtesy of the Frederick C. Crawford Auto-Aviation Museum of the Western Reserve Historical Society; 1930 Model 733 roadster courtesy of A. N. Rodway, photograph by Russel Berry; 1928 Model 443 custom phaeton courtesy of Robert E. Turnquist, photograph by Tom Burnside. Pages 92-93: 1930 Model 745 dual cowl phaeton courtesy of A. N. Rodway, photograph by Russel Berry; 1934 Model 1104 convertible victoria courtesy of Paul C. Lamb, photograph by Henry Austin Clark, Jr.; 1930 Model 734 boattail speedster courtesy of Milford H. Gould, photograph by Don Vorderman. Pages 94-95: 1936 convertible coupé courtesy of the Brooks Stevens Automotive Museum, photograph by Tom Burnside; 1937 convertible coupé courtesy of W. W. Walmsley, photograph by Rick Lenz; 1937 Model 1507 club sedan courtesy of Lt. Col. Thomas E. Hauss, photograph by Tom Burnside. Pages 96-97: 1941 Model 120 sedan courtesy of Dr. Gerald Dahlen, photograph by Rick Lenz; 1940 Darrin Super 8 victoria courtesy of Irving Rothman, photograph by Don Vorderman. Pages 98-99: 1948 Custom Eight limousine courtesy of Calvin Soest, photograph by Rick Lenz; 1951 Patrician sedan courtesy of D. F. Rook, photograph by Richard M. Langworth. Pages 100-101: 1956 Patrician sedan courtesy of Fred R. Mauck, photograph by Rick Lenz; 1953 Caribbean convertible courtesy of Homer W. Forrer, 1955 Caribbean convertible courtesy of W. W. Tilden, photographs by Richard M. Langworth.

THE DOBLE STEAM CAR

Pages 102-103: 1925 Series E-23 phaeton courtesy of Harrah's Automobile Collection, photograph by Don Vorderman. Pages 104-105: 1925 Series E-20 roadster courtesy of Richard L. Hempel, photograph by M. J. Andresen. Page 105: 1925 Series E-24 coupé courtesy of Harrah's Automobile Collection, photograph by Don Vorderman.

PLYMOUTH

Page 107: 1929 Model U rumble-seat roadster courtesy of Jay M. Fisher, 1931 Model PA business coupé courtesy of H. Ray Mark. Pages 108-109: 1932 Model PB convertible sedan courtesy of Earl Buton, Jr. Pages 110-111: 1931 Model PA sedan courtesy of James Skelly; 1933 Model PC convertible coupé courtesy of Stan Marcum. Pages 112-113: 1934 Model PE sedan courtesy of Dr. Richard Rhodes; 1939 Model P-8 sedan courtesy of E. N. Hagaman; 1941 Model P-12 club coupé courtesy of John J. Dyson. All photographs by Stanley Rosenthall.

THE ECCENTRIC MASTERPIECES OF ETTORE BUGATTI

ages 114-117: "Black Bess," "Toast Rack," and Type 13 courtesy of C. W. Hampton, photographs by Tom Burnside. Pages 118-119: Type 44 courtesy A. N. Rodway, Type 46 courtesy of S. Ten Cate, Type 43 courtesy of uillaume J. M. J. Prick, photographs by Tom Burnside. Pages 120-121: ype 57SC courtesy of Vojta Mashek, photograph by Tom Burnside; Type ›B courtesy of Jack R. Harvey, photograph by Don Vorderman; Type 55 urtesy of Miles Coverdale, photograph by Norman Willock. Pages 122-123: ype 41 *La Royale* by Weinberger courtesy of the Henry Ford Museum, Type . *La Royale* by Kellner courtesy of the Briggs Cunningham Automotive Mu-um, photographs by Tom Burnside; Type 50 courtesy of Harrah's Automo-le Collection, photograph by Alexandre Georges. Pages 124-125: Type 59 urtesy of H. Dieter Holterbosch, photograph by Henry Austin Clark, Jr.

AUBURN

age 127: 1921 Model 6-39R roadster courtesy of Harrah's Automobile Col-ction, photograph by Tom Burnside; 1929 Model 8-120 speedster courtesy Page Wensel, photograph by L. Scott Bailey. Pages 128-129: 1927 Model 88 sedan courtesy of Jack Greenleaf, 1933 Model 8-100 sedan courtesy of herrell L. Van Curen, 1931 Model 8-98 phaeton courtesy of C. E. Marting, iotographs by L. Scott Bailey. Pages 130-131: 1932 Model 8-100 sport coupé urtesy of Thurston C. Davis, 1934 Model 850 phaeton sedan courtesy of loyd L. McWilliams, 1936 Model 852 convertible courtesy of J. R. Johnson, iotographs by L. Scott Bailey. Pages 132-133: 1934 V-12 boattail speedster urtesy of Harold A. Smith, photograph by L. Scott Bailey; 1935 Model ›1 speedster courtesy of Russ Strauch, photograph by Don Vorderman.

PUNGS-FINCH INDEED!

ages 134-137: Courtesy of the Long Island Automotive Museum, photographs / Don Vorderman.

ROLLS-ROYCE: THE IMMORTAL LINEAGE

ages 138-139: 1905 30 H.P. two-seater courtesy of S. E. Sears, photograph / Thomas Photos; 1907 Silver Ghost tourer courtesy of Millard Newman, iotograph by L. Scott Bailey; 1912 Silver Ghost limousine courtesy of S. E. ars, photograph by Tom Burnside. Pages 140-141: Silver Ghost/20 H.P. urtesy of S. E. Sears, photograph by Tom Burnside; 1914 Silver Ghost uring courtesy of Carl Anderson, photograph by L. Scott Bailey. Pages ›2-143: 1925 Phantom I boattail speedster courtesy of the Vintage Car Store, iotograph by Alexandre Georges; 1931 Phanton I playboy roadster courtesy David G. Domidion, photograph by Russel Berry. Pages 144-145: 1927 hantom I brougham courtesy of S. E. Sears, photographs by Thomas Photos; lying Lady mascot courtesy of Allen R. Thurn, photograph by Stanley osenthall. Pages 146-147: 1932 20/25 H.P. sports saloon courtesy of S. E. ears, photograph by Tom Burnside; 1930 Phantom II boattail 5/6-seater urtesy of J. K. Acutt, photograph by Don Vorderman. Pages 148-149: 1938 hantom III town car courtesy of the Vintage Car Store, photograph by on Vorderman; 1938 Phantom III close-coupled saloon and 1939 Wraith orts saloon courtesy of S. E. Sears, photographs by Tom Burnside. Pages ›0-151: 1955 Phantom IV limousine courtesy of the Vintage Car Store, 1957 lver Wraith saloon, photographs by Don Vorderman.

CHADWICK: REMEMBER THE NAME

ages 152-159: Courtesy of the Pollock Automotive Museum, photographs by on Vorderman.

DUESENBERG

age 161: Model A roadster courtesy of Harrah's Automobile Collection, iotograph by Mike Roberts; Model J convertible berline courtesy of the intage Car Store, photograph by Stanley Rosenthall. Page 152: Model J nvertible coupé courtesy of George W. Hueguely, photograph by L. Scott ailey; Model J club sedan courtesy of Harrah's Automobile Collection, iotograph by Alexandre Georges. Page 163: Model SJ convertible coupé urtesy of Irving Tuschinsky, photograph by L. Scott Bailey. Pages 164-165: lodel SJ convertible coupé, Model J/SJ dual cowl phaeton and Model SJ eedster courtesy of Harrah's Automobile Collection, photographs by Alex-idre Georges. Pages 166-167: Model SJ speedster courtesy of Bill Brewster, ecial record car courtesy of Royce Kershaw, photographs by Tom Burnside.

LAGO-TALBOT

ages 168-169: 1939 Type 150C-SS coupé courtesy of Vojta Mashek. Pages '0-171: 1939 Type 150C-SS coupé courtesy of the Brooks Stevens Automo-ve Museum; 1937 Type 150-SS cabriolet courtesy of Vojta Mashek. Pages '2-173: 1950 Grand Sport, 1948 competition-type tourismo courtesy of Vojta lashek. All photographs by Tom Burnside.

HENRY'S "T" AND EDSEL'S "A"

Pages 174-175: 1910 Model T town car courtesy of Richard E. Williams, photograph by Charles Miller; 1914 Model T speedster courtesy of Robert Corson, photograph by Stanley Rosenthall. Pages 176-177: 1909 Model T touring courtesy of the Henry Ford Museum, photograph by Charles Miller; 1926 Model T tudor sedan courtesy of Robert E. Crane, photograph by L. Scott Bailey. Pages 178-179: 1928 Model A phaeton courtesy of Leslie R. Henry, photograph by Charles Miller; 1929 Model A station wagon courtesy of Richard E. Williams, photograph by Carl Malotka. Pages 180-181: 1931 Model A convertible victoria and 1931 Model A convertible sedan courtesy of A. N. Rodway, photographs by Russel Berry; 1931 Model A deluxe roadster courtesy of Nick Timon, photograph by Carl Malotka.

LAGONDA LG6

Pages 182-185: Courtesy of Mr. and Mrs. Gerald P. Roeser, photographs by Don Vorderman. Painting by John Hanna.

MODULO BY PININFARINA

Pages 186-187: Courtesy of Carrozzeria Pininfarina, photographs by Don Vorderman.

THE REMARKABLE RUXTON

Pages 188-189: Production roadster courtesy of A. N. Rodway; "Alligator" courtesy of Delyle G. Beyer. Pages 190-191: Production sedan courtesy of Harrah's Automobile Collection. Pages 192-193: Custom-built phaeton courtesy of Russell Strauch. All photographs by Don Vorderman.

MARMON: A QUEST FOR PERFECTION

Pages 194-195: 1912 Model 32 speedster courtesy of Herbert Royston, photograph by Ralph Poole; 1914 Model 41 speedster courtesy of the Brooks Stevens Automotive Museum, photograph by Philip Newton; 1920 Model 34 roadster courtesy of the Brooks Stevens Automotive Museum, photograph by Alexandre Georges. Pages 196-197: 1925 Model 74 speedster courtesy of William Raithel, photograph by L. Scott Bailey; 1926 Model 75 roadster courtesy of A. N. Rodway, photograph by Russel Berry; 1927 Model 75 coupé courtesy of Harrah's Automobile Collection. Pages 198-199: 1931 Sixteen Model 141 coupé courtesy of Dr. Ivor D. Harris; 1932 Sixteen Model 147 limousine courtesy of Kenneth Fahnestock, photographs by L. Scott Bailey. Pages 200-201: 1932 Sixteen open phaeton courtesy of Edmund L. Robinson, photograph by Stanley Rosenthall; 1933 Sixteen Model 149 sedan courtesy of Bernard T. Welsh, photograph by A. B. Veirs; 1933 Sixteen Model 149 sedan courtesy of Harrah's Automobile Collection; 1933 V-12 prototype courtesy of the Brooks Stevens Automotive Museum, photograph by Philip Newton.

SYDNEY ALLARD'S FABULOUS J2X

Pages 202-203: Courtesy of W. E. Bridgeforth, Jr., photographs by Don Vorderman.

PIERCE-ARROW: THE AMERICAN ARISTOCRAT

Pages 206-207: Photograph by L. Scott Bailey and Tom Burnside. Pages 208-209: 1903 Motorette and 1909 Great Arrow courtesy of Burton H. Upjohn, 1914 Model 38 touring courtesy of Arnold Carlson, photographs by Henry Austin Clark, Jr.; 1905 Great Arrow courtesy of Dr. Samuel Scher, photograph by L. Scott Bailey; 1910 Model 38-UU runabout courtesy of G. Whitney Snyder, photograph by Henry Austin Clark, Jr. Pages 210-211: 1917 Model 66 touring courtesy of Seth H. Ely, Jr., photograph by Don Vorderman; 1915 Model 48 rumble-seat roadster courtesy of the Briggs Cunningham Automotive Museum, photograph by Tom Burnside. Pages 212-213: 1924 Series 33 roadster courtesy of Robert D. Thomas, 1920 Series 31 touring courtesy of Benny X. Goldflies, 1922 Series 33 touring courtesy of Robert Lyons, photographs by L. Scott Bailey. Pages 214-215: 1918 Model 48 roadster courtesy of Thomas J. Lester, photograph by Henry Austin Clark, Jr.; 1928 Series 81 sports roadster courtesy of N. O. Geisinger, 1930 Model B rumble-seat roadster courtesy of Charles A. Spross, photographs by L. Scott Bailey; 1929 Model 133 dual cowl phaeton courtesy of A. N. Rodway, photograph by Russel Berry. Pages 216-217: 1932 Model 54 club brougham courtesy of Harris Wichard, photograph by Don Vorderman; 1933 Model 1247 convertible sedan courtesy of Maurice G. Weinstein, 1931 43 rumble-seat coupé courtesy of Harley Frye, photographs by L. Scott Bailey. Pages 218-219: 1933 Silver Arrow courtesy of the Long Island Automotive Museum, photograph by Henry Austin Clark, Jr.; 1936 Model 1602 salon twelve courtesy of Rosen Novak, photograph by Alexandre Georges; 1935 Model 845 production Silver Arrow courtesy of Edmund L. Gibes, photograph by Tom Burnside.

AUTOMOBILE QUARTERLY PUBLICATIONS

The World's Oldest and Largest Publisher of Automobile History

PERIODICAL

Automobile Quarterly magazine is a hardbound publication devoted to the cars of today, yesterday and tomorrow. Recognized as the most outstanding automobile magazine, it has won awards in virtually every area of publishing, and has set new standards in automotive scholarship, photography, graphics and printing. The stories and photographs in *World of Cars* were derived and selected from previously published issues of *Automobile Quarterly* magazine.

BOOKS

World of Cars by the editors of *Automobile Quarterly* magazine
Great Cars & Grand Marques edited by Beverly Rae Kimes
Corvette: A Piece of the Action by William L. Mitchell and Allan Girdler
The Best of Corvette News edited by Karl Ludvigsen
The Best of Porsche Panorama, the official publication of The Porsche Club of America

LIBRARY SERIES OF MARQUE HISTORY BOOKS

The American Car Since 1775 by the editors of *Automobile Quarterly* magazine
Cadillac: Standard of the World by Maurice D. Hendry
Corvette: America's Star-Spangled Sports Car by Karl Ludvigsen
Ferrari: The Man, The Machines edited by Stan Grayson
The Cars That Henry Ford Built by Beverly Rae Kimes
Kaiser-Frazer: The Last Onslaught on Detroit by Richard M. Langworth
The Golden Anniversary of the Lincoln Motorcar by Beverly Rae Kimes
Mustang! The Complete History of America's Pioneer Ponycar by Gary Witzenburg
Oldsmobile: The First Seventy-Five Years by Beverly Rae Kimes and Richard M. Langworth
Opel: Wheels to the World by Karl Ludvigsen and Paul Frère
Packard: A History of the Motor Car and the Company edited by Beverly Rae Kimes
Porsche: Excellence Was Expected by Karl Ludvigsen
The Buick: A Complete History by Terry B. Dunham and Lawrence R. Gustin
Camaro: A Complete History by Gary Witzenburg

TRANSLATED EDITION SERIES

BMW: A History by Halwart Schrader, translated and adapted by Ron Wakefield

RESTORATION GUIDE SERIES

The Complete Corvette Restoration & Technical Guide, Volume I 1953-1962 by Noland Adams

HOBBY BOOK SERIES

Automobile Quarterly's Complete Handbook of Automobile Hobbies edited by Beverly Rae Kimes

Automobile Quarterly Publications, 245 W. Main St., Kutztown, PA 19530. Telephone: 215-683-8352